Artificial Intelligence

Projects and Practical Book

(As per CBSE Syllabus Code 417)

For Class
9

S P Verma

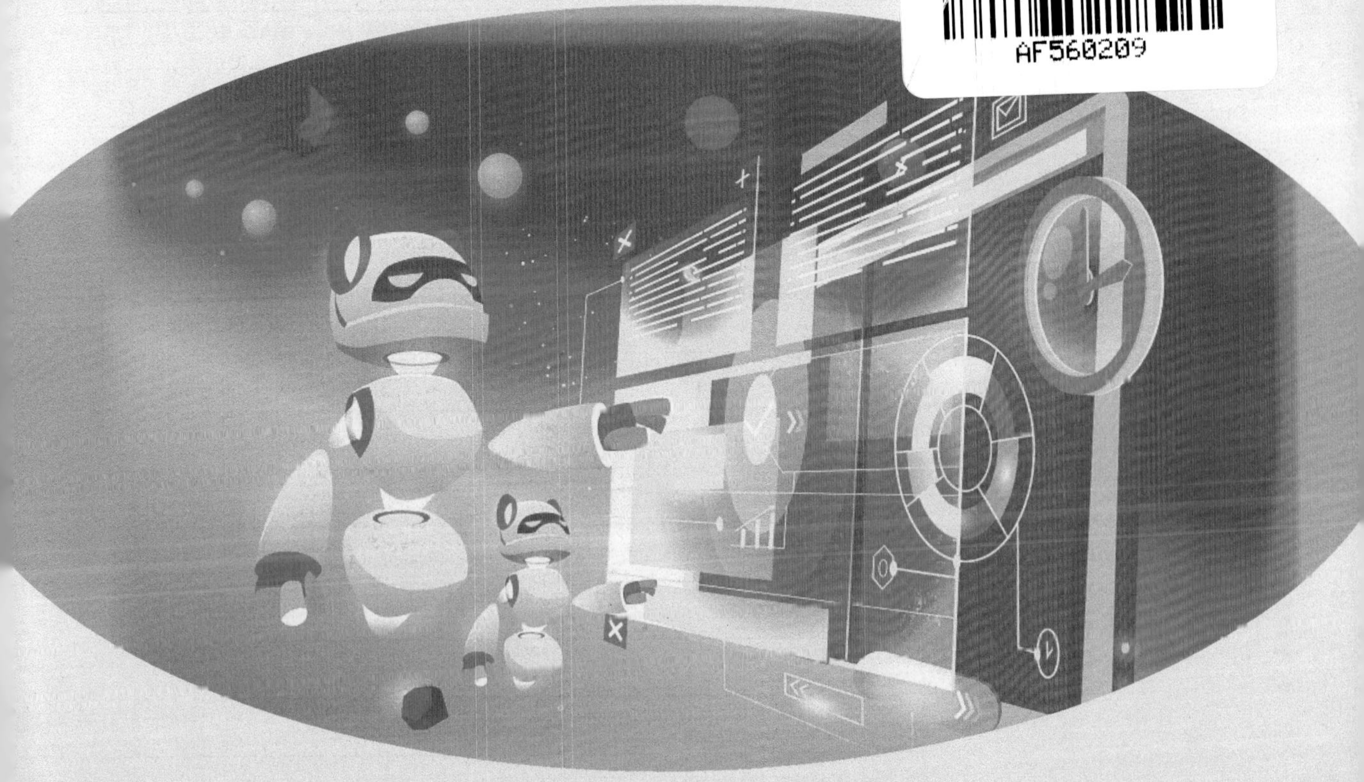

bpb

www.bpbonline.com

FIRST EDITION 2022
REPRINT 2023

ISBN: 978-93-55510-79-2

LIMITS OF LIABILITY AND DISCLAIMER OF WARRANTY

The information contained in this book is true to correct and the best of author's and publisher's knowledge. The author has made every effort to ensure the accuracy of these publications, but publisher cannot be held responsible for any loss or damage arising from any information in this book.

All trademarks referred to in the book are acknowledged as properties of their respective owners but BPB Publications cannot guarantee the accuracy of this information.

CBSE is in no way connected with this book. This Book is written solely for the benefit and guidance of students appearing of CBSE Examination.

Distributors:

BPB PUBLICATIONS
20, Ansari Road, Darya Ganj
New Delhi-110002
Ph: 23254990/23254991

DECCAN AGENCIES
4-3-329, Bank Street,
Hyderabad-500195
Ph: 24756967/24756400

MICRO MEDIA
Shop No. 5, Mahendra Chambers,
150 DN Rd. Next to Capital Cinema,
V.T. (C.S.T.) Station, MUMBAI-400 001
Ph: 22078296/22078297

BPB BOOK CENTRE
376 Old Lajpat Rai Market,
Delhi-110006
Ph: 23861747

Published by Manish Jain for BPB Publications, 20 Ansari Road, Darya Ganj, New Delhi-110002 and Printed by him at Manipal Technologies Limited, Manipal

www.bpbonline.com

Dedicated to

My Parents
(Late Dr. Shiv Swaroop Verma & Mrs. Swaroopi Verma)

My Grandson
(Dearest Atharv Verma)

My Teachers
And

All Learners

About the Author

S P Verma, M.Sc; M.Ed; PGCPM has been working in the field of education since last 35 years. As a seasoned educationist, teacher trainer, career counsellor, academic auditor, motivator, mentor, author and editor, he has authored 55 school books, 6 research papers, 10 research articles, more than 70 articles on career planning; and edited more than 200 educational products. More than 20k educators (teachers and principals) attended his training sessions across the country. More than 200k students were career counselled and inspired to take right career plan by him.

Formerly holding the positions like Principal, Kendriya Vidyalaya Sangathan, New Delhi; Regional Director, TeacherSity, New Delhi; Regional Director, iDC, New Delhi; and Director (School Trg), Vidya Institute of Training and Development, VKP, Meerut; he is now serving as Director (Trg and Innovation), GEM Foundatiions, Bengaluru. Besides Associate Life Member of **Computer Society of India** (CSI), he is associated with a number of professional bodies as Life Member, like Vigyan Parishad, Allahabad; Hindi Vigyan Sahitya Parishad, BARC, Mumbai; InSc, Bengaluru, PTAI, New Delhi, etc.

Acknowledgement

I would like to acknowledge the contributions of all the educationists (teachers and principals), professionals, and reviewers, who provided their feedback and suggestions on the MS of this book. Especially, I am grateful to **Mr. Pavnesh Kumar**, Former Controller of Examinations, CBSE; **Dr. Rajeev Chechi**, Director, Vidya College of Engineering; **Prof. RC Singh**, Controller of Examinations, Sharda University, Greater Noida; **Mr. Akshay Sharma**, B.Tech., ONGC, Mehsana; **Dr. A.K. Sharma**, Former Principal, KVS; **Mr. Shubham Verma**, B.Tech; MBA and Mrs. **Shweta Agrawal**, MCA for their specific suggestions.

It's my proud privilege to put on record my sincere gratitude to my publisher **M/s BPB Publications, New Delhi**, for accepting my vision and plan of writing AI Project books for classes IX and X and providing me the opportunity for the same. The initial interaction with **Mr. Manish Jain**, CEO, and **Mr. Varun Jain**, Director was fruitful in making a long-term association and bonding. I am grateful to them and the entire team of BPB Publications for bringing out these publications in a short span of time.

I am grateful to my well-wishers namely **Mr. RL Jamuda**, Former Commissioner KVS; **Dr. MM Swami**, Former Deputy Commissioner, KVS; **Mr. VK Gupta**, Former Deputy Commissioner, KVS; **Mr. DK Saini**, Former Deputy Commissioner, KVS; **Mr. SSL Agrawal**, Founder Director, MAV, Ahmedabad; **Mr. AK Verma,** CEO, Eduwix, New Delhi; **Mr. NK Verma,** AGM, BHEL HQ; **Mr. AK Pattnaik, Sr. GM** (Academic), Kalorex Group of Institutions, Ahmedabad; **Mr. Vipin Agrawal; Mr. Matin Ahmed, Mr. NK Giri, Mr. NK Bansal** and **Mr. SC Sharma** for their constant support, help and motivation to do something good to the society.

I am touched by the love, patience and tolerance shown, during the completion of this project, by my family members: **Mrs. Rekha Verma** (Life Partner), **Sqn Ldr Anuj Verma** (Son), **Atharv Verma** (Grandson) and **Mrs. Shelja Sharma**, B.Tech. (Daughter in Law). I am grateful to them as well as to all my friends and relatives supporting me in all the creative tasks.

While preparing the manuscript of this book, I have gone through a number of books and different websites. I am grateful to all those authors, contributors, editors, freelancers whose articles are read and used in one or another way in this book.

And last but not the least, I am indebted to God for keeping my brain alive and my health sound even at the time of the Covid Pandemic so that He could complete this task through me. He is the only DOER. Thank God for all the opportunities.

Preface

It gives me immense pleasure to put the first edition of **"Artificial Intelligence Projects and Practical Book for CLASS IX"** before the enthusiastic learners. Artificial intelligence is getting more attention in the world day by day. It touches almost all fields related to the development of the human race. AI Technology is changing at a very fast pace, and its applications in day-to-day life is also increasing exponentially. AI is now used in almost all fields, be it education, transport management, air traffic control, medicine manufacturing, space research, customer care, pandemic control, or entertainment.

After understanding the importance and demand of AI, the Govt of India, through CBSE, has launched Skills Development subjects, including Artificial Intelligence, in classes VI to XII. This book is written according to the latest syllabus of AI (code 417) as prescribed by CBSE. The main objective of writing this book is to provide technical knowledge with all practical aspects of AI and Basics of Python language to the learners so that they may become fully competent to face the challenges of living in an AI-based applications-equipped futuristic society. Moreover, emphasis on the development of 21st Century Life Skills is laid down through a variety of activities, practical and projects.

The book contains seven chapters and two annexures. The salient features of the book are:

- It is written by following the AI syllabus (code 417) as prescribed by CBSE.
- It explains the concepts of Python Advance with proper examples in lucid language.
- Simple, easy, and understandable language is used to clarify the content.
- It incorporates a pictorial setup in presenting the content by using tables, charts, graphs, pictures, photographs, etc.
- It illustrates a good number of Solved Python and Jupyter Coding problems with some unsolved problems too.
- It contains Viva questions as well as MCQs (Chapter wise).
- A special chapter for bright learners has been added.
- Activities and projects for inculcating 21st Century Life Skills, including creativity, innovation, critical thinking, team work, working in a diverse environment, etc., have been incorporated.
- Three Annexures providing extra useful information are annexed at the end of the book.

I am sure that the sincere efforts put in by the author and publication team will be well received by the dynamic, dedicated and passionate teachers, and energetic learners. The author will appreciate all sorts of feedback from the readers to improve the quality of the content.

15 November 2021 **SP Verma**

CURRICULUM/TOPICS FOR CLASS IX

	TERM	UNITS	NO. OF HOURS for Theory and Practical	MAX. MARKS for Theory and Practical
PART A	Employability Skills			
	TERM I	Unit 1: Communication Skills-I	10	5
		Unit 2: Self-Management Skills-I	10	
		Unit 3: ICT Skills-I	10	
	TERM II	Unit 4: Entrepreneurial Skills-I	15	5
		Unit 5: Green Skills-I	05	
		Total	50	10
PART B	**Subject Specific Skills**			
	TERM I	Unit 1: Introduction to Artificial Intelligence (AI)		10
		Unit 2: AI Project Cycle		10
	TERM II	Unit 3: Neural Network		5
		Unit 4: Introduction to Python		15
		Total		40
PART C		**Practical Work** • **Unit 4:** Introduction to Python		20
		Practical Examination		10
		Viva Voce		5
		Total		35
PART D		Project Work / Field Visit / Practical File/ Student Portfolio		10
		Viva Voce		5
		Total		15
		GRAND TOTAL	**200**	**100**

DETAILED CURRICULUM/TOPICS FOR CLASS IX

Part-A: EMPLOYABILITY SKILLS

S.No.	Units	Duration in Hours
1	Unit 1: Communication Skills-I	10
2	Unit 2: Self-management Skills-I	10
3	Unit 3: Basic Information and Communication Technology Skills-I	10
4	Unit 4: Entrepreneurial Skills-I	15
5	Unit 5: Green Skills-I	05
	TOTAL	**50**

Note: For Detailed Curriculum/ Topics to be covered under Part A: Employability Skills can be seen or downloaded from CBSE website.

Part-B: SUBJECT SPECIFIC SKILLS

Unit 1: Introduction to Artificial Intelligence (AI)

Unit 2: AI Project Cycle

Unit 3: Neural Network

Unit 4: Introduction To Python

UNIT 1: INTRODUCTION TO ARTIFICIAL INTELLIGENCE (AI)

Sub-Unit	Learning Outcomes	Session/ Activity/ Practical
Excite	To identify and appreciate Artificial Intelligence and describe its applications in daily life.	**Session:** Introduction to AI and setting up the context of the curriculum
		Ice Breaker Activity: Dream Smart Home idea • Learners to design a rough layout of floor plan of their dream smart home.
	To relate, apply and reflect on the Human-Machine Interactions. To identify and interact with the three domains of AI: Data, Computer Vision and Natural Language Processing.	**Recommended Activity:** The AI Game • Learners to participate in three games based on different AI domains. – Game 1: Rock, Paper and Scissors (based on data) – Game 2: Mystery Animal (based on Natural Language Processing - NLP) – Game 3: Emoji Scavenger Hunt (based on Computer Vision - CV)

	To undergo an assessment for analysing progress towards acquired AI-Readiness skills.	Recommended Activity: • AI Quiz (Paper Pen/Online Quiz)
	To imagine, examine and reflect on the skills required for futuristic job opportunities.	Recommended Activity: To write a letter. Writing a Letter to one's future self • Learners to write a letter to self-keeping the future in context. They will describe what they have learnt so far or what they would like to learn someday
Relate	Learners to relate to application of Artificial Intelligence in their daily lives.	Video Session: To watch a video • Introducing the concept of Smart Cities, Smart Schools and Smart Homes
	To unleash their imagination towards smart homes and build an interactive story around it. To relate, apply and reflect on the Human-Machine Interactions.	Recommended Activity: Write an Interactive Story • Learners to draw a floor plan of a Home/School/ City and write an interactive story around it using Story Speaker extension in Google docs.
Purpose	To understand the impact of Artificial Intelligence on Sustainable Development Goals to develop responsible citizenship.	Session: • Introduction to UN Sustainable Development Goals
		Recommended Activity: Go Goals Board Game • Learners to answer questions on Sustainable Development Goals
Possibilities	To research and develop awareness of skills required for jobs of the future. To imagine, examine and reflect on the skills required for the futuristic opportunities. To develop effective communication and collaborative work skills.	**Session:** Theme-based research and Case Studies • Learners will listen to various case-studies of inspiring start-ups, companies or communities where AI has been involved in real-life. • Learners will be allotted a theme around which they need to search for present AI trends and have to visualise the future of AI in and around their respective theme.
		Recommended Activity: Job Ad Creating activity • Learners to create a job advertisement for a firm describing the nature of job available and the skill set required for it 10 years down the line. They need to figure out how AI is going to transform the nature of jobs and create the Ad accordingly.

AI Ethics	To understand and reflect on the ethical issues around AI.	**Video Session:** Discussing about AI Ethics **Recommended Activity:** Ethics Awareness • Students play the role of major stakeholders, and they have to decide what is ethical and what is not for a given scenario.
	To gain awareness around AI bias and AI access.	**Session:** AI Bias and AI Access • Discussing about the possible bias in data collection • Discussing about the implications of AI technology
	To let the students analyse the advantages and disadvantages of Artificial Intelligence.	**Recommended Activity:** Balloon Debate • Students divide in teams of 3 and 2 teams are given same theme. One team goes in affirmation to AI for their section while the other one goes against it. • They have to come up with their points as to why AI is beneficial/ harmful for the society.

UNIT 2: AI PROJECT CYCLE

Sub-Unit	Learning Outcomes	Session/ Activity/ Practical
Problem Scoping	Identify the AI Project Cycle framework.	**Session:** Introduction to AI Project Cycle • Problem Scoping • Data Acquisition • Data Exploration • Modelling • Evaluation
	Learn problem scoping and ways to set goals for an AI project.	**Activity:** Brainstorm around the theme provided and set a goal for the AI project. • Discuss various topics within the given theme and select one. • List down/ Draw a mind map of problems related to the selected topic and choose one problem to be the goal for the project.
	Identify stakeholders involved in the problem scoped. Brainstorm on the ethical issues involved around the problem selected.	Activity: To set actions around the goal. • List down the stakeholders involved in the problem. • Search on the current actions taken to solve this problem. • Think around the ethics involved in the goal of your project.

	Understand the iterative nature of problem scoping for in the AI project cycle. Foresee the kind of data required and the kind of analysis to be done.	Activity: Data and Analysis • What are the data features needed? • Where can you get the data? • How frequent do you have to collect the data? • What happens if you don't have enough data? • What kind of analysis needs to be done? • How will it be validated? • How does the analysis inform the action?
	Share what the students have discussed so far.	Presentation: Presenting the goal, actions and data.
Data Acquisition	Identify data requirements and find reliable sources to obtain relevant data.	Activity: Introduction to data and its types. • Students work around the scenarios given to them and think of ways to acquire data.
Data Exploration	To understand the purpose of Data Visualisation	Session: Data Visualisation • Need of visualising data • Ways to visualise data using various types of graphical tools.
	Use various types of graphs to visualise acquired data.	Recommended Activity: Let's use Graphical Tools • To decide what kind of data is required for a given scenario and acquire the same. • To select an appropriate graphical format to represent the data acquired. • Presenting the graph sketched.
Modelling	Understand, create and Implement the concept of Decision Trees.	Session: Decision Tree • To introduce basic structure of Decision Trees to students.
		Recommended Activity: Decision Tree • To design a Decision Tree based on the data given.
	Understand and visualise computer's ability to identify alphabets and handwritings.	Recommended Activity: Pixel It • To create an "AI Model" to classify handwritten letters. • Students develop a model to classify handwritten letters by diving the alphabets into pixels. • Pixels are then joined together to analyse a pattern amongst same alphabets and to differentiate the different ones.

UNIT 3: NEURAL NETWORK

Learning Outcomes	Session/ Activity/ Practical
Understand and appreciate the concept of Neural Network through gamification.	Session: Introduction to neural network • Relation between the neural network and nervous system in human body • Describing the function of neural network.
	Recommended Activity: Creating a Human Neural Network • Students split in four teams each representing input layer (X students), hidden layer 1 (Y students), hidden layer 2 (Z students) and output layer (1 student) respectively. • Input layer gets data which is passed on to hidden layers after some processing. The output layer finally gets all information and gives meaningful information as output.

UNIT 4: INTRODUCTION TO PYTHON

Note: Python should be assessed through Practicals only and should not be assessed with the Theory Exam.

Learning Outcomes	Session/ Activity/ Practical
Learn basic programming skills through gamified platforms.	Recommended Activity: • Introduction to programming using Online Gaming portals like Code Combat.
Acquire introductory Python programming skills in a very user-friendly format.	Session: • Introduction to Python language • Introducing python programming and its applications
	Practical: Python Basics • Students go through lessons on Python Basics (Variables, Arithmetic Operators, Expressions, Data Types - integer, float, strings, using print() and input() functions) • Students will try some simple problem-solving exercises on Python Compiler.
	Practical: Python Lists • Students go through lessons on Python Lists (Simple operations using list) • Students will try some basic problem-solving exercises using lists on Python Compiler.

Downloading the code bundle and coloured images:

Please follow the link to download the
Code Bundle and the ***Coloured Images*** of the book:

https://rebrand.ly/4b71d4

Errata

We take immense pride in our work at BPB Publications and follow best practices to ensure the accuracy of our content to provide with an indulging reading experience to our subscribers. Our readers are our mirrors, and we use their inputs to reflect and improve upon human errors if any, occurred during the publishing processes involved. To let us maintain the quality and help us reach out to any readers who might be having difficulties due to any unforeseen errors, please write to us at:

errata@bpbonline.com

Your support, suggestions and feedbacks are highly appreciated by the BPB Publications' Family.

BPB is searching for authors like you

If you're interested in becoming an author for BPB, please visit **www.bpbonline.com** and apply today. We have worked with thousands of developers and tech professionals, just like you, to help them share their insight with the global tech community. You can make a general application, apply for a specific hot topic that we are recruiting an author for, or submit your own idea.

The code bundle for the book is also hosted on GitHub at **https://github.com/bpbpublications/Artificial-Intelligence-For-Class-9**. In case there's an update to the code, it will be updated on the existing GitHub repository.
We also have other code bundles from our rich catalog of books and videos available at **https://github.com/bpbpublications**. Check them out!

PIRACY

If you come across any illegal copies of our works in any form on the internet, we would be grateful if you would provide us with the location address or website name. Please contact us at **business@bpbonline.com** with a link to the material.

If you are interested in becoming an author

If there is a topic that you have expertise in, and you are interested in either writing or contributing to a book, please visit **www.bpbonline.com**.

REVIEWS

Please leave a review. Once you have read and used this book, why not leave a review on the site that you purchased it from? Potential readers can then see and use your unbiased opinion to make purchase decisions, we at BPB can understand what you think about our products, and our authors can see your feedback on their book. Thank you!

For more information about BPB, please visit **www.bpbonline.com**.

Contents

1 Concepts of Python Basics

Structure

In this chapter, you will learn:

- Basics of Python
- Run Python for making some code/programs

Introduction

The usage of AI -based devices and applications is increasing by leaps and bound throughout the world. It is clear now that AI will play a crucial role in shaping future global digital economy. AI in the recent few years has gained popularity and geostrategic importance whereas the use of AI-based devices has also been increased many folds in many countries. Many simple and complex problems can be solved by using AI. India identifies AI as an opportunity and solution provider for many complex problems and inclusive economic growth and social development; and more efforts are putting in to develop more skilled manpower in the field of AI and Data Sciences.

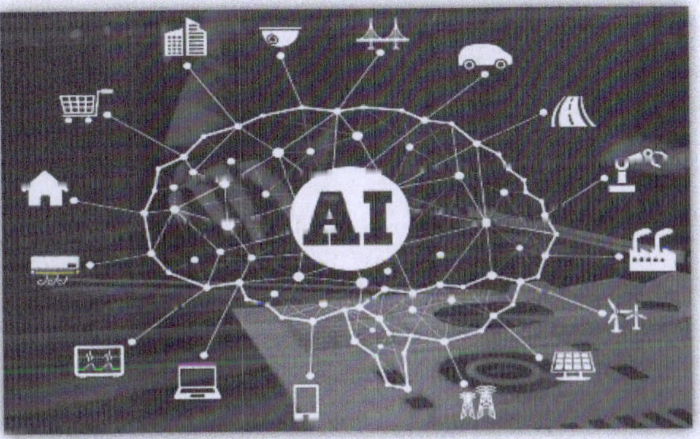

Figure 1.1

Learning Objectives

At the end of this chapter, you will be able to:

- Learn basic programming skills through gamified platforms.
- Acquire introductory Python programming skills in a very user-friendly format.
- Hands- on experience running Python codes.

Python is considered as an OOPs (Object-Oriented Programs) based programming language in many areas, like AI, video games, etc. Moreover, it is a high-level and interpreted programming language. It is a highly useful language that is focused on two principles: Rapid Application Development (RAD) and Don't Repeat Yourself (DRY). It works to connect existing components together. Because of the ease of learning, scalability, and adaptability of Python, it has become one of the fastest-growing languages. Python's support and ever-evolving libraries make it one of the best choices for all sorts of projects, like Web App, Mobile App, IoT, Data Science, AI, etc.

Session 1: Python Basics

Many programming languages are used nowadays whereas Python is gaining momentum for becoming number one programming language due to its many features and specific characteristics. The learning and usage of Python is easy and simple.

1.1 Basic concepts of Python

A programming/coding language is a language that specifies a set of instructions that can be used to produce various kinds of output. In simple words, a programming language is a vocabulary and set of grammatical rules for instructing a computer to perform specific tasks. There are many programming languages, like BASIC, Pascal, C, C++, Java, Haskell, Ruby, Python, etc., but here we will focus on Python only.

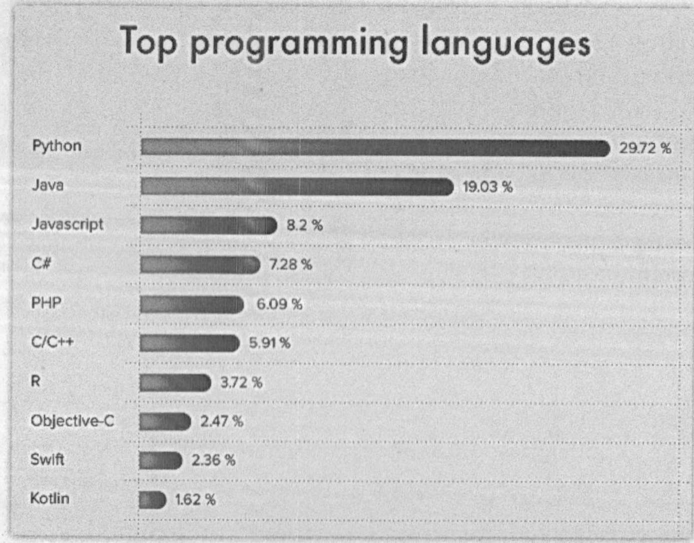

Figure 1.2: *Popular coding languages 2021*

(**Source:** https://www.cleveroad.com/blog/programming-languages-ranking)

1.1.1 What is a program?

A collection of instructions to perform a specific task when executed by a computer is called a program. It is usually written in a specific programming language, like Python. Software development requires many tasks to be incorporated to follow an organised plan and a series of sub-tasks in a well-defined chronological order. The ABCD Rule is followed to better understand the intermediate steps of a computer program before documentation.

A: Analysing the problem:

- Read and understand the basic functionalities of the problem carefully.
- List the inputs required.
- List the required calculations to get the desired output.

B: Broadcasting the developed algorithm:

- Plan all the actions required and their sequence before writing a program.
- Use English language to write a program.

C: Coding the program:

- Convert the plan into the algorithm that is understood by the computer.
- Use a language out of available many programming languages, like C, C++, Java, Python, etc.

D: Testing and debugging the program

- Test the program by giving various inputs and check the outputs for correctness.
- Analyse the syntax errors, if any (No output in case of syntax error in the program)
- Correct the errors logically if the outputs are incorrect.

D: Documentation of the program

1.1.2 Algorithms

In computers, an algorithm means the process required for planning and solving the problems. A sequence of steps to solve any particular problem is called an algorithm. The word "Algorithm" is also related to the name of the mathematician Al-Khwarizmi, which means a procedure or a technique. The pseudocode in computer science is a plain language description of all the steps of an algorithm.

Factz Funda

A recipe is a good example of an algorithm because it describes what must be done, step by step. It takes inputs (ingredients) and produces an output (the completed dish).

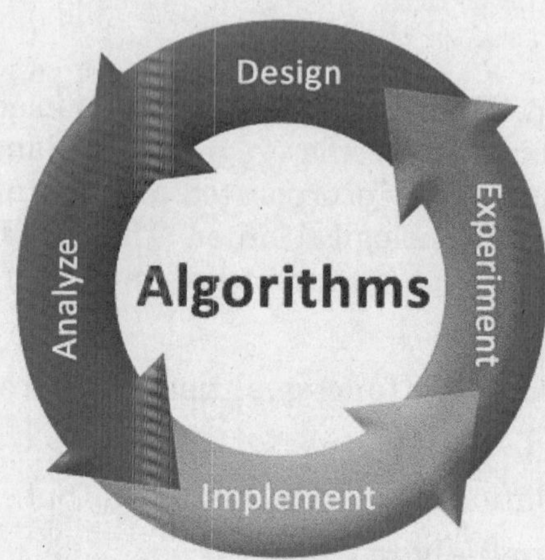

Figure 1.3

1.1.2.1 Types of control structures of an algorithm

An algorithm includes the following three types of control structures:

a. **Sequence**: In coding/programming, sequence means to place statements one after the other in order, and the execution of the program takes place starting from top to bottom.

b. **Branching (Selection)**: There is some condition in-branch control, and as per the condition, a decision of either TRUE or FALSE is evaluated. In the case of the TRUE condition, one out of the two given options is mentioned, while in the case of the FALSE condition, the other alternative is used.

c. **Loop (Repetition)**: The Loop or Repetition control allows a statement(s) to be executed repeatedly a number of times based on certain loop conditions, like WHILE, FOR loops.

1.1.2.2 Steps to write algorithms

Step 1: **Define the inputs for the algorithm:** Define the inputs required for the algorithm. Various algorithms take in data for processing. For example, while calculating the area of a circle, input will be the radius.

Step 2: **Define the variables:** Variables in an algorithm may be used by the user for more than one place, and hence, variables are to be defined. While calculating the area and circumference of a circle, we need to define radius (variable).

Step 3: **Outline the algorithm's operations:** Outlining the operations of the algorithm is required to input variables for computation purposes. For example, to find the area of a circle, multiply the value of pie (3.14) with radius * radius is defined.

Step 4: **Output the results of the operations of the algorithm:** Outline the result(s) of the operations of the algorithm. In the case of the area of a circle, the output will be the value stored in the variable AREA.

1.1.3 Flowchart

A flowchart is a programming tool that uses different symbols to design a solution to a problem. The first design of a flowchart was given away by John Von Neumann in 1945. A flowchart is often considered as a blueprint of a design used for solving any specific problem.

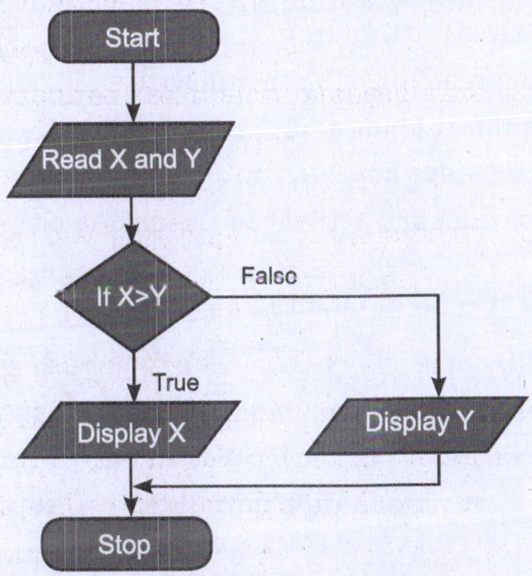

***Figure 1.4:** Flowchart*

To draw a flowchart, various standard symbols as enlisted in Table 1.1 are used.

***Table 1.1:** Standard symbols used in the flowchart*

Symbol Name	Symbol	Function
(i) Oval		Used to represent the start and the end of flowchart.
(ii) Rectangle		Processing: Used for arithmetic operations and data-manipulations.
(iii) Diamond		Decision-making: Used to represent the operation in which there are two/three alternatives, true and false etc.
(iv) Circle		Page connector.
(v) Parallelogram		Used for input and output operation.
(vi) Arrows		Flowline is used to indicate the flow of logic by connecting symbols.

1.1.3.1 Characteristics of a flowchart

- It represents a workflow or process in a diagrammatic representation.
- It consists of standardised and acceptable symbols.
- It exhibits the sequence of instructions/happenings in a single program.
- It shows the logic of an algorithm from start to end.
- It has short, clear, and readable statements written inside the symbols.
- It should have a clear start point and End/Finish point.
- It shows the individual steps and their interconnections.
- It exhibits the control from one activity to the next one.

Steps for drawing flowchart

- Input to the flowchart
- Type of process required
- Decision to be taken
- The output to be produced after processing

Input:

Input means taking data from the user. It is important to know, how many and what type of Inputs are required.

Processing:

It is used for performing calculations and storing the results of calculation. These may include increasing/decreasing a value.

Figure 1.5

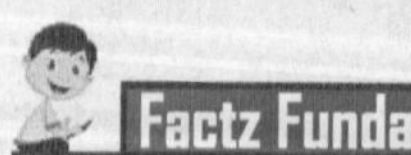

Google algorithms are changed almost 500 times per year.

1.1.3.2 Advantages of flowchart

- The flowchart shows the logic of a program in a simple way.
- It is easy and efficient to analyse the problem using a flowchart.
- The flowchart makes program or system maintenance easier.
- It is easy to convert the flowchart into any programming language code.
- A flowchart is a diagrammatic/graphical representation of a sequence of steps to solve a problem.

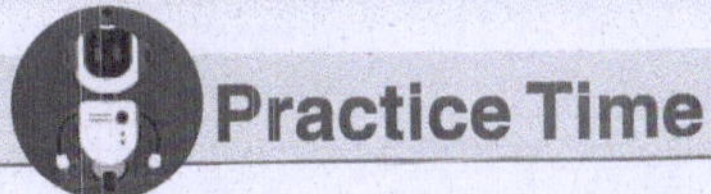

Practice Time

1. Write an algorithm and draw its Flowchart to find the average of three numbers.

   (a) **Algorithm**

   Step1: Start

   Step 2: Input the first number, say A

   Step 3: Input second number, say B

   Step 4: Input third number, say C

   Step 5: Average = (A + B+C)/3

   Step 6: Print Average

   Step 7: Stop

   (b) **Flowchart**

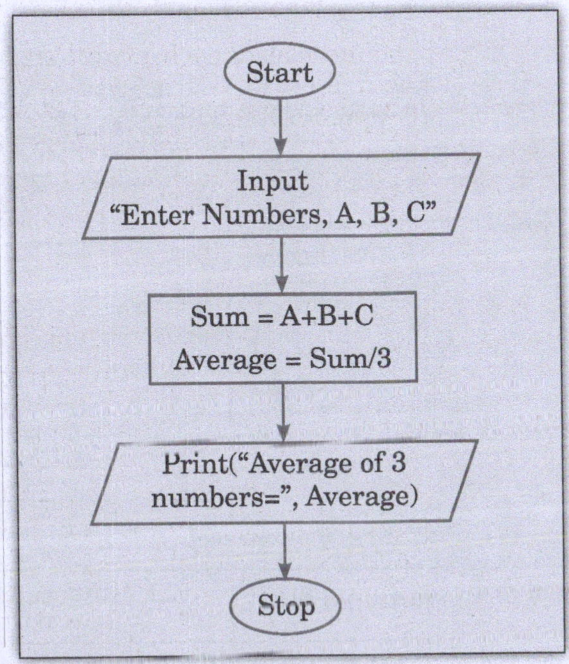

Figure 1.6

2. Write an algorithm and draw its Flowchart to convert feet into centimeters.

   (a) **Pseudocode**

   1. Input the length in feet (Lft).
   2. Process the conversion of feet into centimeters by multiplying Lft with 30.
   3. Print length in centimeters (Lcm).

(b) **Algorithm**

Step1: Start

Step 2: Input the length in feet, say Lft.

Step 3: Lcm = Lft*30

Step 4: Print Lcm

Step 5: Stop

(c) **Flowchart**

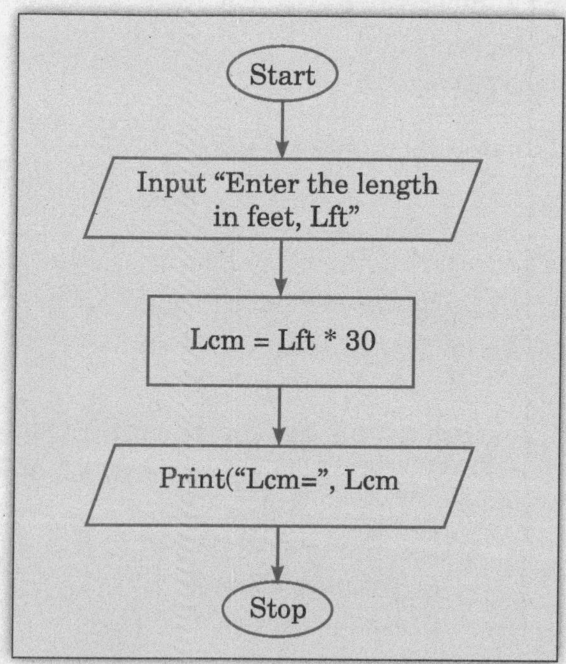

Figure 1.7

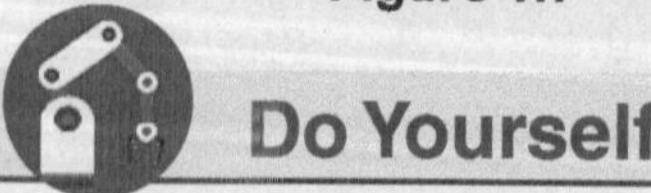

1. Write an algorithm and draw its Flowchart to convert temperature from degree Celsius to degree Fahrenheit.
2. Write an algorithm and draw its flowchart to calculate the Grade (average of marks of five subjects out of 100 maximum marks of a student) and Print PASS in case of getting Grade 35 or more or Print Fail in case of getting Grade less than 35.

1.1.4 What is Python?

Artificial intelligence is nowadays regarded as the future technology of the world. We can see so many AI-Based applications around us that are used by a large number of people daily. If we wish to develop an AI application, then we shall require to know a programming language.

The different programming languages, like Lisp, Prolog, C++, Java, and Python, can be used for developing applications of AI. Python has become a widely used computer programming language nowadays.

Figure 1.8: Python logo

Python is an object-oriented programming language that was created by Guido Rossum in 1989. It is ideally designed for rapid prototyping of complex applications. It has interfaces to many OS system and libraries and is extensible to C or C++. So many large companies like NASA, Google, YouTube, BitTorrent, etc., use the Python programming language.

Python programming is widely used in Artificial Intelligence, Natural Language Generation, Neural Networks, Data Science, and other advanced fields of Computer Science. Python had deep focus on code readability.

1.1.4.1 Features and characteristics of Python

Python has the following important features and characteristics:

a. Python is a case-sensitive language. 'A' and 'a' in Python are different and carry not the same meaning.
b. Python is Interpreted. Python is processed at runtime by the interpreter. The user does not need to compile our program before executing it.
c. Python is Interactive that allows interacting testing and debugging of snippets of code. We can actually work at Python prompt and interact with the interpreter directly to write our programs.
d. Python is Object-Oriented. Python supports Object-Oriented style or technique programming that encapsulates code within objects.
e. Python provides rich data types and easier to read syntax than any other programming languages
f. Python is a very simple high-level language with a vast library of add-on modules.
g. Learning and using Python is easy.
h. Python is a platform independent scripted language with full access to operating system API's.
i. As compared to other programming languages, Python allows more run-time flexibility.
j. Python programs are easily readable and understandable.

k. Python is portable.
l. A module in Python may contain one or more classes and free functions.
m. For building large applications, Python can be compiled to byte-code.
n. Python codes are short.
o. In Python, editing, debugging and testing is fast.

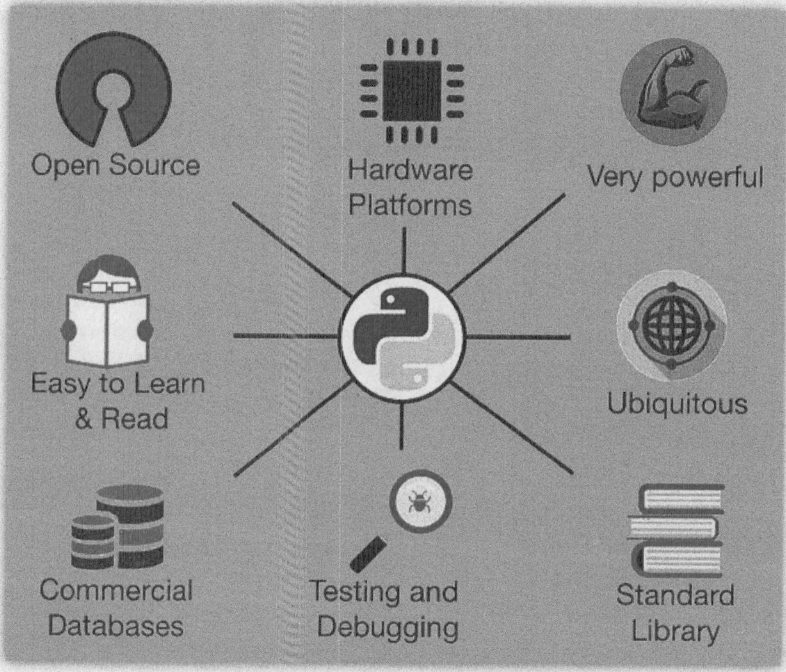

Figure 1.9: Python features

1.1.5 Python and AI

Various programming languages, like Lisp, Prolog, C++, Java, Python, etc., are used for developing applications of AI.

Out of these languages, Python gains maximum popularity because of the following reasons:

a. **Less Code**: Python helps in the easy writing and execution of codes. It is capable of implementing the same logic with about 1/5th of code as compared to other coding (OOPs) languages. The interpreted approach of Python enables check as you code methodology.

b. **Platform Independence**: Python provides the flexibility to provide an API from an existing language which indeed provides extreme flexibility. It is also platform-independent. With just a few changes in codes, we can get our app up and running in a new OS. This saves developers time in testing on different platforms and migrating code.

c. **Prebuilt Libraries**: Python has a number of libraries required for every AI project. Few examples include NumPy for scientific computation, SciPy for advanced computing, and PyBrain for machine learning.

d. **Flexibility:** Flexibility is one of the salient advantages of Python. With the option to choose between the OOPs approach and scripting, Python is suitable for every purpose. It works as a perfect backend and is also suitable for linking different data structures altogether. The option to check the validity of code in the IDLE is also a big plus point for developers who are struggling between different algorithms.

e. **Support**: Python is an open-source resource with a great community. The host of resources available can get any developer to speed up in no time. Also, there is a huge community of active coders willing to help programmers in every stage of the developing cycle.

f. **Popularity**: Python is winning the heart of millions of people. Its ease of learning is attracting millions of people. It is practically easier to find Python developers than LISP or Prolog programmers. Its extended libraries and active community have led it to be one of the best languages today.

***Table 1.2:** Reasons for selection of python for AI projects*

- Availability of packages like NumPy, Matplotlib, Scikit-learn, IPython Notebook to form the basis to start the AI project
- Flexibility
- Readability
- A great AI library ecosystem, like AIMA, Simple AI, Open CV, Easy AI, etc.
- A low entry barrier
- The least code
- Platform independence
- NLTK modules for natural language processing and text analytics
- Good visualisation options
- Community support
- Growing popularity

***Figure 1.10:** Some famous companies that use Python*

1.1.6 Applications of Python

Python is used for a large number of applications. Some of them are mentioned below:

- Web and Internet Development
- Desktop GUI Applications
- Build Artificial Intelligence algorithms
- Business Applications
- Software Development
- Program video games
- 3D Graphics
- Database Access
- Programs: various scientific programs such as statistical models

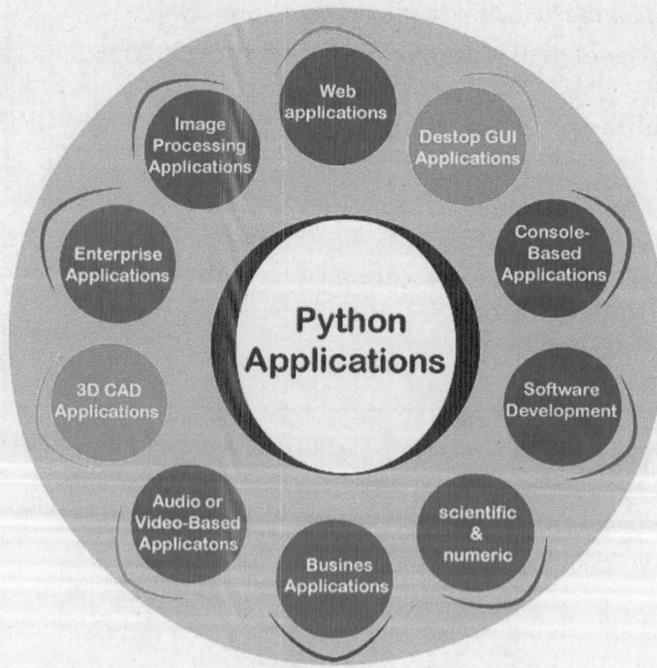

Figure 1.11: *Python applications*

Activity 1.1

Learning programming through Gaming

Introduction to programming using Online Gaming portals like Code Combat. Learners will go through the following link and will play few games online to understand the Code Combat games:

https://www.game-accessibility.com/game/

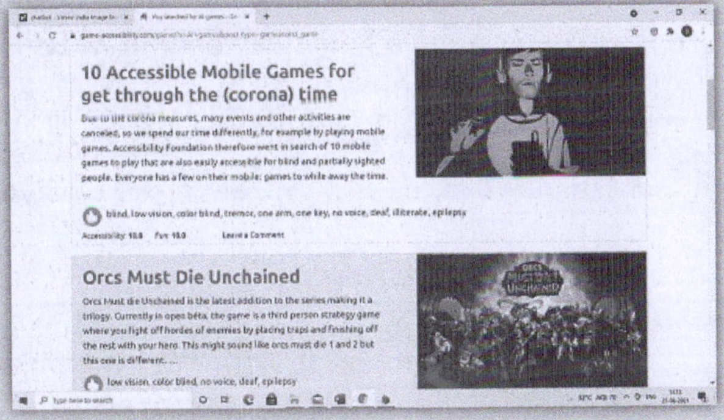

Figure 1.12

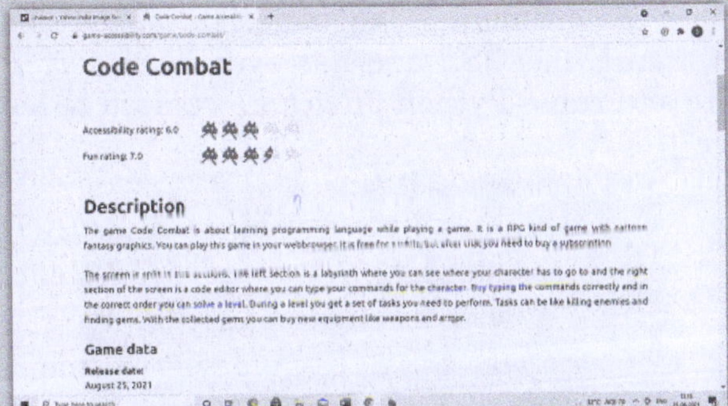

Figure 1.13

The game Code Combat is about learning programming language while playing a game. It is an RPG kind of game with cartoon fantasy graphics. You can play this game in your web browser. It is free for a while, but after that, you need to buy a subscription.

The screen is split into two sections. The left section is a labyrinth where you can see where your character has to go, and the right section of the screen is a code editor where you can type your commands for the character. By typing the commands correctly and in the correct order, you can solve a level. During a level, you get a set of tasks you need to perform. Tasks can be like killing enemies and finding gems. With the collected gems you can buy new equipment like weapons and armour.

How to play?

There is a restricted set of controls you can use to move the character (e.g. self.moveUp (), self.moveLeft(), self.attack, (self.findNearestEnemy()), etc.). You need to type the commands in the correct order on the editor screen. When you run the program you created, you will see your character move through the level in the order you typed the commands. When there is a program error, or you made a wrong order of commands, you will lose lives or die. During the progress of the game, the user will learn new ways to type commands, create loops and logic operators.

Unfortunately, this game cannot be played with a visual/physical/auditory disability. You need to see where the character has to go in order to solve a level.

This game can be hard to play if you have a learning disability. But the whole idea of this game is to learn a programming language in a fun way. Everything the user need to do in this game is explained well, and you can try commands with a trial-and-error method to see if your code is correct.

Gamification is the usage of game concepts in a non-gaming environment.

1.1.7 Getting started with Python

Python is a cross-platform programming language. It means that it runs on multiple platforms, like Windows, Linux, macOS, and has even been ported to the Java and .NET virtual machines. To write and run a Python program, we need to have a Python interpreter installed on our computer.

Figure 1.14: *Chatbot-An application of Python*

Downloading and Setting up Python for use:

Download Python from python.org using link www.python.org/downloads/

Select appropriate download link as per Operating System [Windows 32 Bit/64 Bit, Apple iOS]

For Example:

For Windows 64 Bit OS, select the following link:

https://www.python.org/downloads/windows/

Download Windows x86-64 executable installer

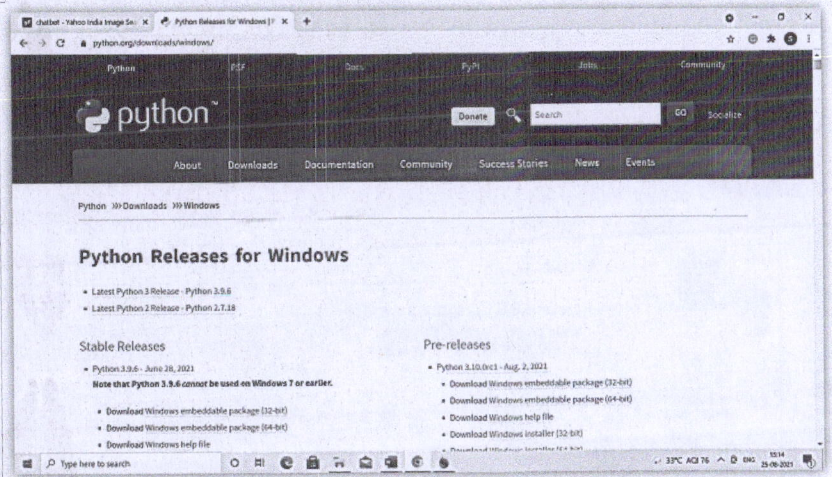

Figure 1.15

1.1.8 Python IDLE installation

Python IDLE installation is done by following the steps as shown here:

Figure 1.16

1.1.8.1 Run in the Integrated Development Environment (IDE)

When we install Python, an IDE named IDLE is also installed. We can use it to run Python on our computers. IDE (GUI integrated) is the standard and the most popular Python development environment. IDE is an acronym for Integrated Development Environment. It allows the user to edit, browse, run, and debug Python Programs from a single interface. This type of arrangement makes it easier to write programs. Python shell can be used in either of two ways: interactive mode and script mode. Interactive Mode allows the user to interact with OS, while script mode create and edit Python source files.

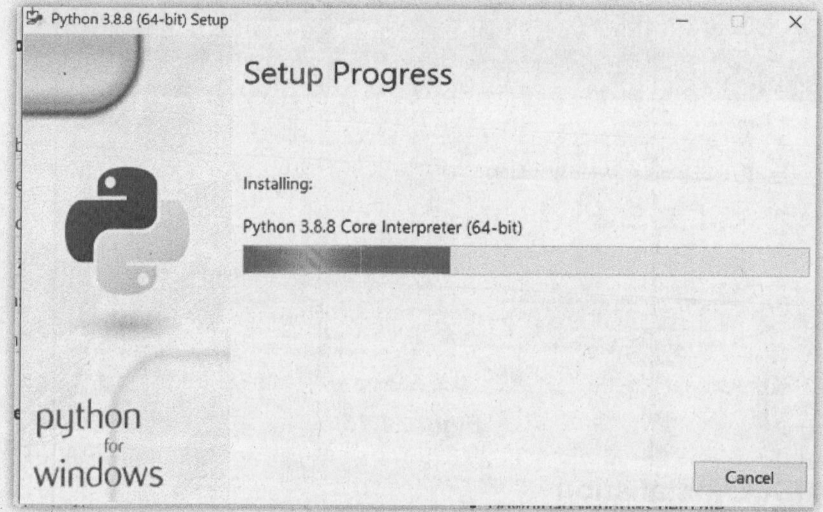

Figure 1.17

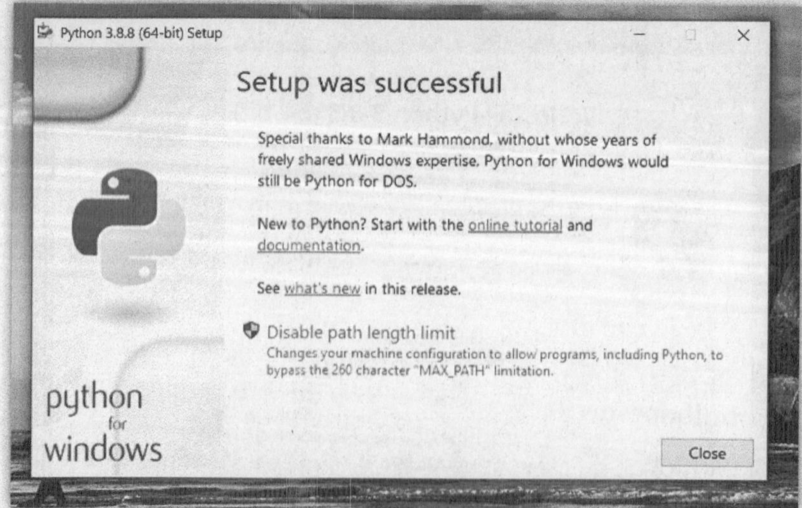

Figure 1.18

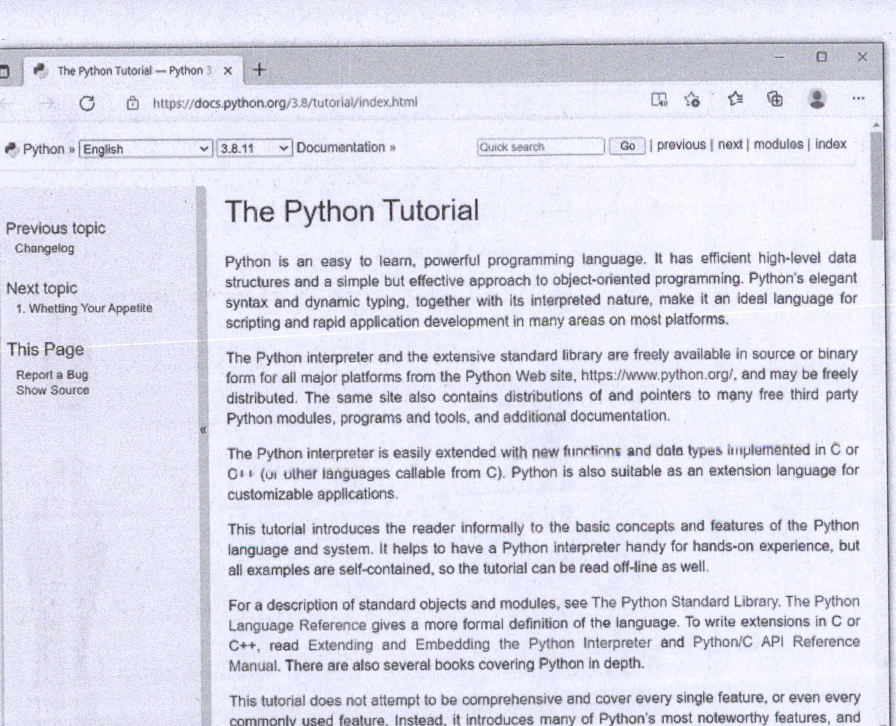

Figure 1.19

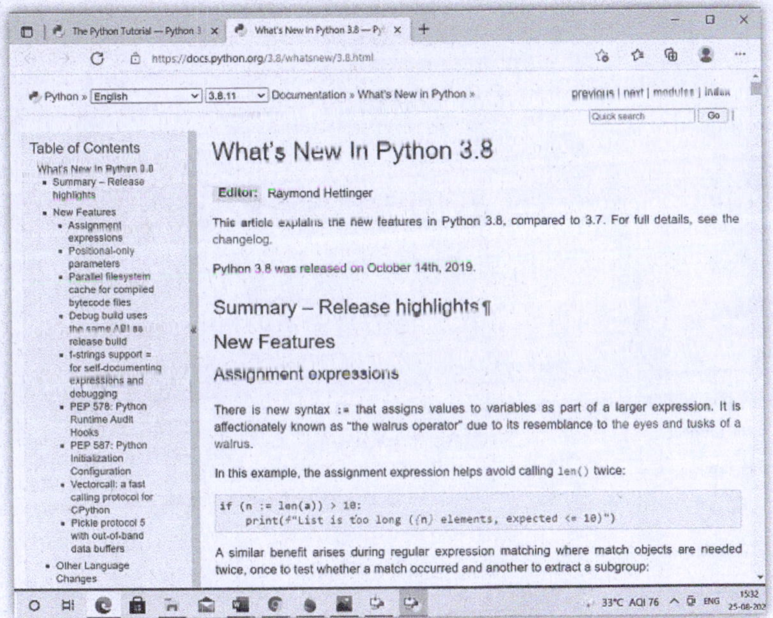

Figure 1.20

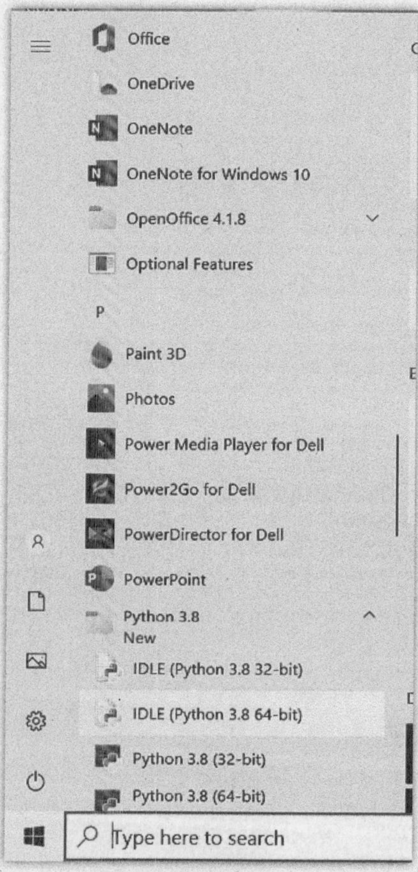

Figure 1.21

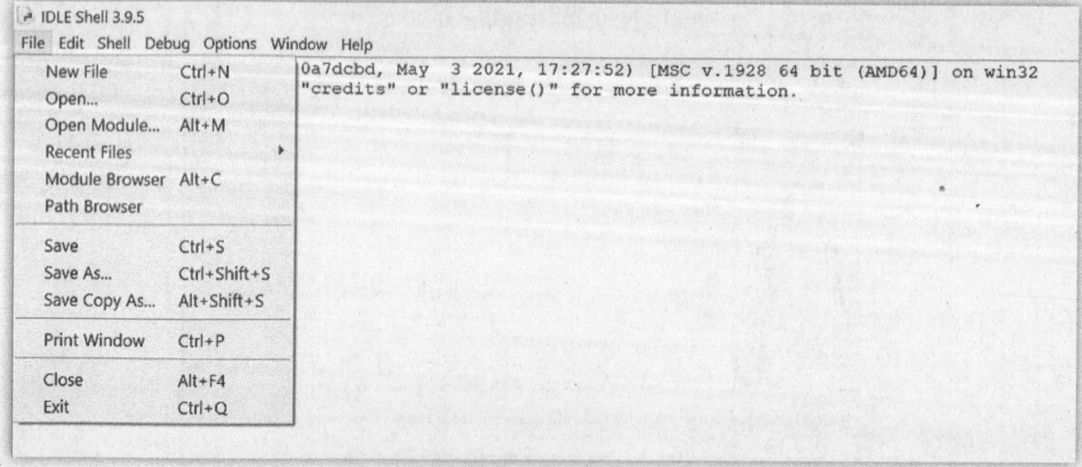

Figure 1.22

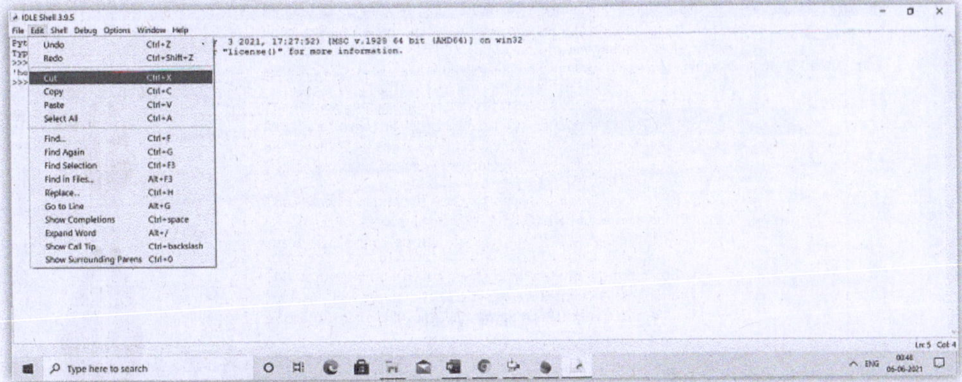

Figure 1.23

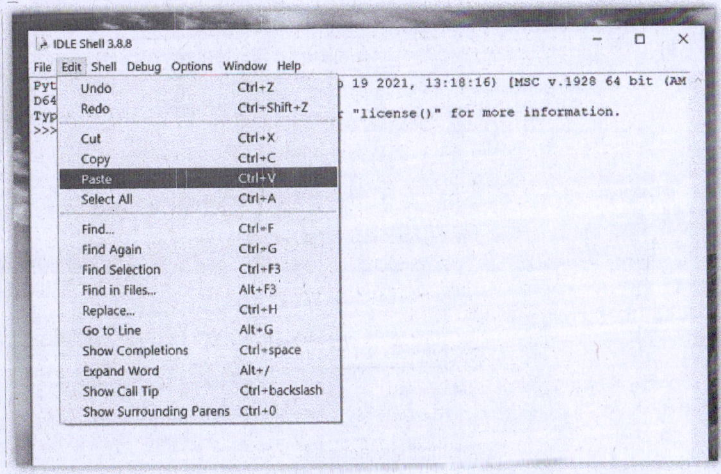

Figure 1.24

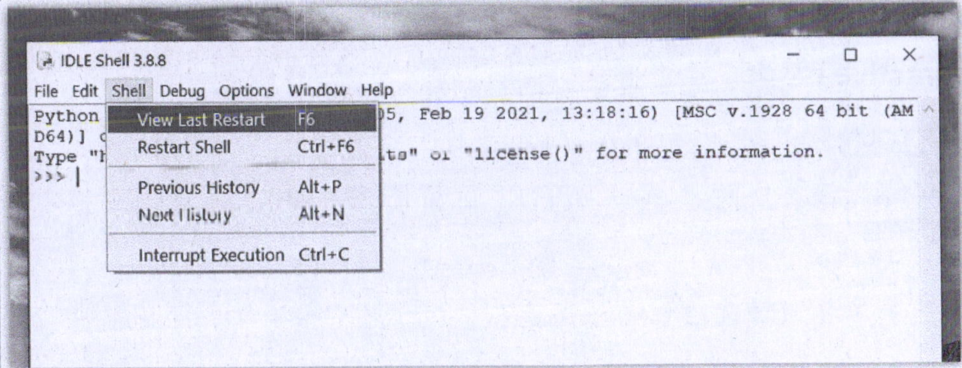

Figure 1.25

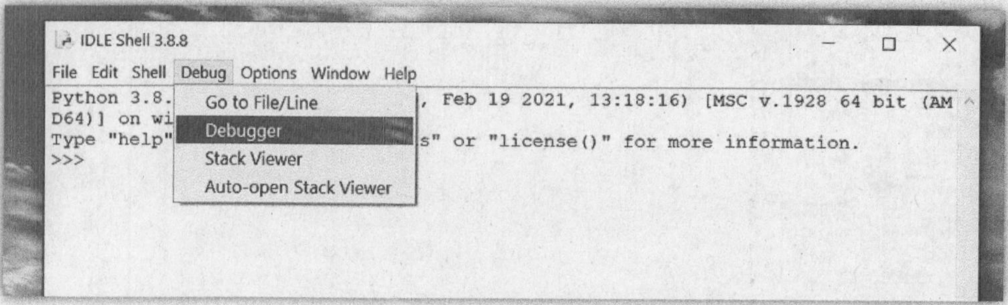

Figure 1.26

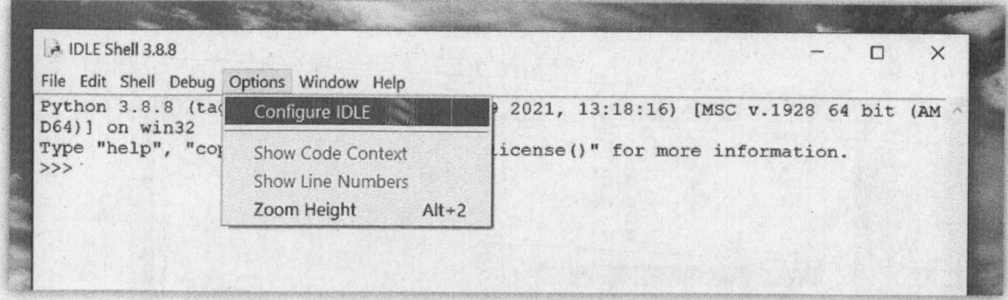

Figure 1.27

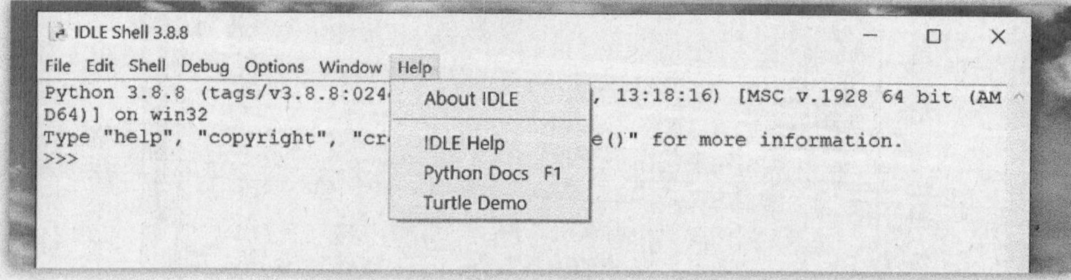

Figure 1.28

1.1.9 Interactive mode

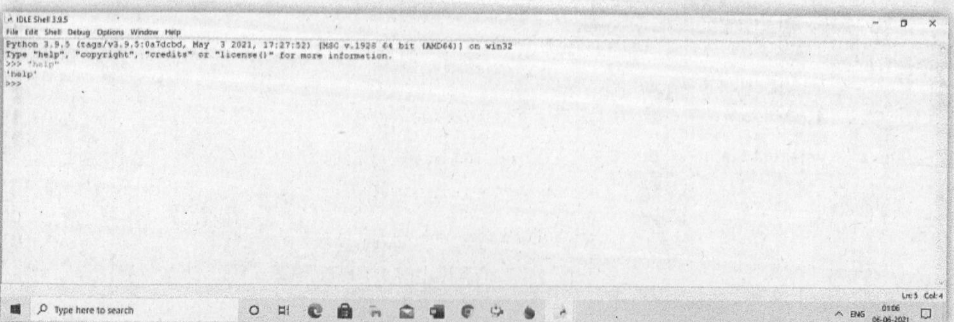

Figure 1.29: *Interactive mode programming*

Python IDLE Shell account has >>> as Python prompt, where simple mathematical expressions and single-line Python commands can be written and can be executed simply by pressing enter.

Practice Time

1. Write the following expressions one by one and press enter after writing each command to get the result.

   Expression 1: 14+614

   Expression 2: 4+6*2

   Expression 3: "Hello, dear friend"

   Expression 4: print("Result:" 8+3*9)

   Expression 5: print("Result:" 15+16*5)

   Expression 6: print("Result:" 4+6*5)

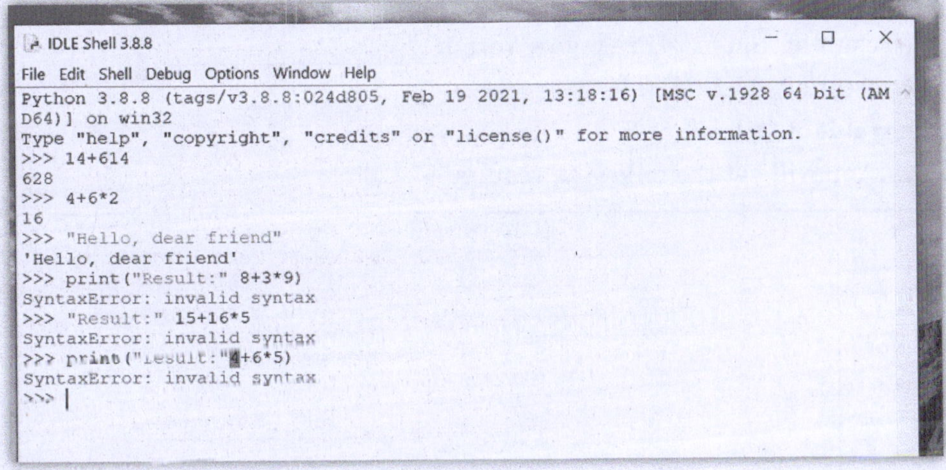

Figure 1.30

The first expression, 14+614 written on the first Python prompt, shows 628 as output in the next line. The second expression 4+6*2 written on the second Python prompt shows 16 as output in the next line. The third statement print("Hello, dear friend") written on the third Python prompt shows Hello, dear friend as output in the next line. The fourth statement print("Result:" 8+3*9) written on the fourth Python prompt, the fifth statement print("Result:" 15+16*5) written on the fifth Python prompt and the sixth statement print("Result:" 4+6*5) written on the sixth Python prompt shows invalid syntax.

Testing Time

1. What is algorithm?
2. Define a flowchart.
3. What do you mean by pseudocode?
4. Which geometrical figure is used to represent an output in a flowchart?
5. Discuss the important characteristics of Python.
6. Name three programming languages.
7. Python is used in making AI programs. Justify the statement.

Do Yourself (Use Python 3.8.3 Shell)

1. Find the multiplication and average of two numbers, 95 and 15.
2. Find the circumference of a circle having a radius (r) of 14 cm (use the formula Area of circle=2*22/7 *r).
3. Find the result of "Satya"+"Prakash+"Verma"."
4. Find the result of "&&&&" + 4
5. Find the result of "&&&&" * 3

Answers: You will get the following results:

```
IDLE Shell 3.8.8
File Edit Shell Debug Options Window Help
Python 3.8.8 (tags/v3.8.8:024d805, Feb 19 2021, 13:18:16) [MSC v.1928 64 bit (AMD64)] on win32
Type "help", "copyright", "credits" or "license()" for more information.
>>> 95*15
1425
>>> (95+15)/2
55.0
>>> 2*22/7*14
88.0
>>> "Satya"+"Prakash"+"Verma"
'SatyaPrakashVerma'
>>> "&&&&"+4
Traceback (most recent call last):
  File "<pyshell#4>", line 1, in <module>
    "&&&&"+4
TypeError: can only concatenate str (not "int") to str
>>> "&&&&"*3
'&&&&&&&&&&&&'
>>> |
```

Figure 1.31

Factz Funda

A list of human-readable instructions that any programmer writes during the development of a program is called source code. A compiler is used to run a source code to convert it into machine code so that it might understood by a computer.

1.1.10 Script mode

In script mode, we type the Python program in a file and then use the interpreter to execute the content from the file. Working in an interactive mode is convenient for beginners and for testing small pieces of code. But for coding more than few lines, we should always save our code so that we may modify and reuse the code.

The result produced by an interpreter in both the modes, viz., Interactive and script mode, is exactly the same.

1.1.11 Python script/program

Python statements written in a particular sequence to solve a problem are known as Python Script/Program.

To write a Python script/program, we need to open a new file - File >> New File, type a sequence of Python statements for solving a problem, save it with a meaningful name - File >> Save, and finally, Run the program to view the output of the program.

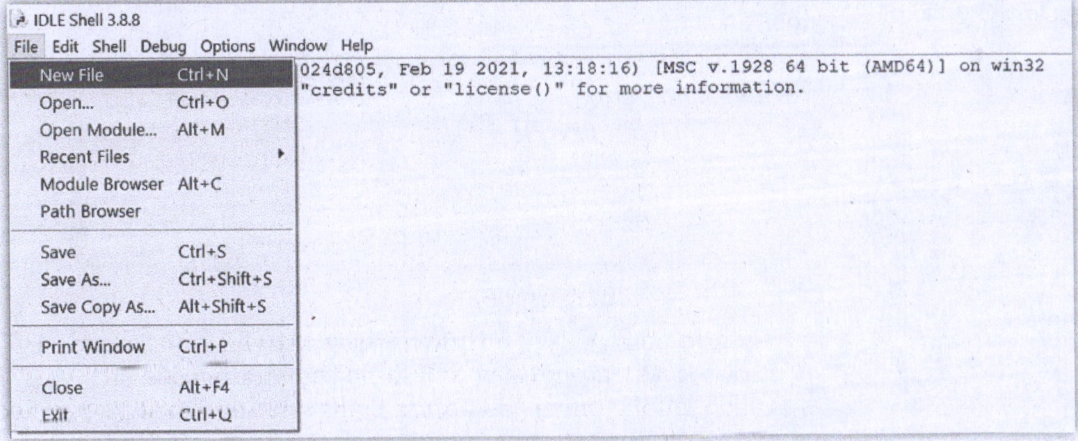

Figure 1.32

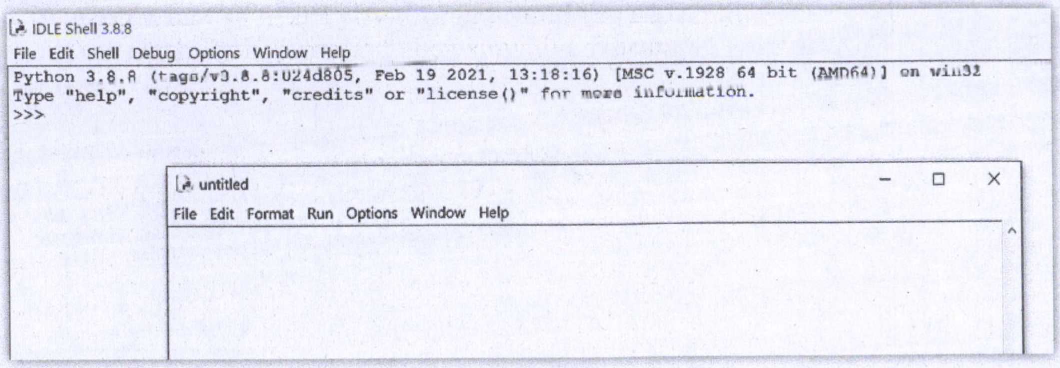

IDLE Shell 3.8.8
File Edit Shell Debug Options Window Help
Python 3.8.8 (tags/v3.8.8:024d805, Feb 19 2021, 13:18:16) [MSC v.1928 64 bit (AMD64)] on win32
Type "help", "copyright", "credits" or "license()" for more information.
>>>
untitled
File Edit Format Run Options Window Help

Figure 1.33

py.1 - D:/BPB projects 2021/IX AI Projects book/source code for python programs/py.1 (3.8.8)

File Edit Format Run Options Window Help

```
n1=23
n2=43
n3=76
sum=n1+n2+n3
print("Sum of three numbers=",sum)
```

Figure 1.34

Figure 1.35

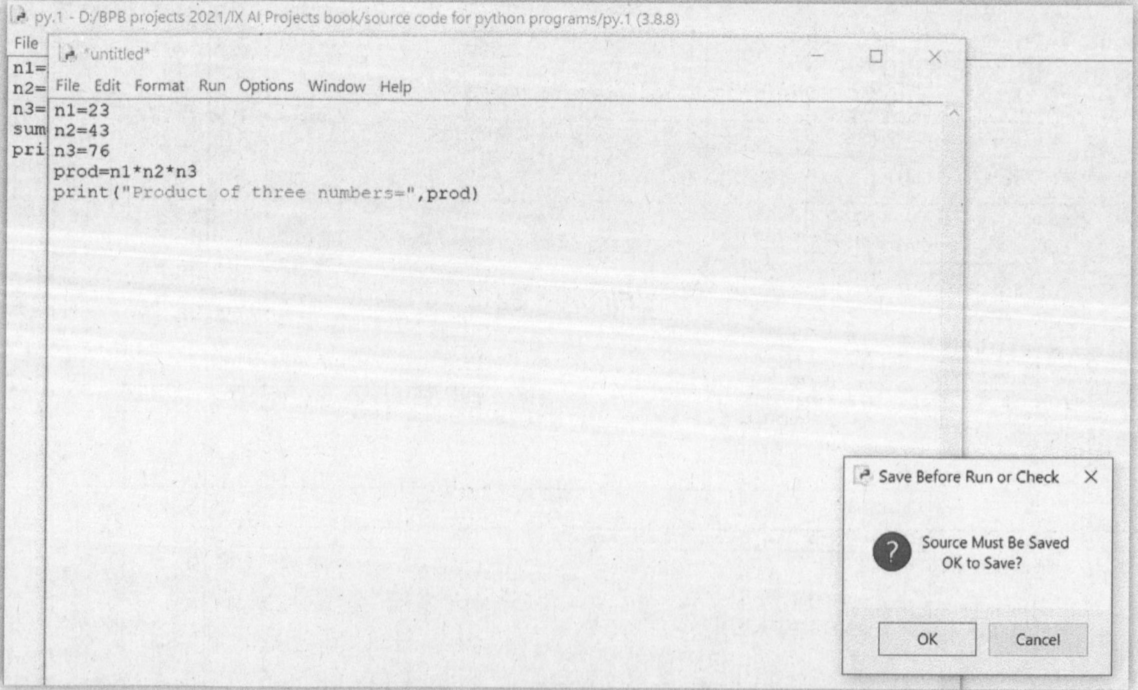

Figure 1.36

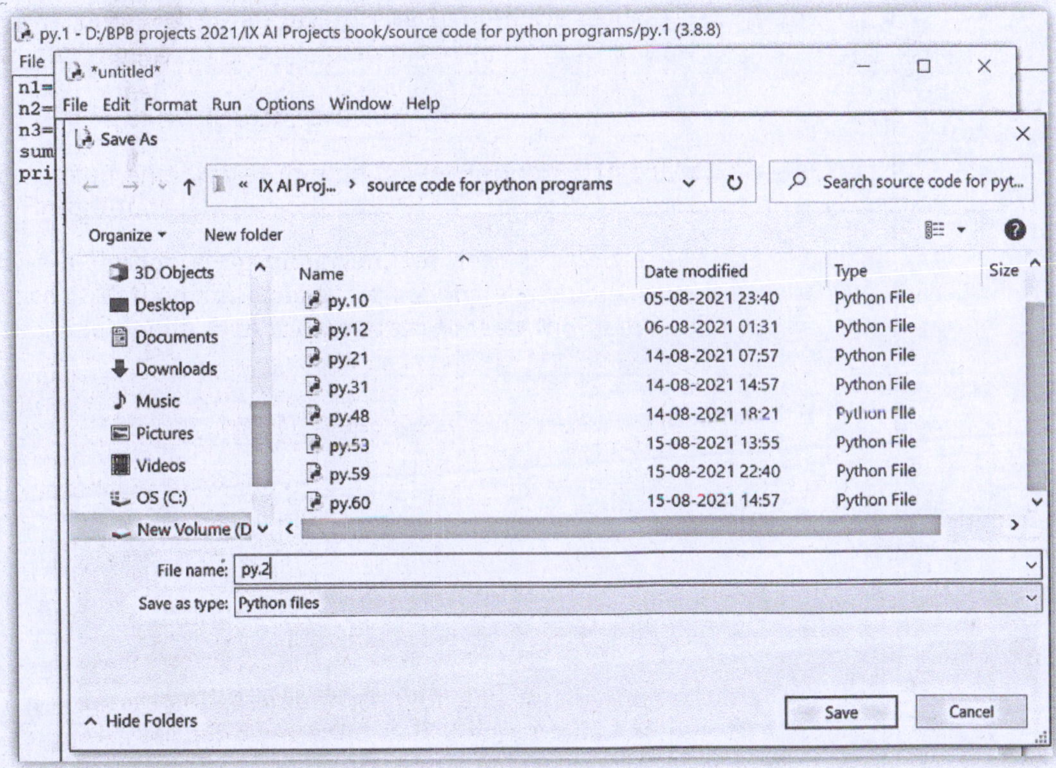

Figure 1.37

py.1 - D:/BPB projects 2021/IX AI Projects book/source code for python programs/py.1 (3.8.8)

File Edit Format Run Options Window Help

```
n1=23
n2=43
n3=76
sum=n1+n2+n3
print("Sum of three numbers=",sum)
```

IDLE Shell 3.8.8

File Edit Shell Debug Options Window Help

```
Python 3.8.8 (tags/v3.8.8:024d805, Feb 19 2021, 13:18:16) [MSC v.1928 64 bit (AM
D64)] on win32
Type "help", "copyright", "credits" or "license()" for more information.
>>>
= RESTART: D:/BPB projects 2021/IX AI Projects book/source code for python progr
ams/py.1
Sum of three numbers= 142
>>>
```

Figure 1.38

Now, type and run your first Python Program.

(*For example:* Find the product of four numbers. You may have the following program and output. Change the numbers as you want to make new program and then run it.)

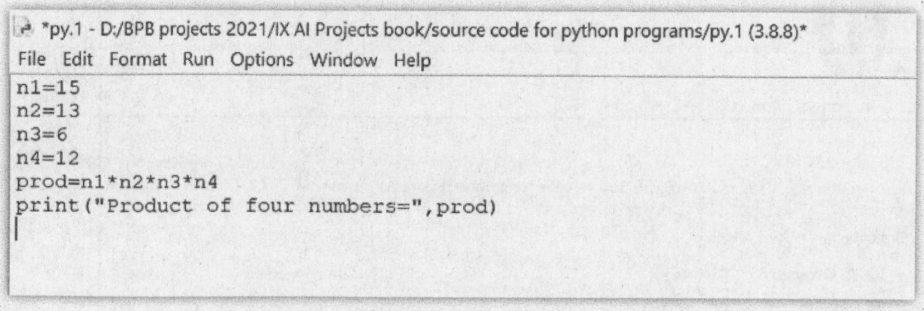

```
*py.1 - D:/BPB projects 2021/IX AI Projects book/source code for python programs/py.1 (3.8.8)*
File Edit Format Run Options Window Help
n1=15
n2=13
n3=6
n4=12
prod=n1*n2*n3*n4
print("Product of four numbers=",prod)
```

***Figure 1.39:** Code*

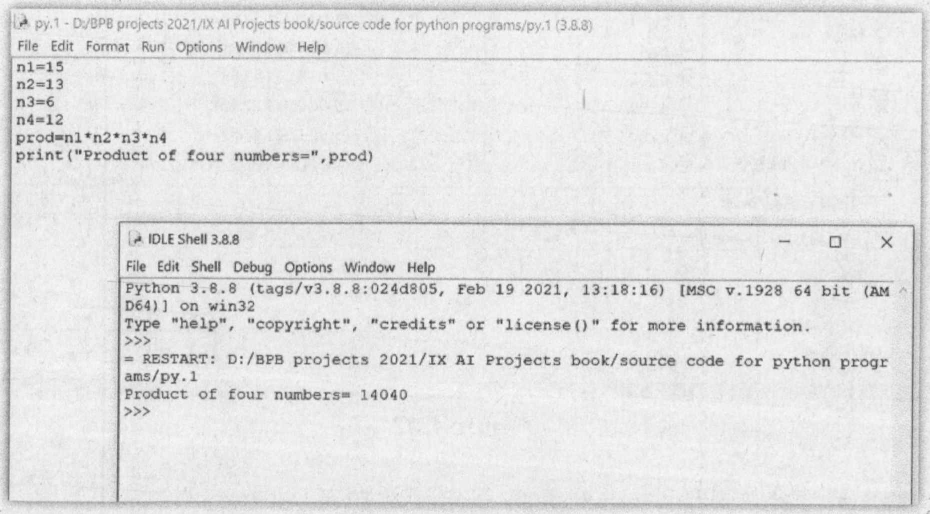

```
py.1 - D:/BPB projects 2021/IX AI Projects book/source code for python programs/py.1 (3.8.8)
File Edit Format Run Options Window Help
n1=15
n2=13
n3=6
n4=12
prod=n1*n2*n3*n4
print("Product of four numbers=",prod)
```

```
IDLE Shell 3.8.8
File Edit Shell Debug Options Window Help
Python 3.8.8 (tags/v3.8.8:024d805, Feb 19 2021, 13:18:16) [MSC v.1928 64 bit (AM
D64)] on win32
Type "help", "copyright", "credits" or "license()" for more information.
>>>
= RESTART: D:/BPB projects 2021/IX AI Projects book/source code for python progr
ams/py.1
Product of four numbers= 14040
>>>
```

***Figure 1.40:** Output*

1.1.12 Explanation of an example

Write a Python Code for ***"Calculating product of five integers"***.

Code:

```
#Calculating product of five integers.
n1=-4
n2=5
n3=-2
n4=10
n5=-145
prod=n1*n2*n3*n4*n5
print("Product of five entered numbers=",prod)
```

Explanation:

Line 1 in the above code starting with # is a comment line, which means the line is nonexecutable and it is only for the programmer's reference.

Line 2, 3,4,5 and 6 defines five integers. (Three numbers are negative integers)

Line 7 defines the formula for the product of five integers.

Line 8 display the print command.

The code and output in Python IDLE will appear like as shown in Figure 1.41.

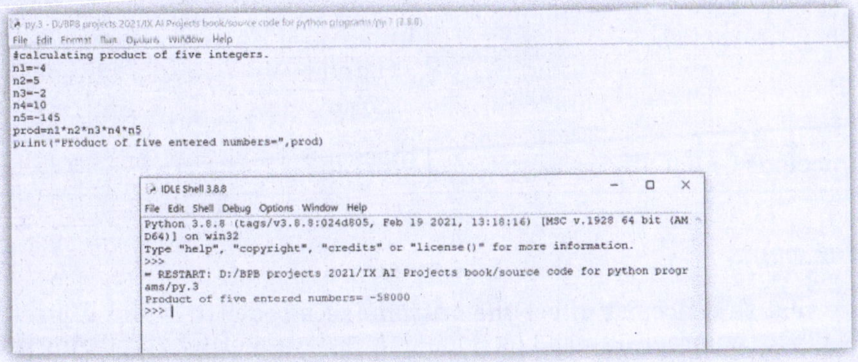

```
#calculating product of five integers.
n1=-4
n2=5
n3=-2
n4=10
n5=-145
prod=n1*n2*n3*n4*n5
print("Product of five entered numbers=",prod)
```

```
Python 3.8.8 (tags/v3.8.8:024d805, Feb 19 2021, 13:18:16) [MSC v.1928 64 bit (AM
D64)] on win32
Type "help", "copyright", "credits" or "license()" for more information.
>>>
= RESTART: D:/BPB projects 2021/IX AI Projects book/source code for python progr
ams/py.3
Product of five entered numbers= -58000
>>>
```

Figure 1.41

1.1.13 Python statement and comments

Now, we will learn about Python statements, indentation, and their importance, and user comments in programming.

(a) Python statement

Statements are the instructions written in the source code for execution. There are various types of statements in the Python programming language, like Assignment statements, Conditional statements, Looping statements, etc. These statements help the user to get the required output. For example, n = 50 is an assignment statement.

(i) Single-line statement

The statements that are expressed in a single line are called single-line statements. Python statements are normally written in a single line. However, the long statement can be divided into multiple lines by using the line continuation character (\).

(ii) Multi-line statement

In Python, the end of a statement is represented by a newline character (\n). However, Statements in Python can be extended to one or more lines using parentheses (), braces {}, square brackets [], semi-colon (;), and continuation character slash (\). When we need to do long calculations and cannot fit these statements into one line, we can use any of these characters.

Table 1.3: Examples of multi-line statements

Type of Multi-line Statement	Usage
(a) Using Continuation Character slash (\)	= 1 + 9 + \ 4 + 5 + 6 + \ 7 + 8 + 2+10\ 14+17
(b) Using Parentheses ()	n = (2 * 5 * 7 +9 –2)
(c) Using Square Brackets []	Indians = ['Kovind' ,'Dhoni', 'Kohli', 'Modi N', , 'Saina']
(d) Using braces {}	x = {15 + 37 +27 + 15 +76 + 11 + 47 }
(e) Using Semicolons (;)	ropes = 5; coins =53; hockey sticks=27.

(b) Python comments

A comment is a text that doesn't affect the outcome of a code. It is just a piece of text to let someone know what the programmer has done in a program or what is being done in a block of code. In Python, the hash (#) symbol is used to start writing a comment.

(i) Single line comments

Python single-line comments start with a hashtag symbol (#) with no white spaces and may last till the end of the line. When the comment exceeds one line, then put a hashtag on the next line and continue the comment. Python's single-line comments are proved useful for supplying short explanations for variables, function declarations, and expressions.

Example:

```
# This is a comment
# Print "SheljaAnuj"
print("SheljaAnuj")
```

```
IDLE Shell 3.8.8
File Edit Shell Debug Options Window Help
Python 3.8.8 (tags/v3.8.8:024d805, Feb 19 2021, 13:18:16) [MSC v.1928 64 bit (AMD64)] on win32
Type "help", "copyright", "credits" or "license()" for more information.
>>> # This is a comment
# Print "SheljaAnuj"
print("SheljaAnuj")

SheljaAnuj
>>>
```

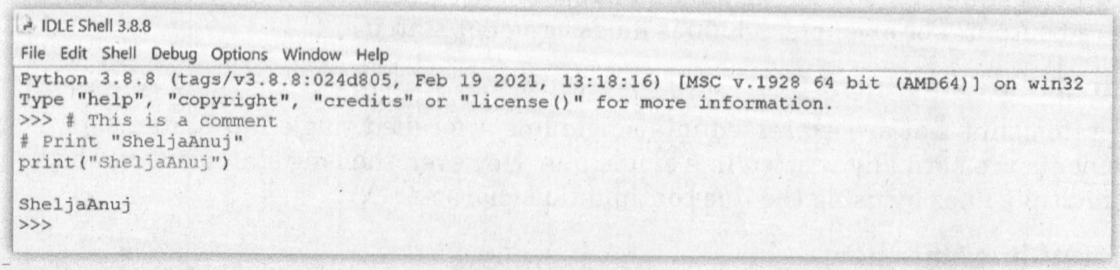

Figure 1.42: Output

(ii) Multi-line comments

Python multi-line comments are pieces of text enclosed in a delimiter (""") on each end of the comment. Moreover, there should not be any white space between delimiter ("""). These comments are useful when the comment text does not fit into one line and needs to spread across lines. Multi-line comments or paragraphs are used as documentation for others to read the code.

Example:

"""

#This is a multi-line comment in Python that has several lines and describes SatyaRekhaAnuj.com

An AI Quiz portal for the students of the whole world. It contains well written,

well thought and well-explained AI Quiz questions and exercises

and some AI programming articles,

worksheets, projects, and much more.

...

"""

print("SatyaRekhaAnuj.com")

```
py.4.py - D:/BPB projects 2021/IX AI Projects book/source code for python programs/py.4.py (3.8.8)
File Edit Format Run Options Window Help
"""
#This is a multi-line comment in Python that has several lines and describes SatyaRekhaAnuj.com
An AI Quiz portal for the students of the whole world. It contains well written, well thought
and well-explained AI Quiz questions and exercises
and some AI programming articles,
worksheets, projects, and much more.
...
"""
print("SatyaRekhaAnuj.com")
```

```
IDLE Shell 3.8.8
File Edit Shell Debug Options Window Help
Python 3.8.8 (tags/v3.8.8:024d005, Feb 19 2021, 13:18:16) [MSC v.1928 64 bit (AM
D64)] on win32
Type "help", "copyright", "credits" or "license()" for more information.
>>>
= RESTART: D:/BPB projects 2021/IX AI Projects book/source code for python progr
ams/py.4.py
SatyaRekhaAnuj.com
>>>
```

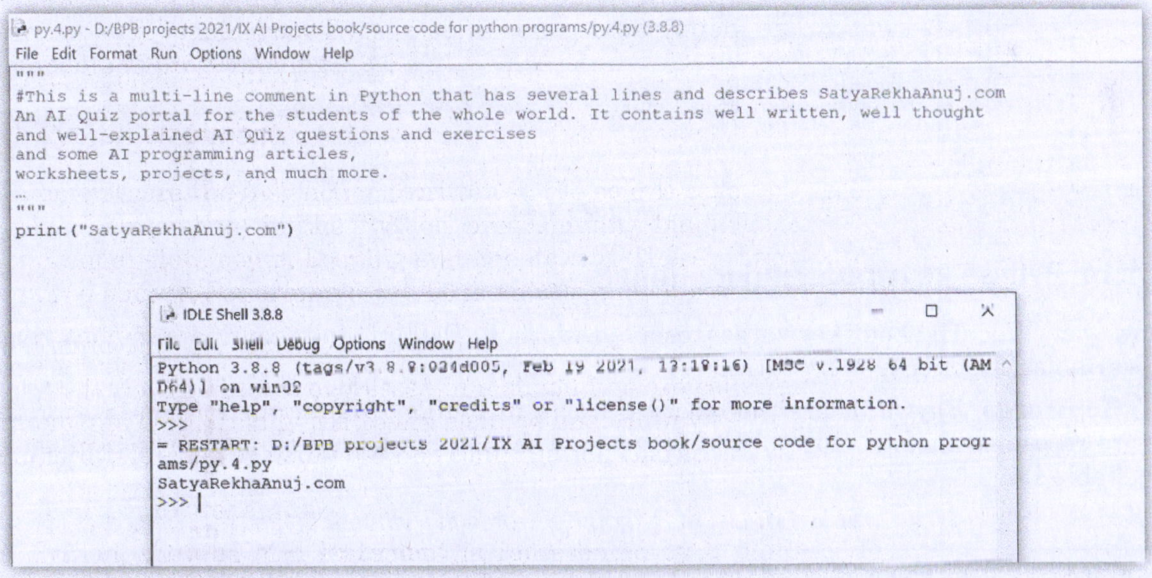

Figure 1.43: *Output*

(iii) Docstring comments

Docstring is an in-built feature of Python that is used to associate documentation written with Python modules, functions, classes, and methods. These comments are added right below the functions, classes or modules to describe what they do. In Python, the docstring is made available via the __doc__ attribute.

Example:

```
def multiply(x, y):
```

```
    """Multiplies the value of x and y"""
    return x*y

# Print the docstring of multiply function
print(multiply.__doc__)
```
Output:

```
Multiplies the value of x and y
```

```
py.5.py - C:/Users/S.P VERMA/AppData/Local/Programs/Python/Python38/py.5.py (3.8.8)
File Edit Format Run Options Window Help
def multiply(x, y):
    """Multiplies the value of x and y"""
    return x*y

# Print the docstring of multiply function
print(multiply.__doc__)

IDLE Shell 3.8.8
File Edit Shell Debug Options Window Help
Python 3.8.8 (tags/v3.8.8:024d805, Feb 19 2021, 13:18:16) [MSC v.1928 64 bit (AM
D64)] on win32
Type "help", "copyright", "credits" or "license()" for more information.
>>>
== RESTART: C:/Users/S.P VERMA/AppData/Local/Programs/Python/Python38/py.5.py ==
Multiplies the value of x and y
>>> |
```

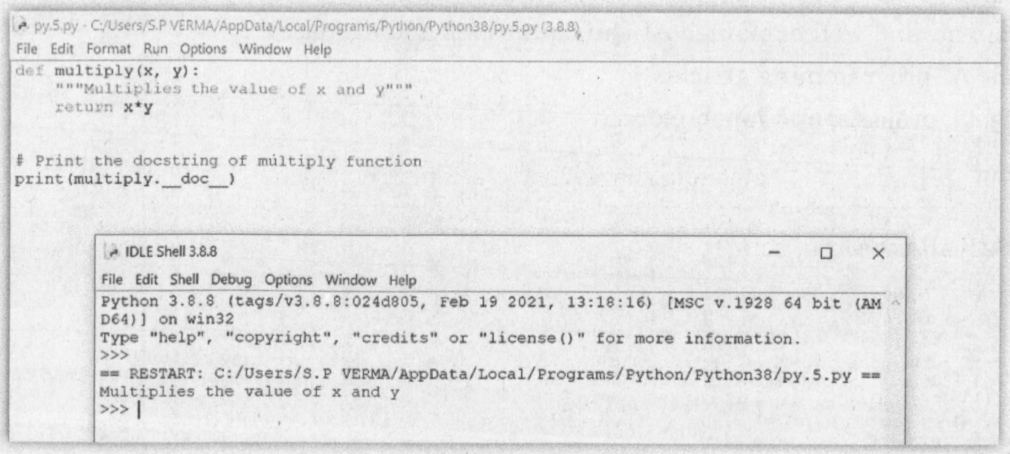

Figure 1.44

1.1.14 Python keywords and identifiers

Now, we will learn about keywords (reserved words in Python) and identifiers (names given to variables, functions, etc.).

(a) Keywords: Keywords are the reserved words in Python used by the Python interpreter to recognise the structure of the program. The List of all Python keywords is given in Table 1.4.

Table 1.4: *List of Python Keywords in Python 9.5.1*

False	Class	Finally	Is	Return	None
Try	Continue	True	And	As	Aasert
Break	Def	Del	Elif	Else	Except
For	From	Global	If	Import	In
Nonlocal	Lambda	Not	Or	Pass	Raise
While	With	Yield			

(b) Identifiers: An identifier is a user-defined name to represent a variable, a function, a module, a class, or any other object. It is a programmable entity with a name in Python. A name given to the fundamental building block in a program is called an identifier.

Here are few conventions used for Python identifiers:

a. An identifier starts either with a letter A to Z or a to z or an underscore (followed by 0 or more letters) or underscores and digits (0 to 9).

b. Python does not allow punctuation characters, like @, $, and % within identifiers.

c. Python is a case-sensitive programming language. Thus, 'Sample' and 'sample' are two different identifiers in Python.

d. An uppercase letter is used to start class names, whereas all other identifiers start with a lowercase letter.

e. When we start an identifier with a single leading underscore, it indicates that the identifier is private.

f. Starting an identifier with two leading underscores informs that it is a strongly private identifier.

g. When the identifier also ends with two trailing underscores, then the identifier is a language-defined special name.

1.1.14.1 Properties of identifiers

The important properties of identifiers are listed as follows:

- Python identifier may contain letters in a small case (a-z), upper case (A-Z), digits (0-9), and/ underscore (_).
- Identifier's name can't begin with a digit.
- Keywords cannot be used as identifiers.
- Python identifier can't contain only digits.
- Special symbols, like !, @, #, $, %, ^, &, etc cannot be used in the identifier.
- Python identifier's name may start with an underscore.

The identifier can be of any length.

Always name identifiers that make sense. While c = 10 is valid, writing count = 10 would make correct sense, and it would be easier to figure out what was it meant even when we look at our code after a long gap. Multiple words can be separated by using an underscore. *Example:*

This_is_a_long_variable

Factz Funda

When solving a problem is difficult and the problem can be changed, then it is divided into simpler problems that are easier to solve, then this process is called recursion.

1.1.15 Variables and datatypes

(a) Variables

A variable is a named location that is used to store data in the memory of the computer. It is like that variable as a container that holds data that can be changed later throughout programming. For example,

```
x = 57
y = 73
z= 91
```

These declarations make sure that the program reserves memory for three variables with the names x, y and z. The variable names stand for the memory location. It's like the three shoeboxes. These shoe boxes are labeled with x, y and z, and the corresponding values are stored in the shoeboxes. Like the three shoeboxes, the memory is empty as well at the beginning.

It is interesting to note that the Assignment operator is used in Python to assign values to variables. For example, a = 5 is a simple assignment operator that assigns the value five on the right to the variable 'a' on the left.

***Table 1.5:** Examples of variables*

Task	Sample code	Output
Assigning a value to a variable	Website = "cafelittlemonk.com" print(Website)	cafelittlemonk.com
Changing value of a variable	Website = "cafesoul.com" print(Website) Website1 = "davuni.ac.in" print(Website1)	cafesoul.com davuni.ac.in
Assigning different values to different variables	a, b, c=75, 21, 69 d="Hello Dear Jaadu" print(d) print(a) print(b) print(c)	Hello Dear Jaadu 75 21 69
Assigning same value to different variable	x=y=z= "Mona " print(x) print(y) print(z)	Mona Mona Mona

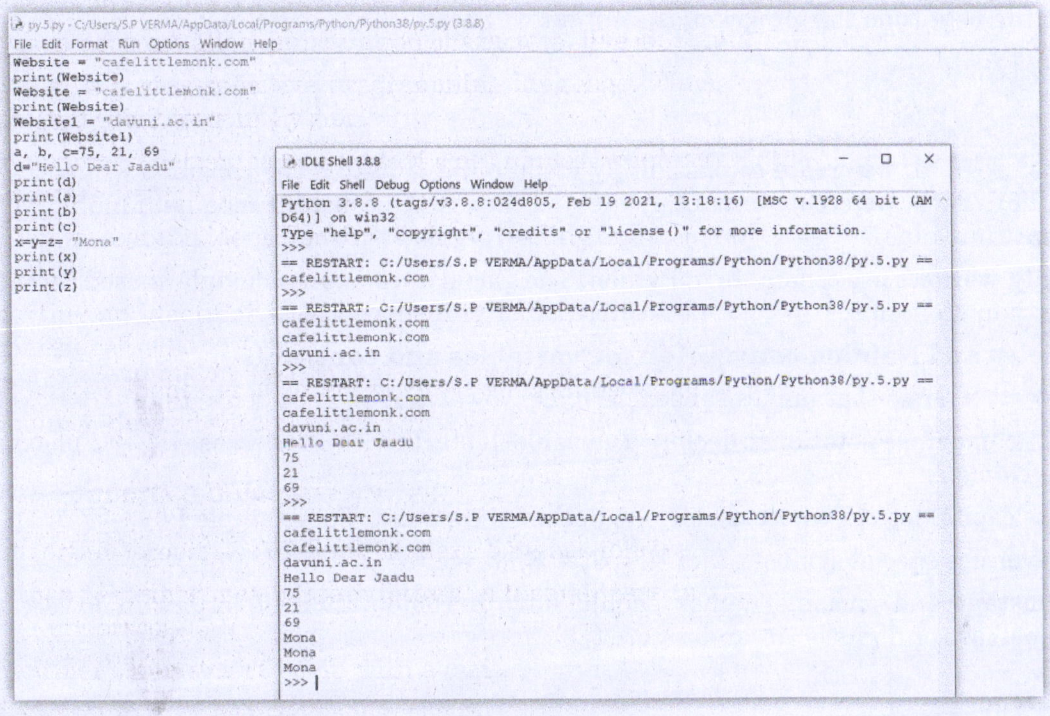

Figure 1.45: Output

(i) Constants

A variable whose value cannot be changed even later on, is called a 'Constant.' Non technically, we can think of constant as a shoebox with a fixed size of shoe kept inside, which cannot be changed after that.

Assigning value to a constant in Python

In Python, constants are generally declared and assigned on a module. A module means a new file containing variables, functions, etc., that is imported to the main file. , Constants inside the module are written in all capital letters, and underscores are used for separating the words.

Example: Declaring and assigning value to a constant

- Create a info.py

```
NAME = "Imran"
AGE = 37
```

- Create a main.py

```
import info
print(info.NAME)
print(info.AGE)
```

When the user runs this program, the output will be:

```
Imran

37
```

In this program, we create a constant.py module file to assign the constant value to PI and GRAVITY. Then, we create a main.py file and import the constant module. Finally, we print the constant value.

Actually, we don't use constants in Python. The global or constants module is used throughout the Python programs.

(ii) Rules and Naming convention for variables and constants

- Create a name that makes sense. *Example:* vowel makes more sense than v.
- Use camelCase notation to declare a variable. It starts with a lowercase letter. For example, myName
- Use capital letters where possible to declare a constant. For example PI
- Never use special symbols, like * , !, @, #, $, %, etc.
- Constant and variable names should have a combination of letters in lowercase or uppercase or digits or an underscore (_).

(b) Data types

Every value in Python has a datatype. Because everything is an object in Python programming, data types are actually classes, and variables are instances (object) of these classes. There are various data types in Python. Some of the important data types are mentioned in Table 1.6.

***Table 1.6:** Data types in Python*

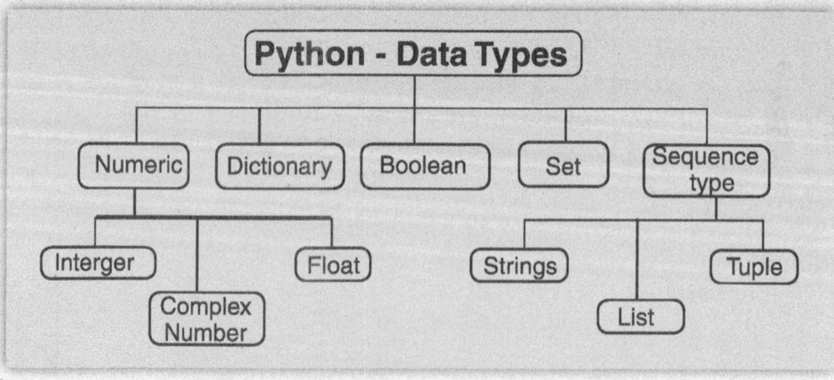

(a) Python numbers

Number data type stores Numerical Values. These are of three different types:

- Integer and Long Integer

- Float / floating-point number
- Complex numbers

(i) **Integer and long integer:** The range of an integer in Python can be from -2147483648 to 2147483647, and a long integer has an unlimited range subject to available memory.

Integers are the whole numbers having + or – sign, like 1000, -56, 0, 17. While writing a large integer value, don't use commas to separate digits. Also, integers should not have leading zeros.

(ii) **Float and floating-point number:** Float () is a built-in Python function that converts a number or a string to a float value and returns the result. When it fails for any invalid input, then an appropriate exception occurs. Numbers with fractions or decimal points are called floating-point numbers. A floating-point number will consist of a sign (+,-) sequence of decimals digits and a dot, like 0.0, -21.9, 0.98333328, 15.2963, etc. These numbers may also be used to represent a number in engineering/ scientific notation.

-3.0×10^7 will be represented as $-3.0e^7$

4.3×10^{-3} will be $4.3e^{-3}$

(iii) **Complex numbers**: A complex number is represented by the general formula "x + yi." Python converts the real numbers x and y into complex numbers using the function complex(x,y). The real part may be accessed using the function real(), and the imaginary part may be represented by image().

Factz Funda

'None' is a special data type with a single value and represented by None. It is used to represent the absence of value/falseness in a situation.

(b) Sequence

A sequence is defined as an ordered collection of items indexed by positive integers. A sequence may be a combination of mutable and non-mutable data types. Three kinds of sequence data types available in Python are Strings, Lists, and Tuples.

(i) **String:** A string is defined as an ordered sequence of letters/characters. Strings are enclosed in single quotes (' ') or double quotes (" "). The quotes are not part of any string, but they only tell the computer where the string begins and ends. They can have any character or sign, including space in them.

Thus, strings in Python are identified as a continuous set of characters represented in the quotation marks. Subsets or a part of strings can be taken using the slice operator ([] and [:]) with indexes starting at 0 at the beginning of the string. The plus (+) sign is the string concatenation operator, and the asterisk (*) is the repetition operator.

(ii) **Lists:** Lists are an important data type of Python. The List is a sequence of values of any type. The values in a List are known as elements or items. These are indexed/ordered. The List is enclosed in square brackets. A list contains items that are separated by commas, and each item is enclosed within a square bracket([]).

The values stored in a list can be accessed using the slice operator ([ ] and [:]) with indexes starting at 0 at the beginning of the list and working the way to end -1. The plus (+) sign represents that the list is the concatenation operator, and the asterisk (*) is the sign of the repetition operator.

Example: dob = [13,"May",1987]

(iii) Tuples: A tuple is also a sequence data type that is similar to the list. Tuples are defined as a sequence of values of any type, and these are indexed by integers. They are immutable. Tuples are enclosed in ().

The two main differences between a list and a tuple are as follows:

Lists are enclosed in big brackets or square brackets ([ ]), and their elements and size may be changed, whereas tuples are enclosed in parentheses (( )) and cannot be updated.

Tuples are non-mutable, but lists are mutable.

Example:

t = ((3,'program',5.3), 4)

(c) Sets

A set is defined as an unordered and mutable collection of values of any type, with no duplicate entry.

Example: >>> a = {1,2,2,3,3,3} >>> a = {1,2,3}

(d) Mapping

This data type is unordered. Dictionaries fall under Mappings.

1.1.16 Python dictionary

A Python Dictionary contains an unordered collection of key-value pairs. Python's dictionaries are a kind of table type where a key and its value are entered. Dictionaries are enclosed by curly braces ({ }), and the values can be assigned and accessed using square braces ([ ]). Dictionaries have no concept of any order among elements. We cannot say that the elements are "out of order"; they are actually unordered.

A Python dictionary is used while dealing with a huge amount of data. Dictionaries are optimised for retrieving data. The key to retrieve the value should be known to the user. Dictionaries in Python are defined within braces {} with each item being a pair in the form "key: value." Here, key and value may be of any type.

Example:

```
>>> d = {2:'Sanjana','key':3}
>>> type(d)
<class 'dict'>
```

1.1.17 Type conversion

The process of conversion of the value of one data type (integer, string, float, etc.) to another data type is called type conversion. Python has two types of type conversion.

- Implicit type conversion
- Explicit type conversion

(i) **Implicit type conversion:** In Implicit type conversion, Python converts one data type to another data type automatically. This process doesn't need any user involvement.

Example:

```
# Code to calculate the Simple Interest.
principle_amount = 15000
roi = 3.0
time = 5
simple_interest = (principle_amount * roi * time)/100
print(“datatype of principle amount : “, type(principle_amount))
print(“datatype of rate of interest : “, type(roi))
print(“value of simple interest : “, simple_interest)
print(“datatype of simple interest : “, type(simple_interest))
```

When we run the above-mentioned program after saving the source code, the output we get is:

```
datatype of principle amount :  <class ‘int’>
datatype of rate of interest :  <class ‘float’>
value of simple interest :  2250.0
datatype of simple interest :  <class ‘float’
>>>
```

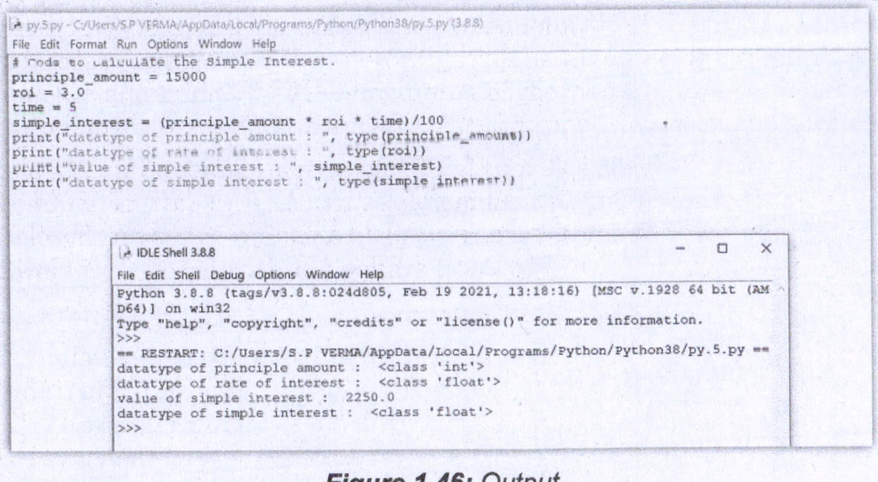

```
py.5.py - C:/Users/S.P VERMA/AppData/Local/Programs/Python/Python38/py.5.py (3.8.8)
File Edit Format Run Options Window Help
# Code to calculate the Simple Interest.
principle_amount = 15000
roi = 3.0
time = 5
simple_interest = (principle_amount * roi * time)/100
print("datatype of principle amount : ", type(principle_amount))
print("datatype of rate of interest : ", type(roi))
print("value of simple interest : ", simple_interest)
print("datatype of simple interest : ", type(simple_interest))

IDLE Shell 3.8.8
File Edit Shell Debug Options Window Help
Python 3.8.8 (tags/v3.8.8:024d805, Feb 19 2021, 13:18:16) [MSC v.1928 64 bit (AM
D64)] on win32
Type "help", "copyright", "credits" or "license()" for more information.
>>>
== RESTART: C:/Users/S.P VERMA/AppData/Local/Programs/Python/Python38/py.5.py ==
datatype of principle amount :  <class 'int'>
datatype of rate of interest :  <class 'float'>
value of simple interest :  2250.0
datatype of simple interest :  <class 'float'>
>>>
```

***Figure 1.46:** Output*

In the above program,

- We calculate the simple interest by multiplying the variable principal amount and ROI with time and then divide it by 100.
- We will look at the data type of all the objects, respectively.
- In the output, we may see the data type of principal amount is an integer,while the datatype of roi is a float.
- Also, we can see the simple interest has float data types because Python always converts smaller data types to larger data types to avoid the loss of data.

Table 1.7: *Example code and sample output with explanation in implicit conversion*

Example code	Sample output	Explanation
a = 15 b = "Hello" print(a+b)	File "C:/Users/S.P VERMA/AppData/Local/Programs/Python/Python38/py.5.py", line 3, in <module> print(a+b) TypeError: unsupported operand type(s) for +: 'int' and 'str'	The output shows an error that says that we cannot add integer and string variable types using implicit conversion.
c = 'Hema' N = 4 print(c*N)	HemaHemaHemaHema	The output shows that the string is printed three times when we use a multiply operator with a string.
x = True y = 30 print(x + y)	31	The output shows that the boolean value x will be converted to an integer and, as it is true, will be considered as 1 and then give the output.
m=True n=36 print(n - m)	35	
m = False n = 58 print(n- m)	58	The output shows that the boolean value m will be converted to an integer and, as it is false, will be considered as 0 and then give the output.

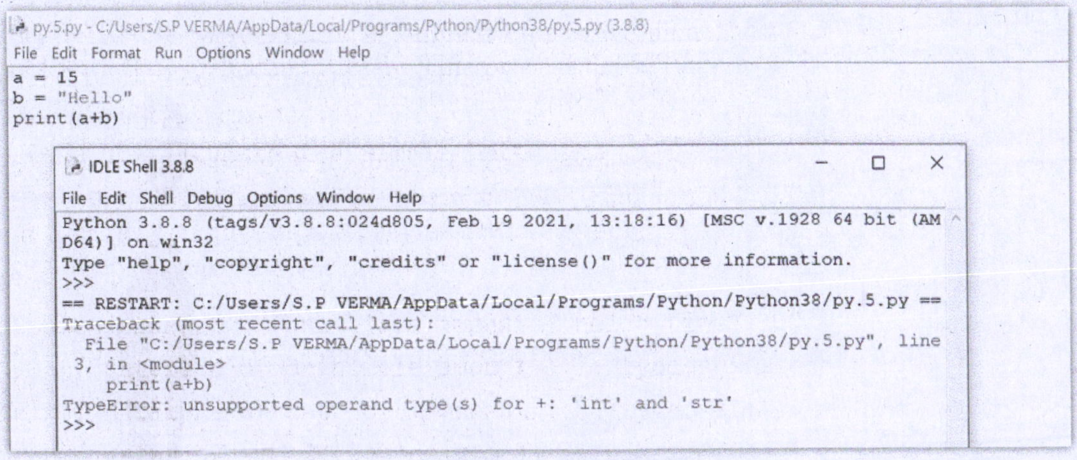

```
py.5.py - C:/Users/S.P VERMA/AppData/Local/Programs/Python/Python38/py.5.py (3.8.8)
File Edit Format Run Options Window Help
a = 15
b = "Hello"
print(a+b)
```

```
IDLE Shell 3.8.8
File Edit Shell Debug Options Window Help
Python 3.8.8 (tags/v3.8.8:024d805, Feb 19 2021, 13:18:16) [MSC v.1928 64 bit (AM
D64)] on win32
Type "help", "copyright", "credits" or "license()" for more information.
>>>
== RESTART: C:/Users/S.P VERMA/AppData/Local/Programs/Python/Python38/py.5.py ==
Traceback (most recent call last):
  File "C:/Users/S.P VERMA/AppData/Local/Programs/Python/Python38/py.5.py", line
 3, in <module>
    print(a+b)
TypeError: unsupported operand type(s) for +: 'int' and 'str'
>>>
```

Figure 1.47: *Output*

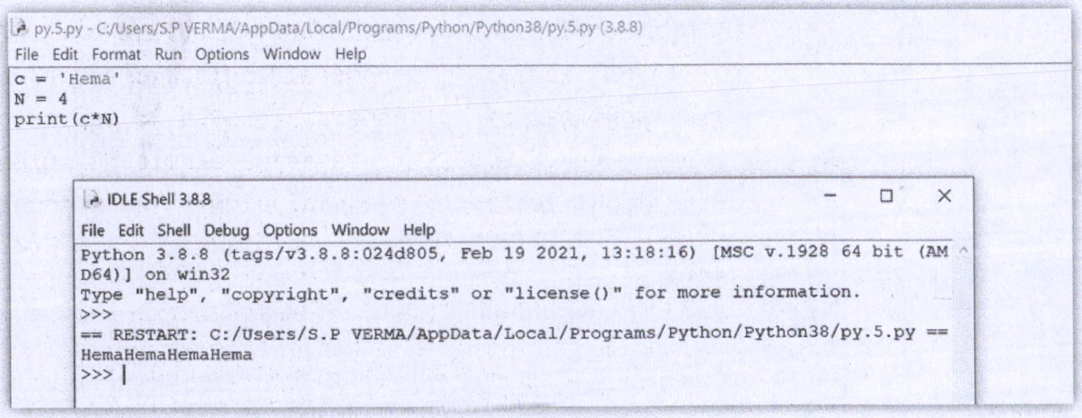

```
py.5.py - C:/Users/S.P VERMA/AppData/Local/Programs/Python/Python38/py.5.py (3.8.8)
File Edit Format Run Options Window Help
c = 'Hema'
N = 4
print(c*N)
```

```
IDLE Shell 3.8.8
File Edit Shell Debug Options Window Help
Python 3.8.8 (tags/v3.8.8:024d805, Feb 19 2021, 13:18:16) [MSC v.1928 64 bit (AM
D64)] on win32
Type "help", "copyright", "credits" or "license()" for more information.
>>>
== RESTART: C:/Users/S.P VERMA/AppData/Local/Programs/Python/Python38/py.5.py ==
HemaHemaHemaHema
>>>
```

Figure 1.48: *Output*

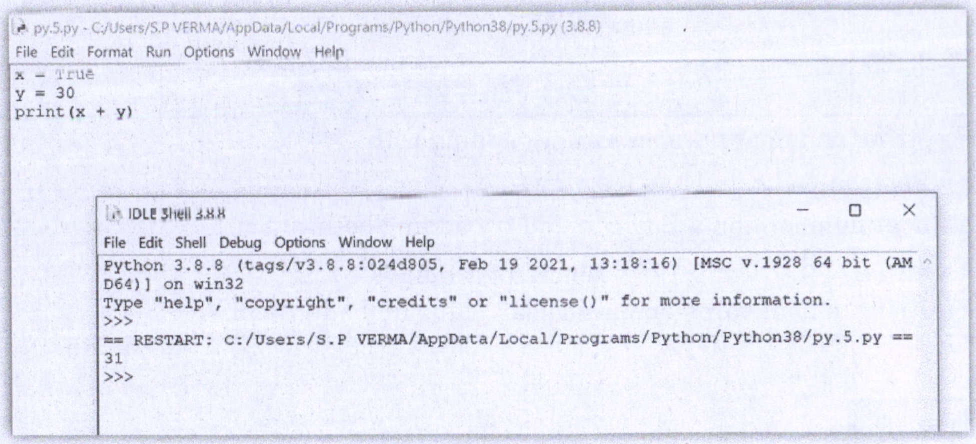

```
py.5.py - C:/Users/S.P VERMA/AppData/Local/Programs/Python/Python38/py.5.py (3.8.8)
File Edit Format Run Options Window Help
x = True
y = 30
print(x + y)
```

```
IDLE Shell 3.8.8
File Edit Shell Debug Options Window Help
Python 3.8.8 (tags/v3.8.8:024d805, Feb 19 2021, 13:18:16) [MSC v.1928 64 bit (AM
D64)] on win32
Type "help", "copyright", "credits" or "license()" for more information.
>>>
== RESTART: C:/Users/S.P VERMA/AppData/Local/Programs/Python/Python38/py.5.py ==
31
>>>
```

Figure 1.49: *Output*

py.5.py - C:/Users/S.P VERMA/AppData/Local/Programs/Python/Python38/py.5.py (3.8.8)

File Edit Format Run Options Window Help

```
m=True
n=36
print(n - m)
```

IDLE Shell 3.8.8

File Edit Shell Debug Options Window Help

```
Python 3.8.8 (tags/v3.8.8:024d805, Feb 19 2021, 13:18:16) [MSC v.1928 64 bit (AM
D64)] on win32
Type "help", "copyright", "credits" or "license()" for more information.
>>>
== RESTART: C:/Users/S.P VERMA/AppData/Local/Programs/Python/Python38/py.5.py ==
35
>>> |
```

***Figure 1.50:** Output*

py.5.py - C:/Users/S.P VERMA/AppData/Local/Programs/Python/Python38/py.5.py (3.8.8)

File Edit Format Run Options Window Help

```
m = False
n = 58
print(n- m)
```

IDLE Shell 3.8.8

File Edit Shell Debug Options Window Help

```
Python 3.8.8 (tags/v3.8.8:024d805, Feb 19 2021, 13:18:16) [MSC v.1928 64 bit (AM
D64)] on win32
Type "help", "copyright", "credits" or "license()" for more information.
>>>
== RESTART: C:/Users/S.P VERMA/AppData/Local/Programs/Python/Python38/py.5.py ==
58
>>>
```

***Figure 1.51:** Output*

Do Yourself

1. Take a string and float number and try adding both.
2. Take a Boolean value and add a string to it.
3. Take a float number and a Boolean and try adding both.
4. Take a string and Boolean value and try adding both.
5. Take a string, a float value and a Boolean value and add them.

Factz Funda

In Python, everything is done by reference as it doesn't support pointers.

(ii) Explicit type conversion: In Explicit Type Conversion, the users convert the data type of an object to the required data type by using predefined functions, like int(), float(), str(), etc. Moreover, this type of conversion is known as typecasting because the user casts (changes) the data type of the objects.

Syntax:

(required_datatype)(expression)

Typecasting may be done by assigning the required data type function to the expression.

Example: Adding of string and an integer using explicit conversion.

```
Birth_day = 21
Birth_month = "June"
print("data type of Birth_day before type casting :", type(Birth_day))
print("data type of Birth_month: ", type(Birth_month))
Birth_day = str(Birth_day)
print("data type of Birth_day after type casting:",type(Birth_day))
Birth_date = Birth_day + Birth_month
print("birth date of the student: ", Birth_date)
print("data type of Birth_date: ", type(Birth_date))
```

When we run the above-mentioned program, the output will be:

```
the data type of Birth_day before typecasting: <class 'int'>
data type of Birth_month:  <class 'str'>
the data type of Birth_day after typecasting: <class 'str'>
birth date of the student: 21 June
data type of Birth_date:  <class 'str'>
>>>
```

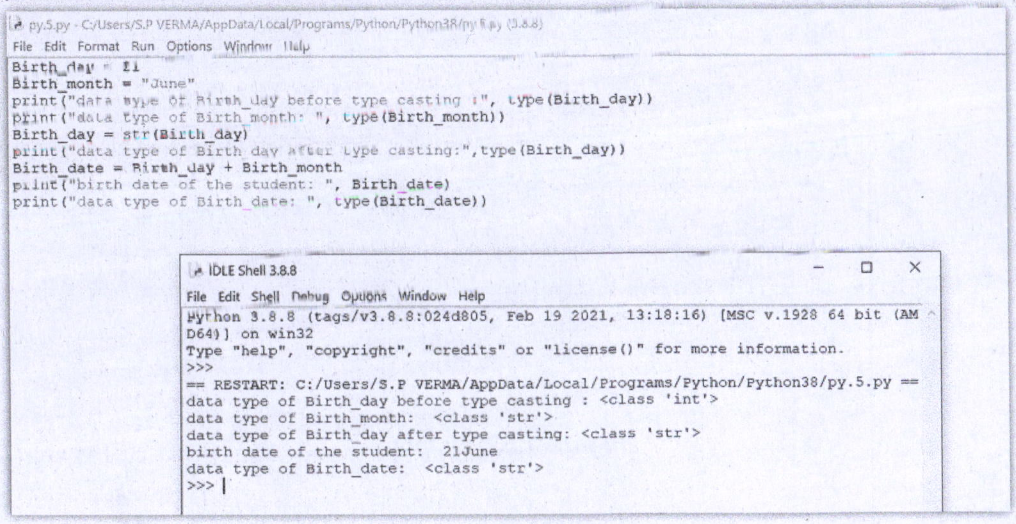

```
py.5.py - C:/Users/S.P VERMA/AppData/Local/Programs/Python/Python38/py.5.py (3.8.8)
File  Edit  Format  Run  Options  Window  Help
Birth_day = 21
Birth_month = "June"
print("data type of Birth_day before type casting :", type(Birth_day))
print("data type of Birth_month: ", type(Birth_month))
Birth_day = str(Birth_day)
print("data type of Birth_day after type casting:",type(Birth_day))
Birth_date = Birth_day + Birth_month
print("birth date of the student: ", Birth_date)
print("data type of Birth_date: ", type(Birth_date))
```

```
IDLE Shell 3.8.8
File  Edit  Shell  Debug  Options  Window  Help
Python 3.8.8 (tags/v3.8.8:024d805, Feb 19 2021, 13:18:16) [MSC v.1928 64 bit (AM
D64)] on win32
Type "help", "copyright", "credits" or "license()" for more information.
>>>
== RESTART: C:/Users/S.P VERMA/AppData/Local/Programs/Python/Python38/py.5.py ==
data type of Birth_day before type casting : <class 'int'>
data type of Birth_month:  <class 'str'>
data type of Birth_day after type casting: <class 'str'>
birth date of the student:  21June
data type of Birth_date:  <class 'str'>
>>>
```

***Figure 1.52:** Output*

In the above program,

- We add Birth_day and Birth_month variables.
- We converted Birth_day from integer(lower) to string(higher) type using str() function to perform the addition.
- We got the Birth_date value and data type to be a string.

***Table 1.8:** Example code and sample output with explanation in implicit conversion*

Example code	Sample output	Explanation
a = 18 b = "Mangoes" print(str(a)+ b)	18 Mangoes	Writing str(a) will convert an integer into a string and then will add to the string b.
x = 9.2 y = 31 print(int(x) + y)	40	Writing int(x) will convert a float number to an integer by just considering the integer part of the number and then perform the operation.
m = False n = 7 print(n + m)	7	Writing Bool() will convert the integer value to Boolean. If it is zero, then it is converted to False, else to True for all other cases.

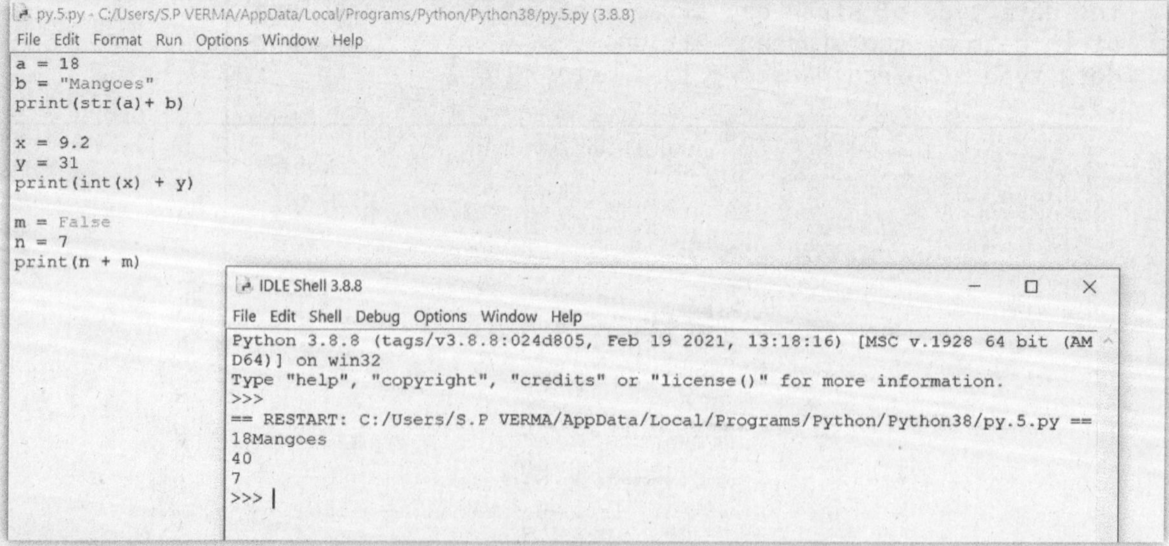

***Figure 1.53:** Output*

Activity 1.1

- Participate in this individual activity.
- Use Python 3.8.3 Shell to test the following:
  a. Take a Boolean value "True" and a floating-point number "56.9" and perform the AND operation on both.
  b. Take a Boolean value "False" and a float number "53.7" and perform the AND operation on both.
  c. Take a string " Zero" and a Boolean value " True" and try adding both by using the Bool() function.
  d. Take the string "Evening" and the float value "60.3" and try to add both of them by using the float() function.
- After performing the above-mentioned exercise, write down your observations and discuss them in the class.

There is no difference in a single or double-quoted string. Both representations can be used interchangeably. When either a single or double quote is a part of the string itself, then the string should be placed in double or single quotes, respectively.

1.1.18 Python operators I

Operators are special symbols that represent computation. They are applied to operand(s), which can be values or variables. Same operators can behave differently on different data types. Operators, when applied to operands, form an expression. Operators are categorized as Arithmetic, Relational, Logical, and Assignment. Value and variables, when used with the operator, are known as operands.

Table 1.9: Arithmetic operators

Operator	Meaning	Expression	Result
+	Addition	5 + 45	50
–	Subtraction	75 – 20	55
*	Multiplication	40 * 12	480
/	Division	75 / 15	5.0
		1 / 2	0.5
//	Integer Division	24 // 10	2
		1 // 2	0
%	Remainder	55 % 10	5
**	Raised to power	6 ** 2	36

Python input and output

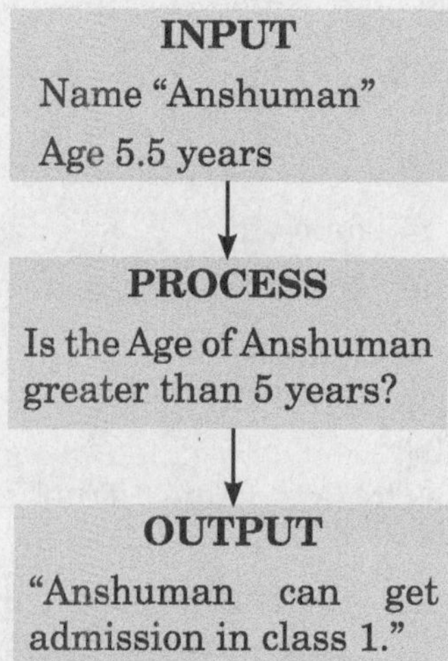

1.1.19 Python output using print() function

The print() function is used to get output data to the standard output device (screen). The output data can be taken to a file also. An example is given below.

```
a = "Hello Universe!"
print(a)
```

The output of this code will be:

```
Hello Universe!
```

```
py.5.py - C:/Users/S.P VERMA/AppData/Local/Programs/Python/Python38/py.5.py (3.8.8)
File Edit Format Run Options Window Help
a = "Hello Universe!"
print(a)
```

```
IDLE Shell 3.8.8
File Edit Shell Debug Options Window Help
Python 3.8.8 (tags/v3.8.8:024d805, Feb 19 2021, 13:18:16) [MSC v.1928 64 bit (AM
D64)] on win32
Type "help", "copyright", "credits" or "license()" for more information.
>>>
== RESTART: C:/Users/S.P VERMA/AppData/Local/Programs/Python/Python38/py.5.py ==
Hello Universe!
>>>
```

Figure 1.54: *Output*

***Table 1.10:** Some examples of code and output*

Example code	Output
a = 75 b = 40 print(a + b)	115
print(105 + 45)	150
print("My name is Guru Gendalal Sarwar.")	My name is Guru Gendalal Sarwar.
a = "Saumya" print("My name is :",a)	My name is Saumya
x = 3.7 print("x = /n", x)	x= /n 3.7

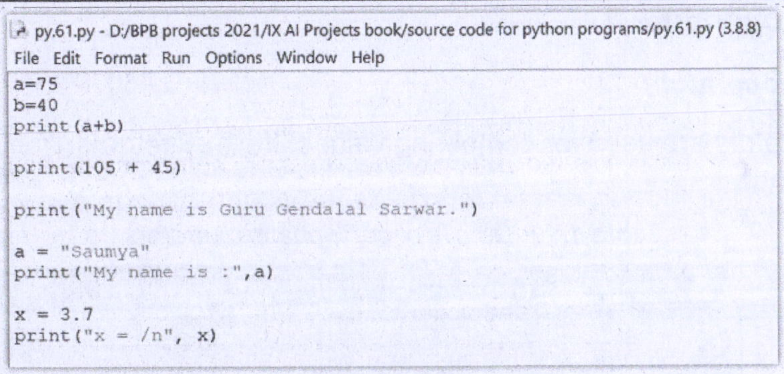

```
py.61.py - D:/BPB projects 2021/IX AI Projects book/source code for python programs/py.61.py (3.8.8)
File Edit Format Run Options Window Help
a=75
b=40
print(a+b)

print(105 + 45)

print("My name is Guru Gendalal Sarwar.")

a = "Saumya"
print("My name is :",a)

x = 3.7
print("x = /n", x)
```

***Figure 1.55:** Codes*

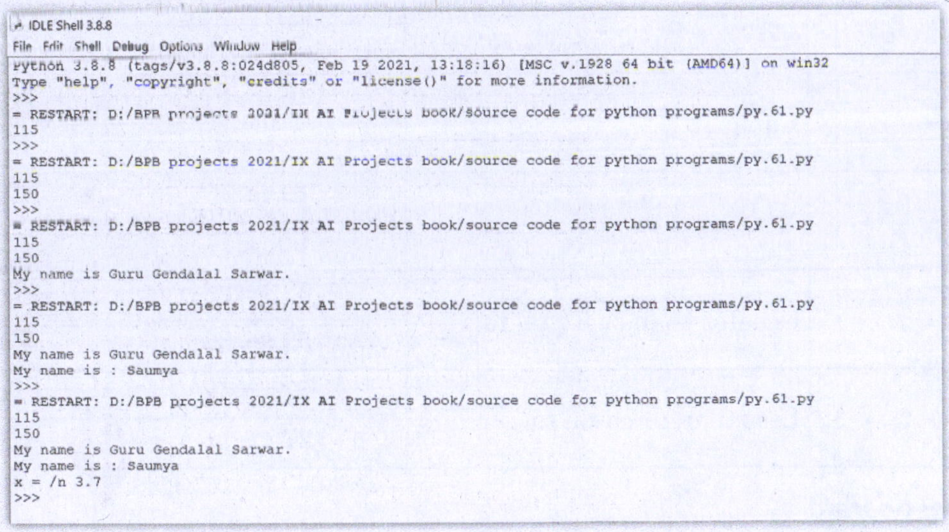

```
IDLE Shell 3.8.8
File Edit Shell Debug Options Window Help
Python 3.8.8 (tags/v3.8.8:024d805, Feb 19 2021, 13:18:16) [MSC v.1928 64 bit (AMD64)] on win32
Type "help", "copyright", "credits" or "license()" for more information.
>>>
= RESTART: D:/BPB projects 2021/IX AI Projects book/source code for python programs/py.61.py
115
>>>
= RESTART: D:/BPB projects 2021/IX AI Projects book/source code for python programs/py.61.py
115
150
>>>
= RESTART: D:/BPB projects 2021/IX AI Projects book/source code for python programs/py.61.py
115
150
My name is Guru Gendalal Sarwar.
>>>
= RESTART: D:/BPB projects 2021/IX AI Projects book/source code for python programs/py.61.py
115
150
My name is Guru Gendalal Sarwar.
My name is : Saumya
>>>
= RESTART: D:/BPB projects 2021/IX AI Projects book/source code for python programs/py.61.py
115
150
My name is Guru Gendalal Sarwar.
My name is : Saumya
x = /n 3.7
>>>
```

***Figure 1.56:** Outputs*

User input

In all the examples till now, we have been using the calculations on known values (constants). Now, let us learn to take the user's input in the program. In Python, the input() function is used for the same purpose.

Table 1.11: *Meaning of some syntax*

Syntax	Meaning
=input()	For string input
=int(input())	For integer input
=float(input())	For float (Real no.) input

1.1.20 Python operators II

(a) Comparison operators

Comparison operators are used for comparing values. It either returns True or False as per the condition.

Table 1.12: *Details of comparison operators*

Operator	Meaning	Expression	Result
>	Greater Than	54 > 11	True
		35 > 46	False
<	Less Than	30 < 45	True
		75 < 19	False
==	Equal To	6 == 6	True
		5 == 9	False
!=	Not Equal to	67 != 35	True
		50 != 50	False
>=	Greater than or Equal to	88 >= 88	True
		53 >= 67	False
<=	Less than or equal to	57 <= 57	True
		27 <= 15	False

(b) Logical operators

Logical operators are three: and, or, not.

Table 1.13: Details of logical operators

Operator	Meaning	Expression	Result
and	And operator	True and True	True
		True and False	False
or	Or operator	True or False	True
		False or False	False
not	Not Operator	not False	True
		not True	False

(c) Assignment operators

Assignment operators are mainly used in Python to assign values to variables.

Table 1.14: Details of assignment operators

Operator	Expression	Equivalent to
=	X = 7	X = 7
+=	X +=5	X = X + 5
-=	X -= 4	X = X – 4
*=	X *= 9	X = X * 9
/=	X /= 3	X = X / 3

(d) Python membership operators

Python's membership operators are used to test for membership in a sequence, like strings, lists, or tuples. There are two membership operators, as explained in Table 1.15.

Table 1.15: Details of membership operators

Operators	Description	Example
In	It evaluates to true if it finds a variable in the specified sequence and false otherwise.	x in y, here 'in' operator results in a 1 when x is a member of sequence y.
Not in	It evaluates to true if it does not find a variable in the specified sequence and false otherwise.	x not in y, here not in operator results in a 1 when x is not a member of sequence y.

(e) Python identify operators

The identity operators compare the memory locations of two objects. There are two identity operators as explained in Table 1.16.

***Table 1.16:** Details of identity operators*

Operators	Description	Example
Is	Evaluates to true if the variables on either side of the operator point to the same object and false otherwise.	x in y, here in operator results in 1 if id (x) equal id (y)
Is not	Evaluates to false if the variables on either side of the operator point to the same object and true otherwise.	x not in y, here is not in operator results in 1 if id(x) is not equal to id(y).

1.1.21 Debugging

A python program having some errors cannot be executed. Python programs may generate wrong output or may not execute when the programmer enters a wrong input, or there is a mistake in source code. Debugging is the process of identifying and removing errors and bugs from a program.

Errors in a program may be of three types:

a. **Syntax Errors:** Syntax errors occur when the rules of the programming language are not followed by the programmer during the development of the program. The python interpreter interprets and executes the statements of a program when it is syntactically correct. In case of any error, the interpreter shows error message(s) and stops the execution.

b. **Logical Errors**: A logical error or semantic error occurs when a statement is syntactically correct but does not do what the programmer intended. This type of program runs without producing error messages but does not do the right thing. Semantic errors occur when the statements are not meaningful.

c. **Runtime Error**: A runtime error is defined as an application error that occurs during the execution of a program. Runtime errors are dynamic errors that cannot be detected by the compiler. A common example of runtime errors includes dividing by zero, calling invalid functions, etc.

1.1.22 Python operator's precedence

While evaluating complex expressions involving different types of operators in Python, like 8+3*7%(3-1), it follows a precedence rule known as PEMDAS. Here,

P = Parenthesis

E = Exponentiation

M = Multiplication

D = Division

A = Addition

S = Subtraction

The precedence of operators is enlisted from high to low. When the operators are of the same precedence and are grouped by parenthesis, the order of execution is based on operator associativity. An operator may be left-associative or right-associative. In the case of a left-associative, the operator falling on the left side will be evaluated first, whereas, in a right-associative, the operator falling on the right will be evaluated first. The right-associative operators are '=' and '**.' The precedence of operators is listed in Table 1.17.

***Table 1.17:** Operator description*

S.No.	Operator and description
1	** Exponentiation (raise to the power)
2	~ + – Complement, unary plus and minus (method names for the last two are + @ and – @)
3	* / % // Multiply, divide, modulo and floor division
4	+ – Addition and subtraction
5	>>, << Right and left bitwise shift
6	& Bitwise 'AND'
7	| Bitwise exclusive OR and regular OR
8	< =, < >, > = Comparison operators
9	<, >, = =, ! = Equality operators
10	=, % =, / =, – =, + =, * =, **= Assignment operators
11	Is, is no Identity operators
12	In, not in Membership operators
13	Not, or, and Logical operators

Understand the following example of coding:

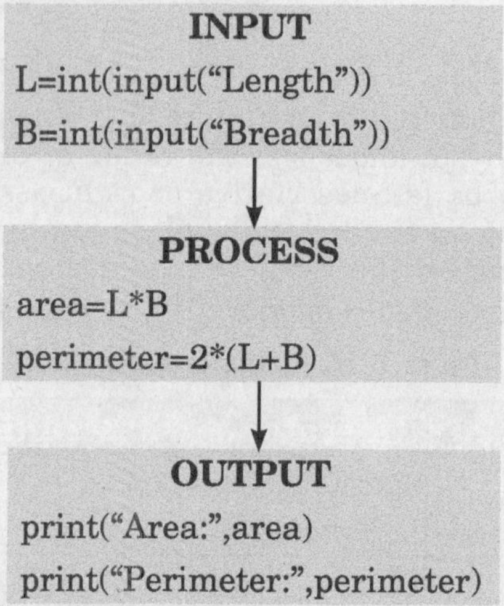

Example:

Python code	Sample output

# To calculate Area and 	
# Perimeter of a rectangle 	
L=int(input("Length"))
B=int(input("Breadth"))
Area=L*B
Perimeter=2*(L+B)
print("Area:",Area)
print("Perimeter:",Perimeter)
	Length:67
	Breadth:45
	Area:3015
	Perimeter:224

py.62.py - D:/BPB projects 2021/IX AI Projects book/source code for python programs/py.62.py (3.8.8)

File Edit Format Run Options Window Help

```
# To calculate Area and
# Perimeter of a rectangle
L=int(input("Length="))
B=int(input("Breadth="))
area=L*B
perimeter=2*(L+B)
print("Area:",area)
print("Perimeter:",perimeter)
```

***Figure 1.57:** Code*

```
IDLE Shell 3.8.8
File Edit Shell Debug Options Window Help
Python 3.8.8 (tags/v3.8.8:024d805, Feb 19 2021, 13:18:16) [MSC v.1928 64 bit (AMD64)] on win32
Type "help", "copyright", "credits" or "license()" for more information.
>>>
= RESTART: D:/BPB projects 2021/IX AI Projects book/source code for python programs/py.62.py
Length=67
Breadth=45
Area: 3015
Perimeter: 224
>>> |
```

Figure 1.58: Output

Practice Time

Write the code for the following problems 1-4:

S.N.	Python code	Sample output
1	# To calculate Area of a triangle # with Base and Height ______________ #Input Base ______________ #Input Height ______________ #Calculate Area ______________ #print Area	Base:40 Height:15 Area:300
2	# To calculating average marks # of 3 main subjects ______________ #Input Maths Marks ______________ #Input Science Marks ______________ #Input SSt Marks ______________ #Calculate Total Marks ______________ #Calculate Average Marks ______________ #print Total Marks ______________ #print Average Marks	Science:65 Maths :55 SSt: 63 Total Marks: 183 Average Marks: 61.0
3	# To calculate discounted amount # with discount % ______________ #Input Amount ______________ #Input Discount% ______________ #Calculate Discount ______________ #Calculate Discounted Amount ______________ #print Discount ______________ #print Discounted Amount	Amount: 7000 Discount%:12 Discount:840 Discounted Amt:6160

4	# To calculate Surface Area and Volume # of a Cuboid ________________ #Input Length ________________ #Input Breadth ________________ #Input Height ________________ #Calculate Surface Area ________________ #Calculate Volume ________________ #print Surface Area ________________ #print Volume	Length:25 Breadth:12 Height:6 Surface Area:1044 Volume:1800

Testing Time

1. What do you mean by stringers in Python?
2. Define comments in Python.
3. Explain key features of Python.
4. Define variables.
5. Mention the different properties of an identifier.

Summary

- Python is a case-sensitive programming language.
- Python is a high-level and interpreted programming language.
- OOPs means Object-Oriented Programs.
- Python's support and ever-evolving libraries make it one of the best choices for all sorts of projects, like Web App, Mobile App, IoT, Data Science, AI, etc.
- The pseudocode in computer science is a plain language description of all the steps of an algorithm.
- A flowchart shows the logic of a program in a simple way.
- A flowchart is an easy and efficient tool to analyse a problem.
- It is easy to convert the flowchart into any programming language code.
- A diagrammatic/graphical representation of a sequence of steps to solve a problem is known as a flowchart.
- Website for installation of Python: https://www.python.org
- Weblink for downloading Python documentation: https://www.python.org/doc

- Python does not allow punctuation/special characters such as @, $, and % within identifiers.
- All other identifiers except class names start with a lowercase letter.
- An identifier starting with a single leading underscore signifies when the identifier is private.
- When an identifier starts with two leading underscores, it indicates that the identifier is a strongly private identifier.
- When the identifier also ends with two trailing underscores, then the identifier is a language-defined special name.
- Strings in Python are identified as a continuous set of characters represented in the quotation marks.
- The plus (+) sign is defined as the string concatenation operator, and the asterisk (*) is the repetition operator.
- Python language supports the operators: Arithmetic Operators, Comparison (Relational) Operators, Assignment Operators, Logical Operators, Bitwise Operators, Membership Operators, Identity Operators.
- Python has two types of type conversion: Implicit Type Conversion and Explicit Type Conversion.

Exercise Time

A. Multiple choice questions

Tick (√) the correct option for each question.

1. Which of the following languages is the most popular language used for AI-based devices nowadays?

   a. Java b. Ruby
   c. C+ d. Python

2. In computer science, a plain language description of all the steps of an algorithm is called:

   a. Pseudocode b. Algorithm
   c. Code d. Output

3. Which of the following in Python are identified as a continuous set of characters represented in the quotation marks?

   a. Lists b. Strings
   c. Floats d. Integers

4. What is the correct syntax to output the type of variable in python?

   a. print(type of x) b. print(type of (x))
   c. print(type (x)) d. print(type x)

5. Which sign is defined as the string concatenation operator?
   a. + b. –
   c. * d. $
6. Which extension is used for Python files?
   a. .px b. .py
   c. *py d. $py
7. Which of the following is used to enclose strings in Python?
   a. Single quote (' ') b. Double quote (" ")
   c. Triple Quote (""" """) d. Any of the above
8. Which sign is used to end all control flow statements in Python?
   a. Full stop (.) b. Semicolon (;)
   c. Colon (:) d. Hash tag (#)
9. Which term is used for special symbols that perform some action on operands?
   a. Operation b. Operators
   c. Floats d. Tuples
10. The remarks that are added by the programmer to understand the code later, are called:
   a. Comments b. Lists
   c. Instructions d. Tuples

Answers: 1.d, 2.a, 3.b, 4.d, 5.a, 6.b, 7.d, 8.c, 9.b, 10.a.

B. State whether the following statements are true/false

1. Flowchart makes program or system maintenance difficult.
2. Python has five standard data types.
3. Class names start with an uppercase letter.
4. The flowchart does not show the logic of a program in a simple way.
5. A diagrammatic/graphical representation of a sequence of steps to solve a problem is known as a flowchart.
6. Lists are enclosed in parenthesis.
7. Python has three types of type conversion.
8. When the identifier also ends with two trailing underscores, then the identifier is a language-defined special name.
9. Strings in Python are identified as a contiguous set of characters represented in the quotation marks.
10. The negative (-) sign is defined as the string concatenation operator.

Answers: 1.F (easier) 2.T 3.T 4.F 5.T 6.T 7.F (two) 8.T 9.T 10.F(plus)

C. Very short answer questions

1. Define Python.
2. What do you mean by a string?
3. Define float.
4. What do you mean by Lists in Python?
5. What is implicit type conversion?

D. Short answer questions

1. Write two uses of NLTK packages in Python.
2. Differentiate among float, string and integer.
3. What are the main applications of a flowchart?
4. Mention two kinds of Type conversion.
5. Write the commands to install Python.

E. Long answer questions

1. List six companies that use Python.
2. List down the various types of comments.
3. Discuss the rules for the naming of variables and constants.
4. What do you mean by type conversion? Explain with the help of examples.
5. Explain python input and output with the help of a code example.
6. Write a program to find numbers that are divisible by 7 and multiple of 5 between 300 and 500.
7. Discuss the main features of Python.

Projects and practical

1. **Debate:**

   Students will participate in the debate on the topic **'Future of Python is not bright'** and present their views either in affirmation to the topic or against it. They have to deliberate with their points about the future of Python in AI projects.

2. **Video session and class discussion**

   Watch a video related to Python on the following topics and have a class discussion after viewing videos on the topics related to Python applications.

   The teacher will play the following video or any other related video, followed by class discussion:

(i) What Can You Do with Python? – The 3 Main Applications
https://www.youtube.com/watch?v=kLZuut1fYzQ

3. **Writing an interactive story**

   Write an interactive story depicting the future AI-based innovative applications in various fields.

4. **Theme-based research and powerpoint presentation**

   Teacher will divide the class into small groups of 4-8 students. Each group will research on the topic "**Future of Programming Languages**" and will prepare a report in the form of a PowerPoint Presentation (10-15 slides). Two representatives from each group will present their report in the seminar. Other children will be allowed to ask questions related to the presentations.

5. **Job ad creating activity**

   Suppose you are running an Ad agency "***Dreamz Unlimited***" in the year 2035 and you have to create a job advertisement for the post of "**Data Analyst**" for one of your clients- '**Atharv AI Solutions'** by describing the nature of the job available and the skill-set required for the job. The client firm has specialisation in creating AI Devices and AI solutions to different types of industries. The ad should be created in about 150-200 words.

6. **Class seminar on AI trends and python**

   Learners will be divided into groups of 4-6 without any bias. Each group will have to search for present AI trends and need to visualise the future of AI and Python in and around the various themes. Two representatives from each group will present the oral report before the full class.

7. **Write the Python codes/programs for the following problems:**

   a. Write a Python Program to enter heights of five persons and calculate the mean height.

   b. Write a program to enter the length, breadth and height of a cuboid and calculate its volume.

   c. Write a program which inputs three sides of a triangle and calculate its perimeter,semi perimeter and area.

   d. Write a Python program to find the sum of all even numbers from1 to 10.

   e. Write a Python program to find the sum of the first 10 odd numbers.

   f. Write a program to find compound interest for entered principal amount, time and rate of interest.

   g. Write a Python program to enter three numbers and find the lowest one.

   h. Write a program to accept a positive value from a user and print the cube of the number.

   i. Find the output of the following Python code:

   ```
   x=2
   y=8
   ```

```
for x in range(1, y):
    print(x,y)
```

j. Find the output of the following Python code:

```
i=1
while True:
    if i%7==0:
        break
    print(i)
    i+=1
```

References and further readings

1. Python_Content_Manual.pdf (cbseacademic.nic.in)
2. https://www.codingdojo.com/blog/top-7-programming-languages
3. https://www.codingdojo.com/blog/top-7-programming-languageshttps://www.w3schools.com/python/python_intro.asp
4. https://www.programiz.com/python-programming/first-program https://www.geeksforgeeks.org/python-programming-language/
5. https://www.edrawsoft.com/explainalgorithm-flowchart.php
6. https://www.w3schools.com/python/python_conditions.asp
7. https://thestempedia.com/blog/simple-ai-and-machine-learning-projects-for-students-and-beginners/
8. https://www.pstanalytics.com/blog/advanced-analytics/python-list-data-science/
9. https://kids.kiddle.co/Algorithm

Notes

2 Guidelines for Conducting Projects, Activities, and Practical

Active participation of students in activities, projects, and practical work is the basis for experiential learning. As NEP 2020 gives emphasis on skills development and technology awareness through learning by doing, the active participation of students in practical activities and projects will provide them an opportunity to explore the world as a whole. Strict planning and choosing the right activities and projects as per the need of the subject by the teachers will create curiosity and interest among students.

An activity is something that one does or something that is going on. According to Merriam -Webster, 'an activity is defined as the quality or state of being active; Behaviour or actions of a particular kind.' In simple words, the participation of an individual or more persons in some action for a purpose is called activity, whereas a project is defined as an undertaking/work carried out individually or collectively by two or more people collaboratively involving some research or design for attaining some aim. Practical involves working actually rather than reading/studying or making something after getting theoretical knowledge.

Three types of Activities /Projects may be organized involving:

- Individual
- Pair
- Group (4-8 students)

Figure 2.1: *Individual work*

Figure 2.2: *Oral presentation*

Figure 2.3: *Pair activity*

Figure 2.4: *Teamwork*

Figure 2.5: *Group activity*

2.1 Instructional methods

Ability is defined as the capacity to do some work, while skill is defined as the capacity to do some work with perfection. Thus, skills are those abilities that are attained by doing more and more practice. When any activity is carried out in the class by a teacher, not only are educational aims achieved by clearing the concepts but a good number of skills are also developed among the learners. Take this example, when a teacher is carrying a 'reading the passage activity' in the class, the main objectives are to develop the reading skills, capturing new words, understanding the meaning of new words, and correlating the meaning of new words in the context of given passage but at the same time the skills among the students developed includes increasing attention capacity, listening capacity (listening is hearing with a purpose), confidence level, removing hesitation to present self before a group, increasing word power, self-awareness (here, how many words an individual knows?), presentation skills, communication skills, listening to others with empathy, etc.

So, during the organization of activities, new and dynamic methods, including the use of elective media, are to be adopted with a view to inculcate skills, like curiosity, life skills, encouraging self-study, and nurture problem-solving skills among students.

(a) Methods/Tools/Techniques involving construction of creative activities

- Poster making
- Creating an advertisement
- Collage making
- Charts
- Scrapbooks
- Preparing PowerPoint Presentation
- Project preparation
- Coding/programming
- Model making
- Story writing
- Case studies (individual working)
- Drawing
- Sketches
- Graphs
- Flannel Board
- Specimen
- Cartoons
- Diagrams

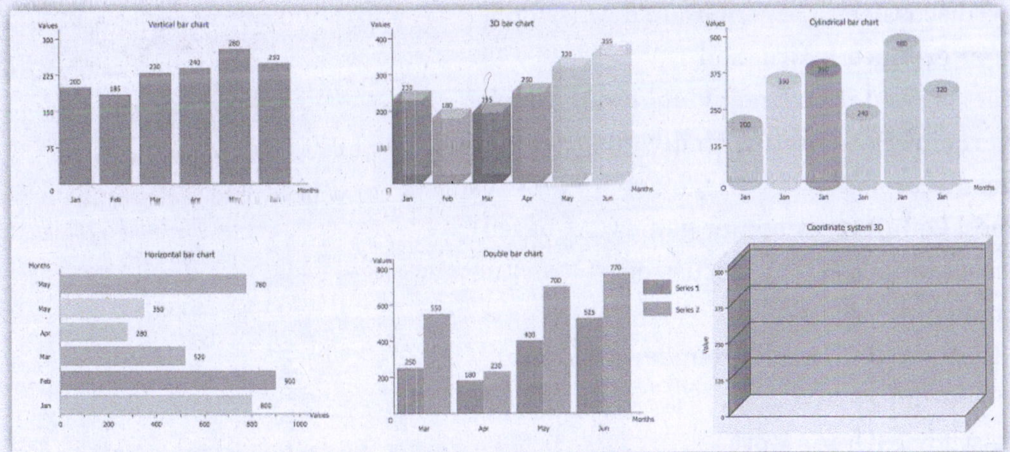

***Figure 2.6:** Graphs*

Figure 2.7: *Flannel Board*

(b) Methods/Tools/Techniques involving participation and observation

- Surveys
- Quiz
- Field visits/ Industrial Visit
- Class seminar
- Role Plays/ Plays
- Debates
- Group Discussion (Small)
- Class discussion / Larger Group discussion
- Computer-aided instruction
- Report presentation (Individual/Pair/Group)
- PowerPoint Presentation (Individual/Pair/Group)
- Panel discussion
- Games/ Online or computer games (AI-based)
- Video show followed by discussion
- Excursions
- Discussions (Pair/small group/larger group)
- Brainstorming
- Case studies (Group work)
- Slide shows (ppt)

Figure 2.8: *Survey*

- Demonstrations
- Mock Interviews
- Experiments
- Study tours
- Inter-school visits
- Lecturers
- Story Telling
- Newspaper reading
- Video Film shows
- Radio programs
- Audio recording & programmes
- Media analysis
- Puppetry
- Dance
- Drama
- Songs
- Poems/Mimes

Figure 2.9: *Field Trip*

2.2 Criteria for selection of activities/projects

While planning an activity/ project for the students, the following criteria may be kept in mind:

a. The activity should be in accordance with the basic concept(s) involving purposive, meaningful, and manual work.

b. It should help the students in nurturing desirable life skills, ethics, and values.

c. It should be best suited to the level of maturity of students.

d. It should be capable of generating enough interest among the students.

e. It should be easy to be organized by using most of the school's resources.

f. It should have the dimensions ,like:

   - Identification and possible solution of a problem;
   - Observation skills;
   - Active participation of students;
   - Presentation skills
   - Cultivation of good habits, values, and attitudes
   - Production of goods/services.

2.3 Life skills

During the organization and participation in activities and projects, some life skills are inculcated among the students. Let's try to understand life skills.

Life skills are those skills that are required to lead a meaningful and successful life by an individual. According to WHO, 'Life skills are defined as the abilities for adaptive and positive behaviour for enabling individuals to deal effectively with the demands and challenges of everyday life.' Life skills are abilities that facilitate the physical, mental and emotional well-being an individual.

Figure 2.10: *WHO*

The following life skills are required to be developed among students during schooling days as per the guidelines of the World Health Organization:

- Self-awareness
- Critical Thinking
- Creativity
- Empathy
- Decision-making
- Problem-solving
- Interpersonal relationship skills
- Intrapersonal relationship skills
- Managing feelings and emotions
- Stress management
- Time management
- Advocacy

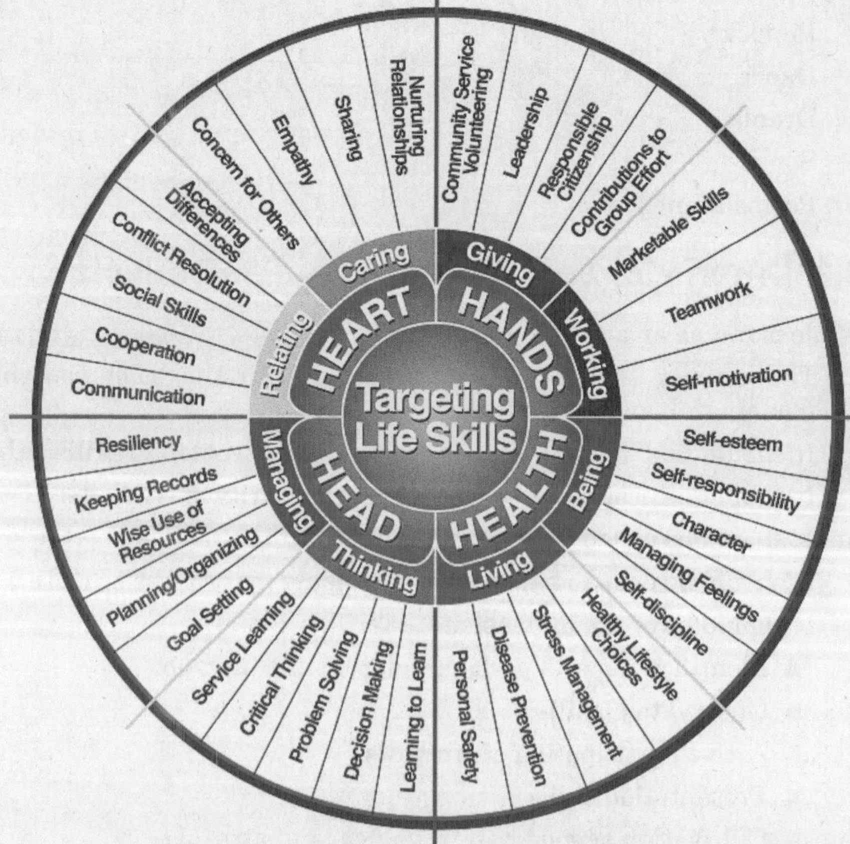

Figure 2.11: *Life skills*

(Picture Courtesy: https://maul15.blogspot.com/2019/02/targeting-life-skills-4-h.html)

2.4 Assessment evaluation tools

The evaluation tools, which can be used include:

- Observation
- Viva/Interview/Oral test
- Group Discussion and Debate
- Written test (Objective type questions)
- Reports
- Work Book
- Feedback Sheets
- Attitude Scales
- Practical Exercises
- Checklist

Sometimes digital tools, as shown in Figure 2.11, may also be used as per the need and requirements.

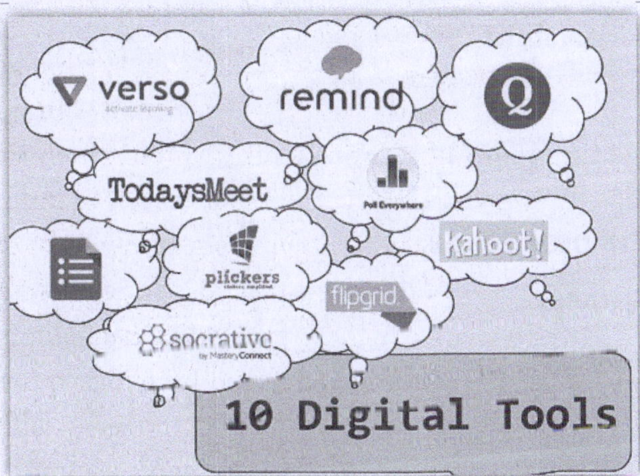

Figure 2.12

(picture courtesy: https://zahnerhistory.com/2015/05/10-digital-tools-for-formative assessments html)

2.5 Preparing for AI project

Identify a local issue affecting your school or community that could be solved using artificial intelligence (AI). While doing this, students will learn more about problems they can solve to improve lives and make the world a better place.

The participants of the group project will learn the following skills:

- Working in a team

- Identifying an issue and who is getting affected (the user)
- Participating in brainstorming to get solutions and select the best one (developing critical thinking and creativity, communication skills)
- Deciding the type of AI useful for your proposed solution (decision-making skills)
- Collecting data ethically (ethics and values)
- Using data to train a computer to help solve the issue (technical skills)
- How to test the prototype with users and use their feedback to improve the solution? (technical skills, problem-solving skills)
- How to pitch the solution to people who will be able to help in taking action? (Empathy, team building, time management)

2.6 Some indicators for assessment of cognitive and non-cognitive learning outcomes

(a) Assessment of a product/Project outcome

- Use of scientific theory/method
- Utility
- Durability
- Presentation

(b) Assessment of the processes

- Imagination and creativity
- Regularity and punctuality
- Orderliness
- Team spirit and cooperativeness
- Patience and tolerance
- Planned and systematic work
- Use of appropriate tools and materials
- Care of tools and leaving them in proper place after work
- Sustainable resource utilization
- Neatness and cleanliness in work
- Positive attitude
- Devotion and honest effort in work
- Perseverance and zeal for perfection
- Self-effort and problem-solving spirit

- Workmanship and skill in the performance of work

The criteria, as listed above, are large in number and varied as many cognitive and non-cognitive capacities are required to be developed and inculcated among the children for their overall personality development and professional growth while participating in activities and projects. For a specific activity, the teacher may identify the selection criteria.

(c) Indicators for assessment of students during a Field-visit

- Discipline and orderly behaviour.
- Seriousness in the purpose of the visit.
- Interest and inquisitiveness.
- Making relevant and probing queries.
- Tactfulness in eliciting information.
- Avoidance of putting embarrassing questions and making humiliating or derogatory comments.
- Showing proper courtesy, respect, and dignity to the people, particularly the workers of the place of visit.
- Avoidance of repetitiveness in making queries.

Figure 2.13

(d) Indicators for assessment of a post-visit discussion/debate

- Sensitivity and insight developed.
- Social awareness reflected.
- Understanding the importance of economic activities.
- Understanding the simple and basic facts of life and living through mutual co-operation, participation and contribution.

- Patiently listening and allowing others to put forward their points of view.
- Presenting own point of view.
- Observance of proper etiquette, courtesy, and respect while interacting with others.

(e) Indicators for assessment of a report of a field visit

- Detailed, thorough, correct, and systematic presentation.
- Understanding of the importance of the role played and contribution made by the centre visited (production or services) for the individuals as well as the society as a whole.
- Sensitivity reflected
- Reflective thinking and feeling developed.
- Care, sincerity, and seriousness in preparing the report.
- Understanding of how various economic activities and public services are going on through the process of their necessary interdependence in the world of work as well as their indispensability individual, society, and national life.

(f) Indicators for assessment of a Log Book/Practical Notebook/ Journal

- Detailed and systematic keeping of records.
- Care and neatness in maintaining the workbook.
- Regularity in maintaining the workbook and getting it regularly checked up by the teacher.

2.7 Tips/guidelines/points for consideration

- Plan the activity/project/ practical work carefully. Make a time schedule.
- Clarify the objectives of the activity/project undertaken to all the participants.
- For any pair activity, always try to make heterogeneous pairs to remove gender bias.
- For any group activity/ work, divide the class into groups randomly without gender bias. All groups should have boys and girls both.
- The process/flow of the activity should be made clear.
- The roles of all group members should be made clear.
- Stick to the plan and timetable that helps you to give the right amount of attention to complete the activity/project within the given time limit.
- Participants should participate in the activities actively and attentively.
- Assessment/evaluation criteria (Rubrics) of the activity should be made clear to all participants by the teacher.
- Emphasis should be given to the participation of all students.
- Efforts of each child should be appreciated as attaining success should not be the sole criteria for getting good marks/grades in the activity. This is the process of learning by doing.

- No one can expect to remember everything. So, note down a summary of what you have done.
- Keep your journal/activity logbook/practical file updated, having details of participation in all activities (date wise).
- Create and keep records of evidence of the activities in the form of pictures, newspaper cuttings, screenshots of posts on social media, etc.

Figure 2.14

Notes

3 Coding Problems and Programs Based on Python

3.1 Python coding problems and programs

Use the following steps to check whether the coding programs written by you are working well or not:

- Read the problem carefully and think about input, process, and output.
- Write the code/program and 'Run' it on IDLE of Python 3.8.3. (Before 'Run' the program, you will be asked to save it on your computer).
- Alternatively, you may check your program on an Online Python Compiler. Click on any of the following websites:

  https://www.programiz.com/python-programming/online-compiler/

  https://www.online-python.com/online_python_compiler

  https://www.onlinegdb.com/

  Write your program in main.py and then click 'Run' to see the results in the python shell. If the program is working well, it will be shown there. In case of some errors in the program, they will be reflected line-wise, which can be rectified easily.

3.1.1 Solved problems

1. **Write a python program to multiply two variables.**

```
A=int(input("Enter the first number:"))
b=int(input("Enter the second number:"))
c=a*b
print("product=", c)
```

py.10.py - D:/BPB projects 2021/IX AI Projects book/source code for python programs/py.10.py (3.8.3)

File Edit Format Run Options Window Help

```
a=int(input("Enter the first number:"))
b=int(input("Enter the second number:"))
c=a*b
print("Product=",c)
```

Figure 3.1 a: Code

```
Python 3.8.3 Shell
File Edit Shell Debug Options Window Help
Python 3.8.3 (tags/v3.8.3:6f8c832, May 13 2020, 22:20:19) [MSC v.1925 32 bit (Intel)] on win32
Type "help", "copyright", "credits" or "license()" for more information.
>>>
= RESTART: D:/BPB projects 2021/IX AI Projects book/source code for python programs/py.10.py
Enter the first number:45
Enter the second number:65
Product= 2925
>>> |
```

***Figure 3.1 b:** Output*

2. Write a python program to accept a positive value from the user and print the cube of the number.

```
a=int(input("Enter the  number:"))
if(a<0):
    print("Number is negative")
else:
    print("The cube of",a,"=",a*a*a)
```

```
py.10.py - D:/BPB projects 2021/IX AI Projects book/source code for python programs/py.10.py (3.8.3)
File Edit Format Run Options Window Help
a=int(input("Enter the  number:"))
if(a<0):
    print("Number is negative")
else:
    print("The cube of",a,"=",a*a*a)
```

***Figure 3.2 a:** Code*

```
Python 3.8.3 Shell
File Edit Shell Debug Options Window Help
Python 3.8.3 (tags/v3.8.3:6f8c832, May 13 2020, 22:20:19) [MSC v.1925 32 bit (Intel)] on win32
Type "help", "copyright", "credits" or "license()" for more information.
>>>
= RESTART: D:/BPB projects 2021/IX AI Projects book/source code for python programs/py.10.py
Enter the  number:7
The cube of 7 = 343
>>> |
```

***Figure 3.2 b:** Output*

```
Python 3.8.3 Shell
File Edit Shell Debug Options Window Help
Python 3.8.3 (tags/v3.8.3:6f8c832, May 13 2020, 22:20:19) [MSC v.1925 32 bit (Intel)] on win32
Type "help", "copyright", "credits" or "license()" for more information.
>>>
= RESTART: D:/BPB projects 2021/IX AI Projects book/source code for python programs/py.10.py
Enter the  number:-8
Number is negative
>>> |
```

***Figure 3.2 c:** Output*

3. **Write a python program for accepting an integer from the user and checking if this number is less than 15.**

```
a=int(input("Enter the first number:"))

print("number =",a)

if(a<15):

    print("Number is less than 15")

else:

    print("Number is greater than 15")
```

```
py.10.py - D:/BPB projects 2021/IX AI Projects book/source code for python programs/py.10.py (3.8.3)
File Edit Format Run Options Window Help
a=int(input("Enter the number:"))
print("number =",a)
if(a<15):
    print("Number is less than 15")
else:
    print("Number is greater than 15")
```

Figure 3.3 a: Code

```
Python 3.8.3 Shell
File Edit Shell Debug Options Window Help
Python 3.8.3 (tags/v3.8.3:6f8c832, May 13 2020, 22:20:19) [MSC v.1925 32 bit (Intel)] on win32
Type "help", "copyright", "credits" or "license()" for more information.
>>>
= RESTART: D:/BPB projects 2021/IX AI Projects book/source code for python programs/py.10.py
Enter the number:66
number = 66
Number is greater than 15
>>>
```

Figure 3.3 b: Output

```
Python 3.8.3 Shell
File Edit Shell Debug Options Window Help
Python 3.8.3 (tags/v3.8.3:6f8c832, May 13 2020, 22:20:19) [MSC v.1925 32 bit (Intel)] on win32
Type "help", "copyright", "credits" or "license()" for more information.
>>>
= RESTART: D:/BPB projects 2021/IX AI Projects book/source code for python programs/py.10.py
Enter the number:-8
number = -8
Number is less than 15
>>>
```

Figure 3.3 c: Output

4. **Write a python program to print the smallest number out of the three numbers entered.**

```
a=int(input("Enter the first number:a="))

b=int(input("Enter the second number:b="))
```

```
c=int(input("Enter the third number:c="))
if(a<=b and a<=c):
    print("a is the smallest number")
elif(b<=a and b<=c):
    print("b is the smallest number")
else:
    print("c is the smallest number")
```

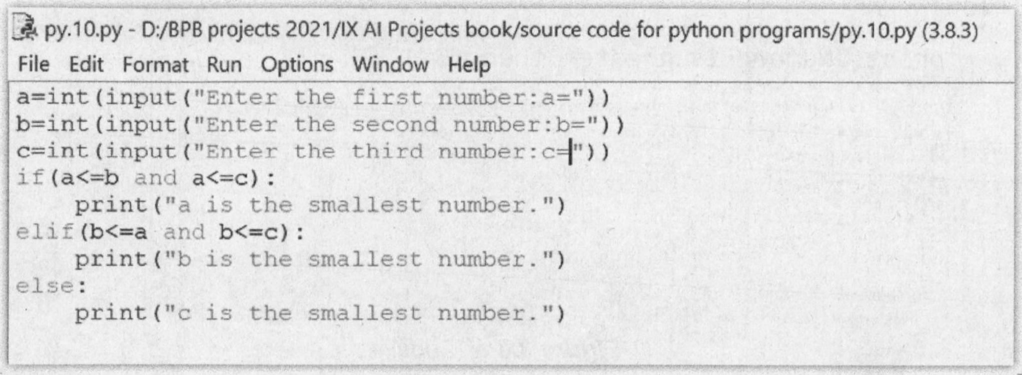

```
py.10.py - D:/BPB projects 2021/IX AI Projects book/source code for python programs/py.10.py (3.8.3)
File Edit Format Run Options Window Help
a=int(input("Enter the first number:a="))
b=int(input("Enter the second number:b="))
c=int(input("Enter the third number:c="))
if(a<=b and a<=c):
    print("a is the smallest number.")
elif(b<=a and b<=c):
    print("b is the smallest number.")
else:
    print("c is the smallest number.")
```

***Figure 3.4 a:** Code*

```
Python 3.8.3 Shell
File Edit Shell Debug Options Window Help
Python 3.8.3 (tags/v3.8.3:6f8c832, May 13 2020, 22:20:19) [MSC v.1925 32 bit (Intel)] on win32
Type "help", "copyright", "credits" or "license()" for more information.
>>>
= RESTART: D:/BPB projects 2021/IX AI Projects book/source code for python programs/py.10.py
Enter the first number:a=76
Enter the second number:b=34
Enter the third number:c=-56
c is the smallest number.
>>>
```

***Figure 3.4 b:** Output*

```
Python 3.8.3 Shell
File Edit Shell Debug Options Window Help
Python 3.8.3 (tags/v3.8.3:6f8c832, May 13 2020, 22:20:19) [MSC v.1925 32 bit (Intel)] on win32
Type "help", "copyright", "credits" or "license()" for more information.
>>>
= RESTART: D:/BPB projects 2021/IX AI Projects book/source code for python programs/py.10.py
Enter the first number:a=-7
Enter the second number:b=-78
Enter the third number:c=-45
b is the smallest number.
>>>
```

***Figure 3.4 c:** Output*

```
Python 3.8.3 Shell
File Edit Shell Debug Options Window Help
Python 3.8.3 (tags/v3.8.3:6f8c832, May 13 2020, 22:20:19) [MSC v.1925 32 bit (Intel)] on win32
Type "help", "copyright", "credits" or "license()" for more information.
>>>
= RESTART: D:/BPB projects 2021/IX AI Projects book/source code for python programs/py.10.py
Enter the first number:a=44
Enter the second number:b=76
Enter the third number:c=93
a is the smallest number.
>>> |
```

Figure 3.4 d: Output

5. **Write a python program to print the area of a triangle when all three sides of a triangle are given.**

```
a=int(input("Enter the first side:"))
b=int(input("Enter the second side:"))
c=int(input("Enter the third side:"))
s=(a+b+c)/2
area=(s*(s-a)*(s-b)*(s-c))**0.5
print("area of triangle =",area)
```

```
py.10.py - D:/BPB projects 2021/IX AI Projects book/source code for python programs/py.10.py (3.8.3)
File Edit Format Run Options Window Help
a=int(input("Enter the first side:"))
b=int(input("Enter the second side:"))
c=int(input("Enter the third side:"))
s=(a+b+c)/2
area=(s*(s-a)*(s-b)*(s-c))**0.5
print("area of triangle =",area)
```

Figure 3.5 a: Code

```
Python 3.8.3 Shell
File Edit Shell Debug Options Window Help
Python 3.8.3 (tags/v3.8.3:6f8c832, May 13 2020, 22:20:19) [MSC v.1925 32 bit (Intel)] on win32
Type "help", "copyright", "credits" or "license()" for more information.
>>>
= RESTART: D:/BPB projects 2021/IX AI Projects book/source code for python programs/py.10.py
Enter the first side:3
Enter the second side:4
Enter the third side:5
area of triangle = 6.0
>>> |
```

Figure 3.5 b: Output

6. **Write a python program to create and print 5,10,15, ... till 35.**

```
num=5
```

```
print("Numbers from 5 to 35 with 5 intervals")
while(num<=35):
    print(num)
 num=num+5
```

```
py.10.py - D:/BPB projects 2021/IX AI Projects book/source code for python programs/py.10.py (3.8.3)
File Edit Format Run Options Window Help
num=5
print("Numbers from 5 to 35 with 5 intervals")
while(num<=35):
    print(num)
    num=num+5
```

Figure 3.6 a: *Code*

```
Python 3.8.3 Shell
File Edit Shell Debug Options Window Help
Python 3.8.3 (tags/v3.8.3:6f8c832, May 13 2020, 22:20:19) [MSC v.1925 32 bit (Intel)] on win32
Type "help", "copyright", "credits" or "license()" for more information.
>>>
= RESTART: D:/BPB projects 2021/IX AI Projects book/source code for python programs/py.10.py
Numbers from 5 to 35 with 5 intervals
5
10
15
20
25
30
35
>>> |
```

Figure 3.6 b: *Output*

7. **Show the output of the following code:**

```
a,b=10,5
x,y=a+b,b-2
z=x-y
print("x:",x,"y:",y,"z:",z)
```

```
py.12.py - D:/BPB projects 2021/IX AI Projects book/source code for python programs/py.12.py (3.8.3)
File Edit Format Run Options Window Help
a,b=10,5
x,y=a+b,b-2
z=x-y
print("x:",x,"y:",y,"z:",z)
```

Figure 3.7 a: *Code*

```
py.10.py - D:/BPB projects 2021/IX AI Projects book/source code for python programs/py.10.py (3.8.3)
File Edit Format Run Options Window Help
a,b=10,5
x,y=a+b,b-2
z=x-y
print("x:",x,"y:",y,"z:",z)
```

Figure 3.7 b: Output

8. **If a three digits number is input through the keyboard, write a program to reverse the digits of the number.**

```
n=int(input("Enter number :"))

rev=0

while(n>0):

    dig = n%10

    rev=rev*10+dig

    n=n//10

print("The reverse of the number:" ,rev)
```

```
py.12.py - D:/BPB projects 2021/IX AI Projects book/source code for python programs/py.12.py (3.8.3)
File Edit Format Run Options Window Help
n=int(input("Enter number :"))
rev=0
while(n>0):
    dig = n%10
    rev=rev*10+dig
    n=n//10
print("The reverse order of digits of the number:" ,rev)
```

Figure 3.8 a: Code

```
Python 3.8.3 Shell
File Edit Shell Debug Options Window Help
Python 3.8.3 (tags/v3.8.3:6f8c832, May 13 2020, 22.20:19) [MSC v.1925 32 bit (Intel)] on win32
Type "help", "copyright", "credits" or "license()" for more information.
>>>
= RESTART: D:/BPB projects 2021/IX AI Projects book/source code for python programs/py.12.py
Enter number :739
The reverse order of digits of the number: 937
>>> |
```

Figure 3.8 b: Output

9. **Write a python program to input a number when the number is even, then print its cube; otherwise, print its square.**

```
n=int(input("Enter a number :"))
if(n%2==0):
    print("The number is even")
    print("The cube of the number is",n*n*n)
else:
    print("The number is odd")
    print("The square of the number is",n*n)
```

```
py.12.py - D:/BPB projects 2021/IX AI Projects book/source code for python programs/py.12.py (3.8.3)
File Edit Format Run Options Window Help
n=int(input("Enter a number :"))
if(n%2==0):
    print("The number is even")
    print("The cube of the number is",n*n*n)
else:
    print("The number is odd")
    print("The square of the number is",n*n)
```

***Figure 3.9 a:** Code*

```
Python 3.8.3 Shell
File Edit Shell Debug Options Window Help
Python 3.8.3 (tags/v3.8.3:6f8c832, May 13 2020, 22:20:19) [MSC v.1925 32 bit (Intel)] on win32
Type "help", "copyright", "credits" or "license()" for more information.
>>>
= RESTART: D:/BPB projects 2021/IX AI Projects book/source code for python programs/py.12.py
Enter a number :27
The number is odd
The square of the number is 729
>>>
```

***Figure 3.9 b:** Output*

```
Python 3.8.3 Shell
File Edit Shell Debug Options Window Help
Python 3.8.3 (tags/v3.8.3:6f8c832, May 13 2020, 22:20:19) [MSC v.1925 32 bit (Intel)] on win32
Type "help", "copyright", "credits" or "license()" for more information.
>>>
= RESTART: D:/BPB projects 2021/IX AI Projects book/source code for python programs/py.12.py
Enter a number :36
The number is even
The cube of the number is 46656
>>>
```

***Figure 3.9 c:** Output*

10. Write a python program to generate and print all even numbers from 1 to 20.

```
print("The even numbers from 1 to 20")
for i in range(2,21,2):
 print(i)
```

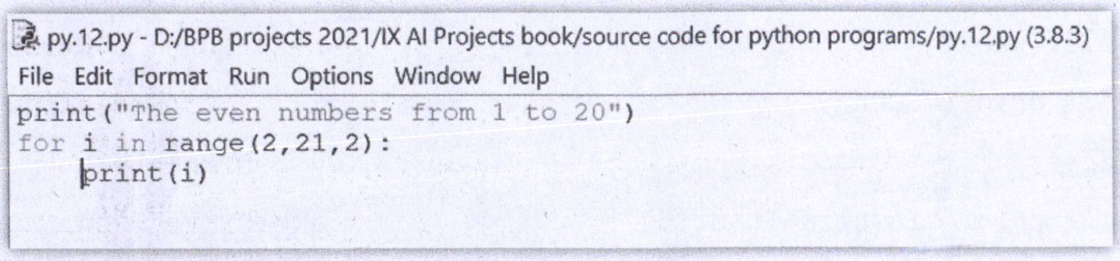

```
py.12.py - D:/BPB projects 2021/IX AI Projects book/source code for python programs/py.12.py (3.8.3)
File Edit Format Run Options Window Help
print("The even numbers from 1 to 20")
for i in range(2,21,2):
    print(i)
```

Figure 3.10 a: Code

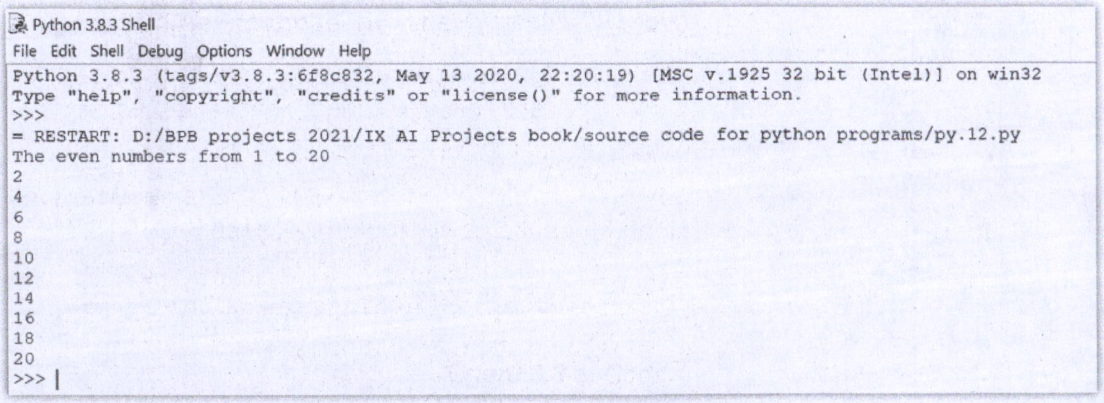

```
Python 3.8.3 Shell
File Edit Shell Debug Options Window Help
Python 3.8.3 (tags/v3.8.3:6f8c832, May 13 2020, 22:20:19) [MSC v.1925 32 bit (Intel)] on win32
Type "help", "copyright", "credits" or "license()" for more information.
>>>
= RESTART: D:/BPB projects 2021/IX AI Projects book/source code for python programs/py.12.py
The even numbers from 1 to 20
2
4
6
8
10
12
14
16
18
20
>>> |
```

Figure 3.10 b: Output

11. Write a python program that will allow an integer from 1 to 7 to be input and the name of the day of the week corresponding to the integer to be output.

```
week=int(input("Enter week number 1-7: "))
if(week == 1):
    print("Monday")
elif(week == 2):
    print("Tuesday")
elif(week == 3):
    print("Wednesday")
elif(week == 4):
    print("Thursday")
```

```
elif(week == 5):
    print("Friday")
elif(week == 6):
    print("Saturday")
elif(week == 7):
    print("Sunday")
else:
    print("Invalid Input!")
```

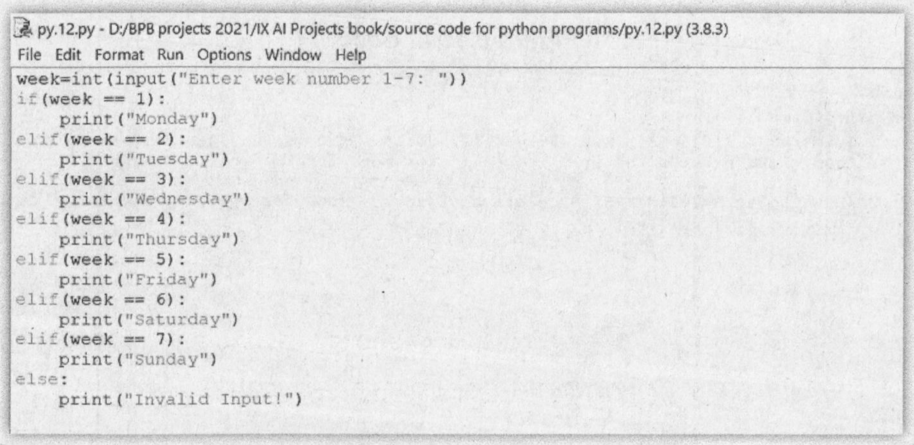

```
py.12.py - D:/BPB projects 2021/IX AI Projects book/source code for python programs/py.12.py (3.8.3)
File Edit Format Run Options Window Help
week=int(input("Enter week number 1-7: "))
if(week == 1):
    print("Monday")
elif(week == 2):
    print("Tuesday")
elif(week == 3):
    print("Wednesday")
elif(week == 4):
    print("Thursday")
elif(week == 5):
    print("Friday")
elif(week == 6):
    print("Saturday")
elif(week == 7):
    print("Sunday")
else:
    print("Invalid Input!")
```

***Figure 3.11 a:** Code*

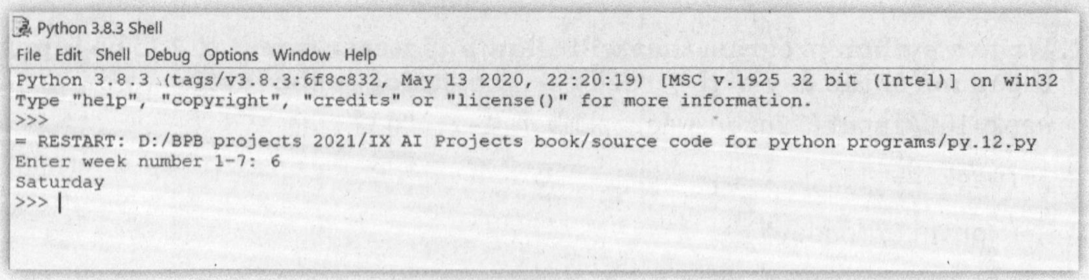

```
Python 3.8.3 Shell
File Edit Shell Debug Options Window Help
Python 3.8.3 (tags/v3.8.3:6f8c832, May 13 2020, 22:20:19) [MSC v.1925 32 bit (Intel)] on win32
Type "help", "copyright", "credits" or "license()" for more information.
>>>
= RESTART: D:/BPB projects 2021/IX AI Projects book/source code for python programs/py.12.py
Enter week number 1-7: 6
Saturday
>>> |
```

***Figure 3.11 b:** Output*

12. Write a python program for the calculation of the area of a parallelogram.

```
base = float(input("Length of base:"))
height = float(input("Measurement of height:"))
area = base * height
print("Area is: ", area)
```

py.12.py - D:/BPB projects 2021/IX AI Projects book/source code for python programs/py.12.py (3.8.3)

File Edit Format Run Options Window Help

```
base = float(input("Length of base:"))
height = float(input("Measurement of height:"))
area = base * height
print("Area =", area)
```

Figure 3.12 a: *Code*

Python 3.8.3 Shell

File Edit Shell Debug Options Window Help

```
Python 3.8.3 (tags/v3.8.3:6f8c832, May 13 2020, 22:20:19) [MSC v.1925 32 bit (Intel)] on win32
Type "help", "copyright", "credits" or "license()" for more information.
>>>
= RESTART: D:/BPB projects 2021/IX AI Projects book/source code for python programs/py.12.py
Length of base:8.5
Measurement of height:3.5
Area = 29.75
>>>
```

Figure 3.12 b: *Output*

13. Write a python program for swapping two variables.

```
var1=int(input("Enter the value of first variable:"))
var2=int(input("Enter the value of second variable:"))
print("After swapping the value of variables")
temp=var1
var1=var2
var2=temp
print("The value of variable 1 is",var1)
print("The value of variable 2 is",var2)
```

py.12.py - D:/BPB projects 2021/IX AI Projects book/source code for python programs/py.12.py (3.8.3)

File Edit Format Run Options Window Help

```
var1=int(input("Enter the value of first variable:"))
var2=int(input("Enter the value of second variable:"))
print("After swapping the value of variables")
temp=var1
var1=var2
var2=temp
print("The value of variable 1 is",var1)
print("The value of variable 2 is",var2)
```

Figure 3.13 a: *Code*

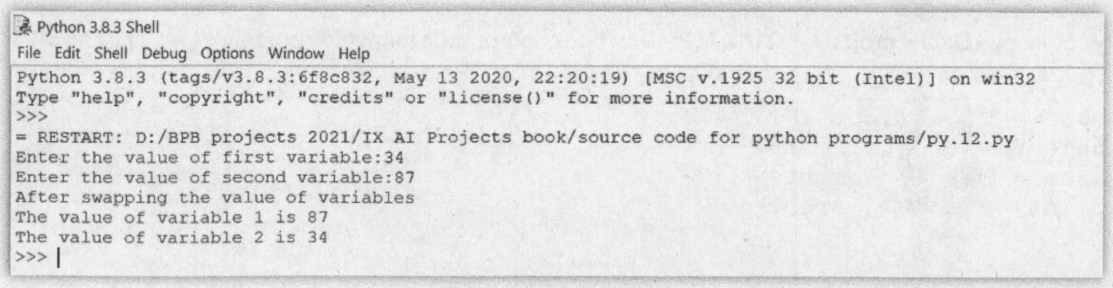

```
Python 3.8.3 Shell
File Edit Shell Debug Options Window Help
Python 3.8.3 (tags/v3.8.3:6f8c832, May 13 2020, 22:20:19) [MSC v.1925 32 bit (Intel)] on win32
Type "help", "copyright", "credits" or "license()" for more information.
>>>
= RESTART: D:/BPB projects 2021/IX AI Projects book/source code for python programs/py.12.py
Enter the value of first variable:34
Enter the value of second variable:87
After swapping the value of variables
The value of variable 1 is 87
The value of variable 2 is 34
>>>
```

Figure 3.13 b: *Output*

14. Write a python program to find simple interests.

```
principal=int(input("Enter the principal amount:"))
rate=int(input("Enter rate of interest:"))
time=int(input("Enter time:"))
SI=(principal*rate*time)/100
print("Simple interest is",SI)
```

```
py.12.py - D:/BPB projects 2021/IX AI Projects book/source code for python programs/py.12.py (3.8.3)
File Edit Format Run Options Window Help
principal=int(input("Enter the principal amount:"))
rate=int(input("Enter rate of interest:"))
time=int(input("Enter time:"))
SI=(principal*rate*time)/100
print("Simple interest is",SI)
```

Figure 3.14 a: *Code*

```
Python 3.8.3 Shell
File Edit Shell Debug Options Window Help
Python 3.8.3 (tags/v3.8.3:6f8c832, May 13 2020, 22:20:19) [MSC v.1925 32 bit (Intel)] on win32
Type "help", "copyright", "credits" or "license()" for more information.
>>>
= RESTART: D:/BPB projects 2021/IX AI Projects book/source code for python programs/py.12.py
Enter the principal amount:500
Enter rate of interest:3
Enter time:5
Simple interest is 75.0
>>>
```

Figure 3.14 b: *Output*

15. Write a python program to display a maximum and minimum of two numbers.

```
num1=int(input("Enter the first number:"))
num2=int(input("Enter the second number:"))
if(num1>num2):
    print("num1 is the maximum number")
```

```
else:
    print("num2 is the minimum number")
```

py.12.py - D:/BPB projects 2021/IX AI Projects book/source code for python programs/py.12.py (3.8.3)

File Edit Format Run Options Window Help

```
num1=int(input("Enter the first number:"))
num2=int(input("Enter the second number:"))
if(num1>num2):
    print("num1 has the maximum value")
else:
    print("num1 has the minimum value")
```

Figure 3.15 a: *Code*

Python 3.8.3 Shell

File Edit Shell Debug Options Window Help

```
Python 3.8.3 (tags/v3.8.3:6f8c832, May 13 2020, 22:20:19) [MSC v.1925 32 bit (Intel)] on win32
Type "help", "copyright", "credits" or "license()" for more information.
>>>
= RESTART: D:/BPB projects 2021/IX AI Projects book/source code for python programs/py.12.py
Enter the first number:66
Enter the second number:12
num1 has the maximum value
>>> |
```

Figure 3.15 b: *Output*

16. A school has the following rules for the grading system. Write a program to ask the user to enter marks of three subjects obtained out of 100 marks, find out the average, and print the corresponding grade as per the following table.

```
Below 25 - F
25 to 32 - E
33 to 45 - D
46 to 60 - C
61 to 80 - B
Above 81- A
print("Enter marks obtained in 3 subjects:")
sub1=input()
sub1=int(sub1)
sub2=int(input())
sub3=int(input())
sum=sub1+sub2+sub3
avg=sum/3
print("Total of marks=",sum)
```

```
print("Average marks=",avg)
if(avg<25):
    print("Your grade is F")
elif(avg>=25 and avg<45):
    print("Your grade is E")
elif(avg>=45 and avg<50):
    print("Your grade is D")
elif(avg>=50 and avg<60):
    print("Your grade is C")
elif(avg>=60 and avg<80):
    print("Your grade is B")
elif(avg>=80):
    print("Your grade is A")
else:
print("Strange grade!!")
```

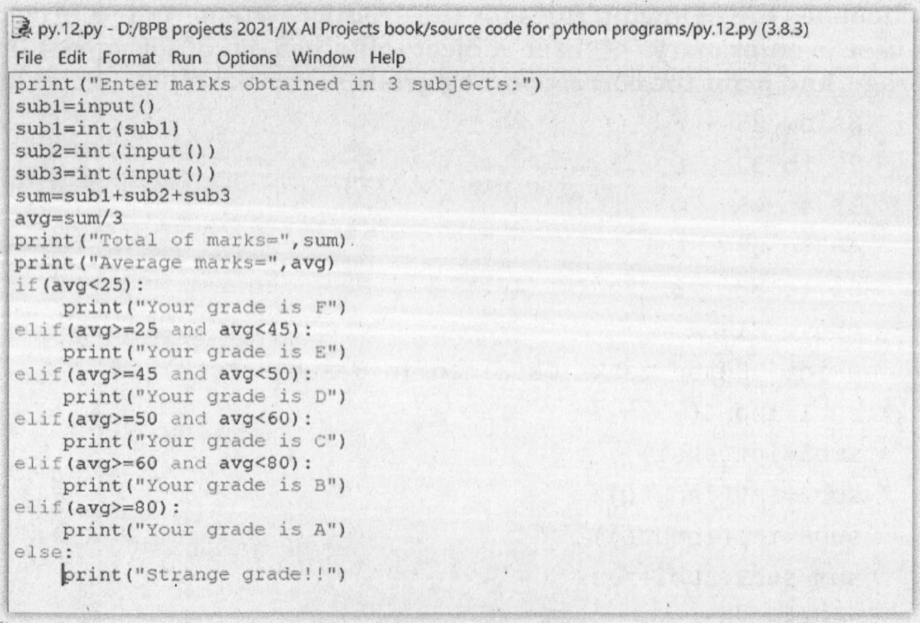

```
py.12.py - D:/BPB projects 2021/IX AI Projects book/source code for python programs/py.12.py (3.8.3)
File Edit Format Run Options Window Help
print("Enter marks obtained in 3 subjects:")
sub1=input()
sub1=int(sub1)
sub2=int(input())
sub3=int(input())
sum=sub1+sub2+sub3
avg=sum/3
print("Total of marks=",sum)
print("Average marks=",avg)
if(avg<25):
    print("Your grade is F")
elif(avg>=25 and avg<45):
    print("Your grade is E")
elif(avg>=45 and avg<50):
    print("Your grade is D")
elif(avg>=50 and avg<60):
    print("Your grade is C")
elif(avg>=60 and avg<80):
    print("Your grade is B")
elif(avg>=80):
    print("Your grade is A")
else:
    print("Strange grade!!")
```

Figure 3.16 a: *Code*

```
Python 3.8.3 Shell
File Edit Shell Debug Options Window Help
Python 3.8.3 (tags/v3.8.3:6f8c832, May 13 2020, 22:20:19) [MSC v.1925 32 bit (Intel)] on win32
Type "help", "copyright", "credits" or "license()" for more information.
>>>
= RESTART: D:/BPB projects 2021/IX AI Projects book/source code for python programs/py.12.py
Enter marks obtained in 3 subjects:
45
89
98
Total of marks= 232
Average marks= 77.33333333333333
Your grade is B
>>>
```

Figure 3.16 b: *Output*

17. Write a program to enter the name and height of the user. Convert the height into inches (1 Foot = 12 inches).

```
print("Input your height: ")
h_ft = int(input("Foot: "))
h_inch = h_ft * 12
print("Your height =",h_inch,"inch")
```

```
py.12.py - D:/BPB projects 2021/IX AI Projects book/source code for python programs/py.12.py (3.8.3)
File Edit Format Run Options Window Help
print("Input your height: ")
h_ft = int(input("Foot: "))
h_inch = h_ft * 12
print("Your height =",h_inch,"inch")
```

Figure 3.17 a: *Code*

```
Python 3.8.3 Shell
File Edit Shell Debug Options Window Help
Python 3.8.3 (tags/v3.8.3:6f8c832, May 13 2020, 22:20:19) [MSC v.1925 32 bit (Intel)] on win32
Type "help", "copyright", "credits" or "license()" for more information.
>>>
= RESTART: D:/BPB projects 2021/IX AI Projects book/source code for python programs/py.12.py
Input your height:
Foot: 8
Your height = 96 inch
>>>
```

Figure 3.17 b: *Output*

18. Write a python program to check whether the entered number is positive or negative.

```
n=int(input("Enter a number: "))
if(n>0):
```

```
    print("Number is positive")
else:
    print("Number is negative")
```

```
py.12.py - D:/BPB projects 2021/IX AI Projects book/source code for python programs/py.12.py (3.8.3)
File Edit Format Run Options Window Help
n=int(input("Enter a number: "))
if(n>0):
    print("Number is positive")
else:
    print("Number is negative")
```

Figure 3.18 a: *Code*

```
Python 3.8.3 Shell
File Edit Shell Debug Options Window Help
Python 3.8.3 (tags/v3.8.3:6f8c832, May 13 2020, 22:20:19) [MSC v.1925 32 bit (Intel)] on win32
Type "help", "copyright", "credits" or "license()" for more information.
>>>
= RESTART: D:/BPB projects 2021/IX AI Projects book/source code for python programs/py.12.py
Enter a number: 7
Number is positive
>>>
```

Figure 3.18 b: *Output*

```
Python 3.8.3 Shell
File Edit Shell Debug Options Window Help
Python 3.8.3 (tags/v3.8.3:6f8c832, May 13 2020, 22:20:19) [MSC v.1925 32 bit (Intel)] on win32
Type "help", "copyright", "credits" or "license()" for more information.
>>>
= RESTART: D:/BPB projects 2021/IX AI Projects book/source code for python programs/py.12.py
Enter a number: -45
Number is negative
>>>
```

Figure 3.18 c: *Output*

19. Write a python program to enter a number n and compute n+nn+nnn.

```
n=int(input("Enter a number n: "))
temp=str(n)
t1=temp+temp
t2=temp+temp+temp
comp=n+int(t1)+int(t2)
print("The value is:",comp)
```

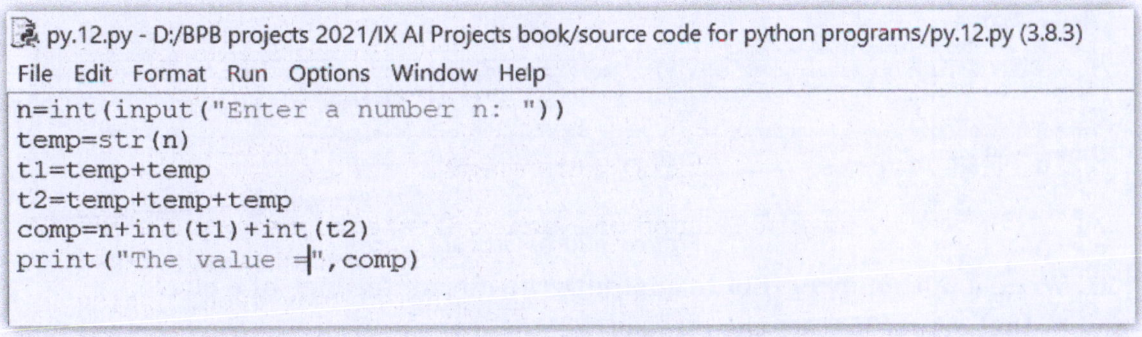

```
py.12.py - D:/BPB projects 2021/IX AI Projects book/source code for python programs/py.12.py (3.8.3)
File Edit Format Run Options Window Help
n=int(input("Enter a number n: "))
temp=str(n)
t1=temp+temp
t2=temp+temp+temp
comp=n+int(t1)+int(t2)
print("The value =",comp)
```

Figure 3.19 a: *Code*

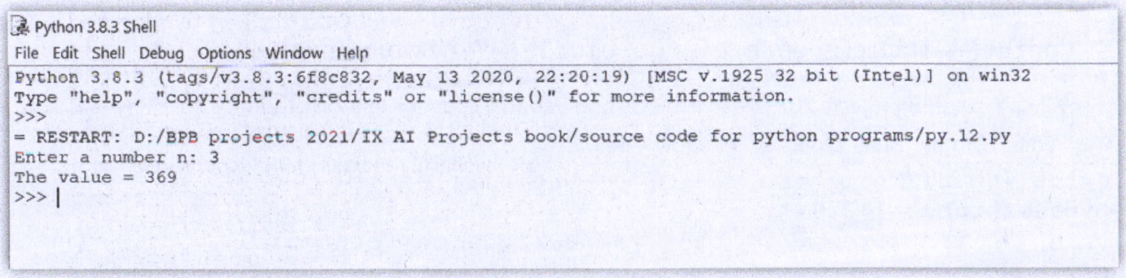

```
Python 3.8.3 Shell
File Edit Shell Debug Options Window Help
Python 3.8.3 (tags/v3.8.3:6f8c832, May 13 2020, 22:20:19) [MSC v.1925 32 bit (Intel)] on win32
Type "help", "copyright", "credits" or "license()" for more information.
>>>
= RESTART: D:/BPB projects 2021/IX AI Projects book/source code for python programs/py.12.py
Enter a number n: 3
The value = 369
>>>
```

Figure 3.19 b: *Output*

20. Write a python program to search the smallest divisor of an integer.

```
n=int(input("Enter an integer:"))

a=[]

for i in range(2,n+1):

    if(n%i==0):

        a.append(i)

a.sort()

print("Smallest divisor is:",a[0])
```

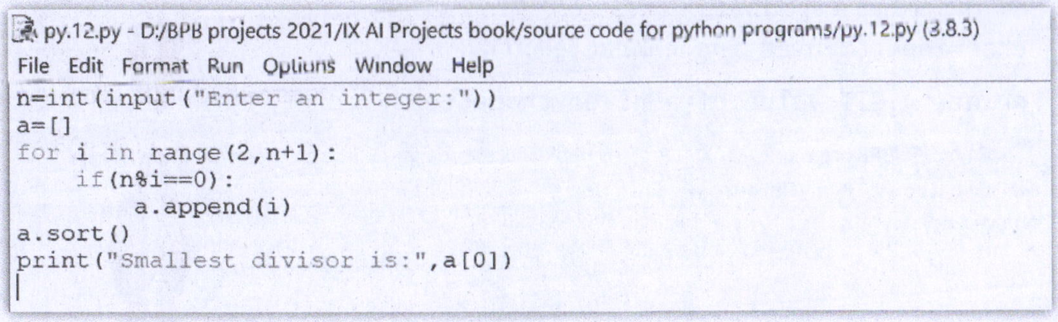

```
py.12.py - D:/BPB projects 2021/IX AI Projects book/source code for python programs/py.12.py (3.8.3)
File Edit Format Run Options Window Help
n=int(input("Enter an integer:"))
a=[]
for i in range(2,n+1):
    if(n%i==0):
        a.append(i)
a.sort()
print("Smallest divisor is:",a[0])
```

Figure 3.20 a: *Code*

```
Python 3.8.3 Shell
File  Edit  Shell  Debug  Options  Window  Help
Python 3.8.3 (tags/v3.8.3:6f8c832, May 13 2020, 22:20:19) [MSC v.1925 32 bit (Intel)] on win32
Type "help", "copyright", "credits" or "license()" for more information.
>>>
= RESTART: D:/BPB projects 2021/IX AI Projects book/source code for python programs/py.12.py
Enter an integer:56565
Smallest divisor is: 3
>>> |
```

Figure 3.20 b: *Output*

21. Write a python program to compute the circumference of a circle.

```
r=int(input("Enter the radius of the circle:"))

circumference=2*3.14*r

print("Circumference of the circle =",circumference)
```

```
py.21.py - D:/BPB projects 2021/IX AI Projects book/source code for python programs/py.21.py (3.8.3)
File  Edit  Format  Run  Options  Window  Help
r=int(input("Enter the radius of the circle:"))
circumference=2*3.14*r
print("Circumference of the circle =",circumference)
|
```

Figure 3.21 a: *Code*

```
Python 3.8.3 Shell
File  Edit  Shell  Debug  Options  Window  Help
Python 3.8.3 (tags/v3.8.3:6f8c832, May 13 2020, 22:20:19) [MSC v.1925 32 bit (Intel)] on win32
Type "help", "copyright", "credits" or "license()" for more information.
>>>
= RESTART: D:/BPB projects 2021/IX AI Projects book/source code for python programs/py.21.py
Enter the radius of the circle:6
Circumference of the circle = 37.68
>>> |
```

Figure 3.21 b: *Output*

22. Write a python program to print the ASCII value of a given character.

(ASCII refers to American Standard Code for Information Interchange, and each character has a specific ASCII value.)

```
char=input("Enter the character:")

print("ASCII value of a given character =",ord(char))
```

```
py.21.py - D:/BPB projects 2021/IX AI Projects book/source code for python programs/py.21.py (3.8.3)
File  Edit  Format  Run  Options  Window  Help
char=input("Enter the character:")
print("ASCII value of the entered character =",ord(char))
```

Figure 3.22 a: *Code*

```
Python 3.8.3 Shell
File Edit Shell Debug Options Window Help
Python 3.8.3 (tags/v3.8.3:6f8c832, May 13 2020, 22:20:19) [MSC v.1925 32 bit (Intel)] on win32
Type "help", "copyright", "credits" or "license()" for more information.
>>>
= RESTART: D:/BPB projects 2021/IX AI Projects book/source code for python programs/py.21.py
Enter the character:t
ASCII value of the entered character = 116
>>>
= RESTART: D:/BPB projects 2021/IX AI Projects book/source code for python programs/py.21.py
Enter the character:a
ASCII value of the entered character = 97
>>>
= RESTART: D:/BPB projects 2021/IX AI Projects book/source code for python programs/py.21.py
Enter the character:A
ASCII value of the entered character = 65
>>> |
```

Figure 3.22 b: *Output*

23. Write a python program to search the power of an entered number using the exponential operator.

```
num=float(input("Enter the number:"))

pow=int(input("Enter the power:"))

result=num**pow

print("Power of the entered number using exponential operator=",result)
```

```
py.21.py - D:/BPB projects 2021/IX AI Projects book/source code for python programs/py.21.py (3.8.3)
File Edit Format Run Options Window Help
num=float(input("Enter the number:"))
pow=int(input("Enter the power:"))
result=num**pow
print("Power of the entered number using exponential operator=",result)
```

Figure 3.23 a: *Code*

```
Python 3.8.3 Shell
File Edit Shell Debug Options Window Help
Python 3.8.3 (tags/v3.8.3:6f8c832, May 13 2020, 22:20:19) [MSC v.1925 32 bit (Intel)] on win32
Type "help", "copyright", "credits" or "license()" for more information.
>>>
= RESTART: D:/BPB projects 2021/IX AI Projects book/source code for python programs/py.21.py
Enter the number:2.5
Enter the power:2
Power of the entered number using exponential operator= 6.25
>>>
= RESTART: D:/BPB projects 2021/IX AI Projects book/source code for python programs/py.21.py
Enter the number:8
Enter the power:4
Power of the entered number using exponential operator= 4096.0
>>> |
```

Figure 3.23 b: *Output*

24. Write a python program to input two numbers and print their quotient and remainder.

```
a=int(input("Enter the first number: "))

b=int(input("Enter the second number: "))

quotient=a//b

remainder=a%b

print("Quotient =",quotient)

print("Remainder =",remainder)
```

```
py.21.py - D:/BPB projects 2021/IX AI Projects book/source code for python programs/py.21.py (3.8.3)
File Edit Format Run Options Window Help
a=int(input("Enter the first number: "))
b=int(input("Enter the second number: "))
quotient=a//b
remainder=a%b
print("Quotient =",quotient)
print("Remainder =",remainder)
```

Figure 3.24 a: *Code*

```
Python 3.8.3 Shell
File Edit Shell Debug Options Window Help
Python 3.8.3 (tags/v3.8.3:6f8c832, May 13 2020, 22:20:19) [MSC v.1925 32 bit (Intel)] on win32
Type "help", "copyright", "credits" or "license()" for more information.
>>>
= RESTART: D:/BPB projects 2021/IX AI Projects book/source code for python programs/py.21.py
Enter the first number: 46
Enter the second number: 5
Quotient = 9
Remainder = 1
>>>
= RESTART: D:/BPB projects 2021/IX AI Projects book/source code for python programs/py.21.py
Enter the first number: 76543
Enter the second number: 8
Quotient = 9567
Remainder = 7
>>>
= RESTART: D:/BPB projects 2021/IX AI Projects book/source code for python programs/py.21.py
Enter the first number: 6548901
Enter the second number: 2356
Quotient = 2779
Remainder = 1577
>>>
```

Figure 3.24 b: *Output*

25. Write a python program for counting the number of digits in a number.

```
n=int(input("Enter a number:"))

count=0

while(n>0):
```

```
    count=count+1
    n=n//10
print("The number of digits in the entered number=",count)
```

```
py.21.py - D:/BPB projects 2021/IX AI Projects book/source code for python programs/py.21.py (3.8.3)
File Edit Format Run Options Window Help
n=int(input("Enter a number:"))
count=0
while(n>0):
    count=count+1
    n=n//10
print("The number of digits in the entered number=",count)
```

Figure 3.25 a: *Code*

```
Python 3.8.3 Shell
File Edit Shell Debug Options Window Help
Python 3.8.3 (tags/v3.8.3:6f8c832, May 13 2020, 22:20:19) [MSC v.1925 32 bit (Intel)] on win32
Type "help", "copyright", "credits" or "license()" for more information.
>>>
= RESTART: D:/BPB projects 2021/IX AI Projects book/source code for python programs/py.21.py
Enter a number:381
The number of digits in the entered number= 3
>>>
= RESTART: D:/BPB projects 2021/IX AI Projects book/source code for python programs/py.21.py
Enter a number:78532065
The number of digits in the entered number= 8
>>> |
```

Figure 3.25 b: *Output*

26. Write a python program for printing the table of a given number.

```
n=int(input("Enter the number to print the tables for:"))
for i in range(1,11):
    print(n,"x",i,"=",n*i)
```

```
py.21.py - D:/BPB projects 2021/IX AI Projects book/source code for python programs/py.21.py (3.8.3)
File Edit Format Run Options Window Help
n=int(input("Enter the number to print the tables for:"))
for i in range(1,11):
    print(n,"x",i,"=",n*i)
```

Figure 3.26 a: *Code*

```
Python 3.8.3 Shell
File Edit Shell Debug Options Window Help
Python 3.8.3 (tags/v3.8.3:6f8c832, May 13 2020, 22:20:19) [MSC v.1925 32 bit (Intel)] on win32
Type "help", "copyright", "credits" or "license()" for more information.
>>>
= RESTART: D:/BPB projects 2021/IX AI Projects book/source code for python programs/py.21.py
Enter the number to print the tables for:31
31 x 1 = 31
31 x 2 = 62
31 x 3 = 93
31 x 4 = 124
31 x 5 = 155
31 x 6 = 186
31 x 7 = 217
31 x 8 = 248
31 x 9 = 279
31 x 10 = 310
>>> |
```

***Figure 3.26 b:** Output*

27. Write a python to input age and check eligibility for voting if the age is equal to or greater than 21 years and print the status.

```
age = int(input("Enter Age : "))
if age>=21:
        status="Eligible"
else:
    status="Not Eligible"
print("You are ",status," for Vote.")
```

```
py.21.py - D:/BPB projects 2021/IX AI Projects book/source code for python programs/py.21.py (3.8.3)
File Edit Format Run Options Window Help
age = int(input("Enter Age : "))
if age>=21:
        status="Eligible"
else:
    status="Not Eligible"
print("You are ",status," for Voting.")
```

***Figure 3.27 a:** Code*

```
Python 3.8.3 Shell
File Edit Shell Debug Options Window Help
Python 3.8.3 (tags/v3.8.3:6f8c832, May 13 2020, 22:20:19) [MSC v.1925 32 bit (Intel)] on win32
Type "help", "copyright", "credits" or "license()" for more information.
>>>
= RESTART: D:/BPB projects 2021/IX AI Projects book/source code for python programs/py.21.py
Enter Age : 55
You are  Eligible  for Voting.
>>>
= RESTART: D:/BPB projects 2021/IX AI Projects book/source code for python programs/py.21.py
Enter Age : 15
You are  Not Eligible  for Voting.
>>>
```

***Figure 3.27 b:** Output*

28. Design a simple calculator using if elif in python.

```
print(“Calculator”)
print(“1.Add”)
print(“2.Substract”)
print(“3.Multiply”)
print(“4.Divide”)
ch=int(input(“Enter Choice(1-4): “))
if ch==1:
    a=int(input(“Enter A:”))
    b=int(input(“Enter B:”))
    c=a+b
    print(“Sum = “,c)
elif ch==2:
    a=int(input(“Enter A:”))
    b=int(input(“Enter B:”))
    c=a-b
    print(“Difference = “,c)
elif  ch==3:
    a=int(input(“Enter A:”))
    b=int(input(“Fnter B:”))
    c=a*b
    print(“Product = “,c)
elif ch--4:
    a=int(input(“Enter A:”))
    b=int(input(“Enter B:”))
    c=a/b
    print(“Quotient = “,c)
else:
    print(“Invalid Choice”)
```

```
py.21.py - D:/BPB projects 2021/IX AI Projects book/source code for python programs/py.21.py (3.8.3)
File Edit Format Run Options Window Help
print("Calculator")
print("1.Add")
print("2.Substract")
print("3.Multiply")
print("4.Divide")
ch=int(input("Enter Choice(1-4): "))
if ch==1:
    a=int(input("Enter A:"))
    b=int(input("Enter B:"))
    c=a+b
    print("Sum = ",c)
elif ch==2:
    a=int(input("Enter A:"))
    b=int(input("Enter B:"))
    c=a-b
    print("Difference = ",c)
elif  ch==3:
    a=int(input("Enter A:"))
    b=int(input("Enter B:"))
    c=a*b
    print("Product = ",c)
elif ch==4:
    a=int(input("Enter A:"))
    b=int(input("Enter B:"))
    c=a/b
    print("Quotient = ",c)
else:
    print("Invalid Choice")
```

Figure 3.28 a: *Code*

```
Python 3.8.3 Shell
File Edit Shell Debug Options Window Help
Python 3.8.3 (tags/v3.8.3:6f8c832, May 13 2020, 22:20:19) [MSC v.1925 32 bit (Intel)] on win32
Type "help", "copyright", "credits" or "license()" for more information.
>>>
= RESTART: D:/BPB projects 2021/IX AI Projects book/source code for python programs/py.21.py
Calculator
1.Add
2.Substract
3.Multiply
4.Divide
Enter Choice(1-4): 3
Enter A:44
Enter B:7
Product =  308
>>>
= RESTART: D:/BPB projects 2021/IX AI Projects book/source code for python programs/py.21.py
Calculator
1.Add
2.Substract
3.Multiply
4.Divide
Enter Choice(1-4): 2
Enter A:6751
Enter B:56
Difference =  6695
>>> |
```

Figure 3.28 b: *Output*

29. Write a python program to print numbers from n to 1.

```
n = int(input("Enter the value of n: "))
if (n<=1):
        print("n should be greater than 1")
        exit()
print("value of n: ",n)
print("numbers from {0} to {1} are: ".format(n,1))
for i in range(n,0,-1):
        print(i)
```

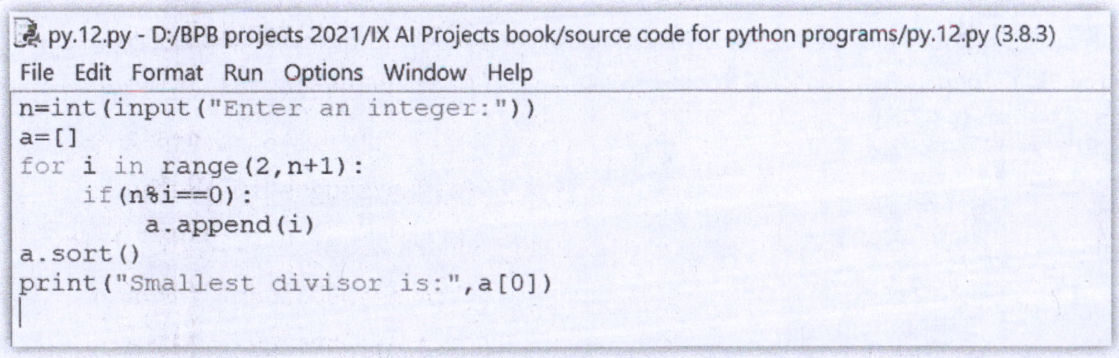

```
py.12.py - D:/BPB projects 2021/IX AI Projects book/source code for python programs/py.12.py (3.8.3)
File Edit Format Run Options Window Help
n=int(input("Enter an integer:"))
a=[]
for i in range(2,n+1):
    if(n%i==0):
        a.append(i)
a.sort()
print("Smallest divisor is:",a[0])
```

Figure 3.29 a: Code

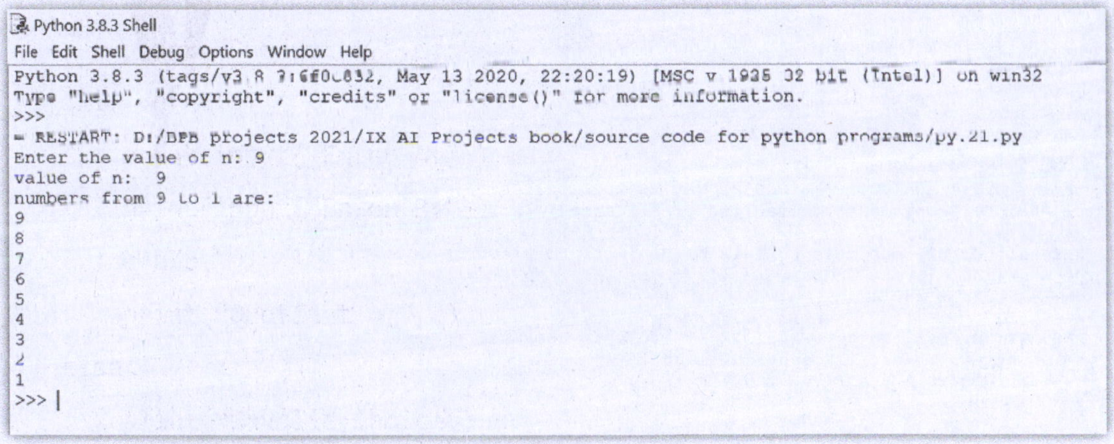

```
Python 3.8.3 Shell
File Edit Shell Debug Options Window Help
Python 3.8.3 (tags/v3.8.3:6f8c832, May 13 2020, 22:20:19) [MSC v.1925 32 bit (Intel)] on win32
Type "help", "copyright", "credits" or "license()" for more information.
>>>
= RESTART: D:/BPB projects 2021/IX AI Projects book/source code for python programs/py.21.py
Enter the value of n: 9
value of n:  9
numbers from 9 to 1 are:
9
8
7
6
5
4
3
2
1
>>> |
```

Figure 3.29 b: Output

30. Write a python program to capitalize the characters of a string without using a function.

```
st = input('Type a string: ')
```

```
out = ‘’
for n in st:
    if n not in ‘abcdefghijklmnopqrstuvwqxyz’:
        out = out + n
    else:
        k = ord(n)
        l = k - 32
        out = out + chr(l)
print(‘------->’, out)
```

```
py.21.py - D:/BPB projects 2021/IX AI Projects book/source code for python programs/py.21.py (3.8.3)
File Edit Format Run Options Window Help
st = input('Type a string: ')
out = ''
for n in st:
    if n not in 'abcdefghijklmnopqrstuvwqxyz':
        out = out + n
    else:
        k = ord(n)
        l = k - 32
        out = out + chr(l)
print('------->', out)
```

Figure 3.30 a: *Code*

```
Python 3.8.3 Shell
File Edit Shell Debug Options Window Help
Python 3.8.3 (tags/v3.8.3:6f8c832, May 13 2020, 22:20:19) [MSC v.1925 32 bit (Intel)] on win32
Type "help", "copyright", "credits" or "license()" for more information.
>>>
= RESTART: D:/BPB projects 2021/IX AI Projects book/source code for python programs/py.21.py
Type a string: lovely india
-------> LOVELY INDIA
>>>
= RESTART: D:/BPB projects 2021/IX AI Projects book/source code for python programs/py.21.py
Type a string: this is a beautiful land.
-------> THIS IS A BEAUTIFUL LAND.
>>>
```

Figure 3.30 b: *Output*

31. Write a python program to search the largest element in an array.

```
def largest(arr,n):
```

```
    max = arr[0]
    for i in range(1, n):
        if arr[i] > max:
            max = arr[i]
    return max
arr = [10, 324, 45, 90, 98,20,108]
n = len(arr)
Ans = largest(arr,n)
print ("Largest in given array is",Ans)
```

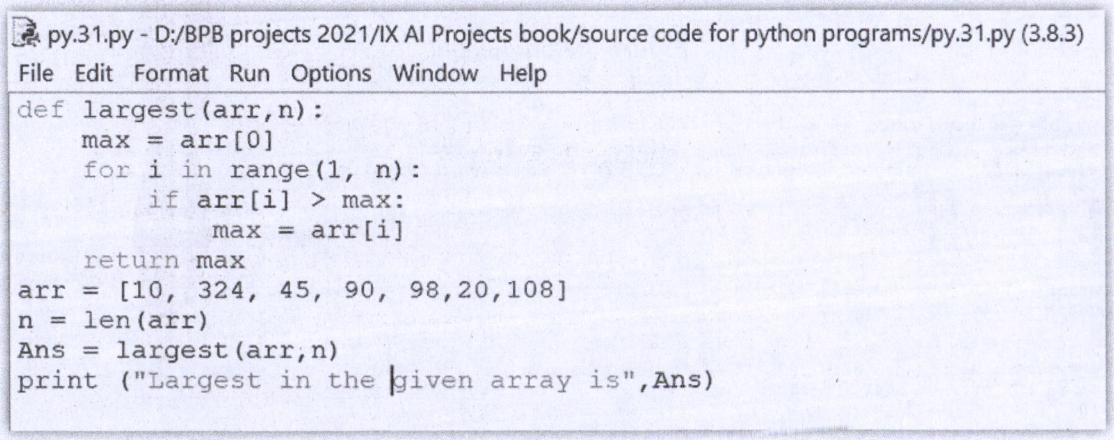

```
py.31.py - D:/BPB projects 2021/IX AI Projects book/source code for python programs/py.31.py (3.8.3)
File Edit Format Run Options Window Help
def largest(arr,n):
    max = arr[0]
    for i in range(1, n):
        if arr[i] > max:
            max = arr[i]
    return max
arr = [10, 324, 45, 90, 98,20,108]
n = len(arr)
Ans = largest(arr,n)
print ("Largest in the given array is",Ans)
```

Figure 3.31 a: *Code*

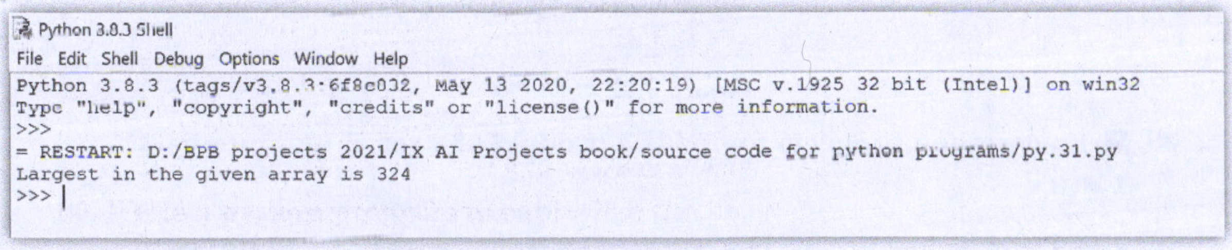

```
Python 3.8.3 Shell
File Edit Shell Debug Options Window Help
Python 3.8.3 (tags/v3.8.3:6f8c832, May 13 2020, 22:20:19) [MSC v.1925 32 bit (Intel)] on win32
Type "help", "copyright", "credits" or "license()" for more information.
>>>
= RESTART: D:/BPB projects 2021/IX AI Projects book/source code for python programs/py.31.py
Largest in the given array is 324
>>> |
```

Figure 3.31 b: *Output*

32. Write a python program for calculating the length of a string.

```
str=input("Enter the string:")
print(len(str))
```

```
py.31.py - D:/BPB projects 2021/IX AI Projects book/source code for python programs/py.31.py (3.8.3)
File Edit Format Run Options Window Help
str=input("Enter the string:")
print(len(str))
```

Figure 3.32 a: *Code*

```
Python 3.8.3 Shell
File Edit Shell Debug Options Window Help
Python 3.8.3 (tags/v3.8.3:6f8c832, May 13 2020, 22:20:19) [MSC v.1925 32 bit (Intel)] on win32
Type "help", "copyright", "credits" or "license()" for more information.
>>>
= RESTART: D:/BPB projects 2021/IX AI Projects book/source code for python programs/py.31.py
Enter the string:The country is surrounded by nine other nations rich in culture and heritage.
77
>>> |
```

Figure 3.32 b: *Output*

```
Python 3.8.3 Shell
File Edit Shell Debug Options Window Help
Python 3.8.3 (tags/v3.8.3:6f8c832, May 13 2020, 22:20:19) [MSC v.1925 32 bit (Intel)] on win32
Type "help", "copyright", "credits" or "license()" for more information.
>>>
= RESTART: D:/BPB projects 2021/IX AI Projects book/source code for python programs/py.31.py
Enter the string:bharat
6
>>>
= RESTART: D:/BPB projects 2021/IX AI Projects book/source code for python programs/py.31.py
Enter the string:lovely
6
>>>
= RESTART: D:/BPB projects 2021/IX AI Projects book/source code for python programs/py.31.py
Enter the string:lovely bharat
13
>>>
= RESTART: D:/BPB projects 2021/IX AI Projects book/source code for python programs/py.31.py
Enter the string:lovelybharat
12
>>>
```

Figure 3.32 c: *Output*

33. Write a python program to find the product of a set of real numbers.

```
i = 0
product = 1
count = int(input("Enter the number of real numbers: "))
for i in range(count):
    x = float(input("Enter a real number: "))
    product = product * x
print("The product of the entered numbers is: ", product)
```

py.31.py - D:/BPB projects 2021/IX AI Projects book/source code for python programs/py.31.py (3.8.3)

File Edit Format Run Options Window Help

```
i = 0
product = 1
count = int(input("Enter the number of real numbers: "))
for i in range(count):
    x = float(input("Enter a real number: "))
    product = product * x
print("The product of the numbers is: ", product)
```

Figure 3.33 a: *Code*

Python 3.8.3 Shell

File Edit Shell Debug Options Window Help

```
Python 3.8.3 (tags/v3.8.3:6f8c832, May 13 2020, 22:20:19) [MSC v.1925 32 bit (Intel)] on win32
Type "help", "copyright", "credits" or "license()" for more information.
>>>
= RESTART: D:/BPB projects 2021/IX AI Projects book/source code for python programs/py.31.py
Enter the number of real numbers: 6
Enter a real number: 3
Enter a real number: 4
Enter a real number: 7
Enter a real number: 2
Enter a real number: 8
Enter a real number: 9
The product of the numbers is:  12096.0
>>>
```

Figure 3.33 b: *Output*

Python 3.8.3 Shell

File Edit Shell Debug Options Window Help

```
Python 3.8.3 (tags/v3.8.3:6f8c832, May 13 2020, 22:20:19) [MSC v.1925 32 bit (Intel)] on win32
Type "help", "copyright", "credits" or "license()" for more information.
>>>
= RESTART: D:/BPB projects 2021/IX AI Projects book/source code for python programs/py.31.py
Enter the number of real numbers: 3
Enter a real number: 2.1
Enter a real number: 3.5
Enter a real number: 7.1
The product of the numbers is:  52.185
>>>
```

Figure 3.33 c: *Output*

34. Write a python program to check whether the given integer is multiple of 6.

```
number = int(input("Enter an integer: "))
if(number%6==0):
    print(number, "is a multiple of 6")
else:
print(number, "is not a multiple of 6")
```

```
py.31.py - D:/BPB projects 2021/IX AI Projects book/source code for python programs/py.31.py (3.8.3)
File Edit Format Run Options Window Help
number = int(input("Enter an integer: "))
if(number%6==0):
    print(number, "is a multiple of 6")
else:
    print(number, "is not a multiple of 6")
```

***Figure 3.34 a:** Code*

```
Python 3.8.3 Shell
File Edit Shell Debug Options Window Help
Python 3.8.3 (tags/v3.8.3:6f8c832, May 13 2020, 22:20:19) [MSC v.1925 32 bit (Intel)] on win32
Type "help", "copyright", "credits" or "license()" for more information.
>>>
= RESTART: D:/BPB projects 2021/IX AI Projects book/source code for python programs/py.31.py
Enter an integer: 672
672 is a multiple of 6
>>>
= RESTART: D:/BPB projects 2021/IX AI Projects book/source code for python programs/py.31.py
Enter an integer: 341
341 is not a multiple of 6
>>>
```

***Figure 3.34 b:** Output*

35. Write a python program to search the smallest element in an array.

```
def smallest(arr,n):
    min = arr[0]
    for i in range(1, n):
        if arr[i] < min:
            min = arr[i]
    return min
arr = [102, 324, 645, 590, 198,203,108]
n = len(arr)
Ans = smallest(arr,n)
print ("The Smallest element in the given array is",Ans)
```

```
py.31.py - D:/BPB projects 2021/IX AI Projects book/source code for python programs/py.31.py (3.8.3)
File Edit Format Run Options Window Help
def smallest(arr,n):
    min = arr[0]
    for i in range(1, n):
        if arr[i] < min:
            min = arr[i]
    return min
arr = [102, 324, 645, 590, 198,203,108]
n = len(arr)
Ans = smallest(arr,n)
print ("The Smallest element in the given array is",Ans)
```

Figure 3.35 a: *Code*

```
Python 3.8.3 Shell
File Edit Shell Debug Options Window Help
Python 3.8.3 (tags/v3.8.3:6f8c832, May 13 2020, 22:20:19) [MSC v.1925 32 bit (Intel)] on win32
Type "help", "copyright", "credits" or "license()" for more information.
>>>
= RESTART: D:/BPB projects 2021/IX AI Projects book/source code for python programs/py.31.py
The Smallest element in the given array is 102
>>> |
```

Figure 3.35 b: *Output*

36. Write a python program to find the geometric mean of n numbers. (Geometric mean is defined as the nth root of the products of n numbers of a series.)

```
c = 0

p = 1.0

count = int(input("Enter the number of values: "))

while(c<count):

    x = float(input("Enter a real number: "))

    c = c+1

    p = p * x

gm = pow(p,1.0/count)

print("The geometric mean is: ",gm)
```

```
py.31.py - D:/BPB projects 2021/IX AI Projects book/source code for python programs/py.31.py (3.8.3)
File Edit Format Run Options Window Help
c = 0
p = 1.0
count = int(input("Enter the number of values: "))
while(c<count):
    x = float(input("Enter a real number: "))
    c = c+1
    p = p * x
gm = pow(p,1.0/count)
print("The geometric mean is: ",gm)
```

***Figure 3.36 a:** Code*

```
Python 3.8.3 Shell
File Edit Shell Debug Options Window Help
Python 3.8.3 (tags/v3.8.3:6f8c832, May 13 2020, 22:20:19) [MSC v.1925 32 bit (Intel)] on win32
Type "help", "copyright", "credits" or "license()" for more information.
>>>
= RESTART: D:/BPB projects 2021/IX AI Projects book/source code for python programs/py.31.py
Enter the number of values: 3
Enter a real number: 4
Enter a real number: 6
Enter a real number: 7
The geometric mean is:  5.517848352762241
>>>
```

***Figure 3.36 b:** Output*

37. Write a python program to implement a linear search.

```
numbers = [4,2,7,1,8,3,6]
f = 0 #flag
x = int(input("Enter the number to be found out: "))
for i in range(len(numbers)):
    if (x==numbers[i]):
        print("Successful search, the element is found at position",i)
        f = 1
        break
if(f==0):
print("Oops! Search unsuccessful")
```

py.31.py - D:/BPB projects 2021/IX AI Projects book/source code for python programs/py.31.py (3.8.3)

File Edit Format Run Options Window Help

```
numbers = [4,2,7,1,8,3,6]
f = 0 #flag
x = int(input("Enter the number to be found out: "))
for i in range(len(numbers)):
    if (x==numbers[i]):
        print("Successful search, the element is found at position",i)
        f = 1
        break
if(f==0):
    print("Oops! Search unsuccessful")
```

Figure 3.37 a: *Code*

Python 3.8.3 Shell

File Edit Shell Debug Options Window Help

```
Python 3.8.3 (tags/v3.8.3:6f8c832, May 13 2020, 22:20:19) [MSC v.1925 32 bit (Intel)] on win32
Type "help", "copyright", "credits" or "license()" for more information.
>>>
= RESTART: D:/BPB projects 2021/IX AI Projects book/source code for python programs/py.31.py
Enter the number to be found out: 54
Oops! Search unsuccessful
>>>
= RESTART: D:/BPB projects 2021/IX AI Projects book/source code for python programs/py.31.py
Enter the number to be found out: 4
Successful search, the element is found at position 0
>>>
```

Figure 3.37 b: *Output*

38. Write a python program to display all the numbers that are multiples of 3 within the range of 20 to 40.

```
for i in range(20,40):
    if (i%3--0):
        print(i)
```

py.31.py - D:/BPB projects 2021/IX AI Projects book/source code for python programs/py.31.py (3.8.3)

File Edit Format Run Options Window Help

```
for i in range(20,40):
    if (i%3==0):
        print(i)
```

Figure 3.38 a: *Code*

```
Python 3.8.3 Shell
File Edit Shell Debug Options Window Help
Python 3.8.3 (tags/v3.8.3:6f8c832, May 13 2020, 22:20:19) [MSC v.1925 32 bit (Intel)] on win32
Type "help", "copyright", "credits" or "license()" for more information.
>>>
= RESTART: D:/BPB projects 2021/IX AI Projects book/source code for python programs/py.31.py
21
24
27
30
33
36
39
>>>
```

***Figure 3.38 b:** Output*

39. Write a python program to display all odd numbers in an array.

```
numbers = [17,11,18,13,19,61,21,14,15,29,6,98]

count = 0

for i in range(len(numbers)):

    if(numbers[i]%2!=0):

        count = count+1

print("The number of odd numbers in the list are: ", count)
```

```
py.31.py - D:/BPB projects 2021/IX AI Projects book/source code for python programs/py.31.py (3.8.3)
File Edit Format Run Options Window Help
numbers = [17,11,18,13,19,61,21,14,15,29,6,98]
count = 0
for i in range(len(numbers)):
    if(numbers[i]%2!=0):
        count = count+1
print("The number of odd numbers in the list are: ", count)
```

***Figure 3.39 a:** Code*

```
Python 3.8.3 Shell
File Edit Shell Debug Options Window Help
Python 3.8.3 (tags/v3.8.3:6f8c832, May 13 2020, 22:20:19) [MSC v.1925 32 bit (Intel)] on win32
Type "help", "copyright", "credits" or "license()" for more information.
>>>
= RESTART: D:/BPB projects 2021/IX AI Projects book/source code for python programs/py.31.py
The number of odd numbers in the list are:  8
>>>
```

***Figure 3.39 b:** Output*

40. Write a python program to insert a number to any position in a list.

```
numbers = [23,14,16,39,6,12,48]

print(numbers)
```

```
x = int(input("Enter the number to be inserted: "))
y = int(input("Enter the position: "))
numbers.insert(y,x)
print(numbers)
```

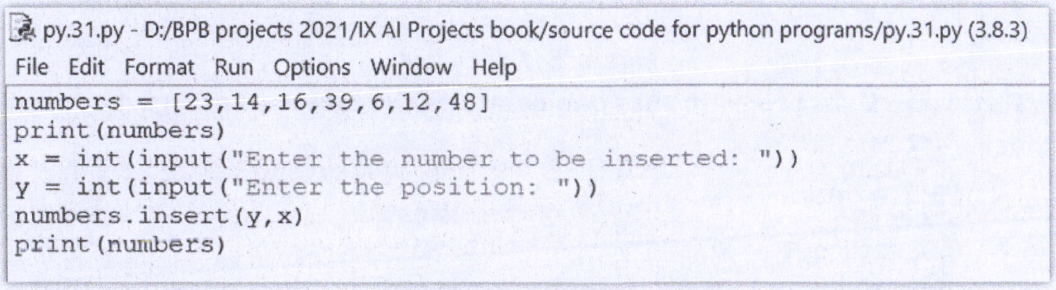

```
py.31.py - D:/BPB projects 2021/IX AI Projects book/source code for python programs/py.31.py (3.8.3)
File Edit Format Run Options Window Help
numbers = [23,14,16,39,6,12,48]
print(numbers)
x = int(input("Enter the number to be inserted: "))
y = int(input("Enter the position: "))
numbers.insert(y,x)
print(numbers)
```

Figure 3.40 a: *Code*

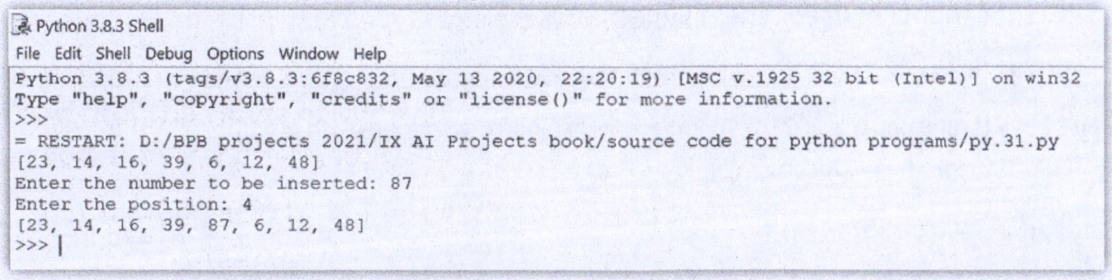

```
Python 3.8.3 Shell
File Edit Shell Debug Options Window Help
Python 3.8.3 (tags/v3.8.3:6f8c832, May 13 2020, 22:20:19) [MSC v.1925 32 bit (Intel)] on win32
Type "help", "copyright", "credits" or "license()" for more information.
>>>
= RESTART: D:/BPB projects 2021/IX AI Projects book/source code for python programs/py.31.py
[23, 14, 16, 39, 6, 12, 48]
Enter the number to be inserted: 87
Enter the position: 4
[23, 14, 16, 39, 87, 6, 12, 48]
>>> |
```

Figure 3.40 b: *Output*

41. Write a python program to delete an element from a list by index.

```
numbers = [16, 13,24,18,29,36,22,18]
print(numbers)
x = int(input("Enter the position of the element to be deleted: "))
numbers.pop(x)
print(numbers)
```

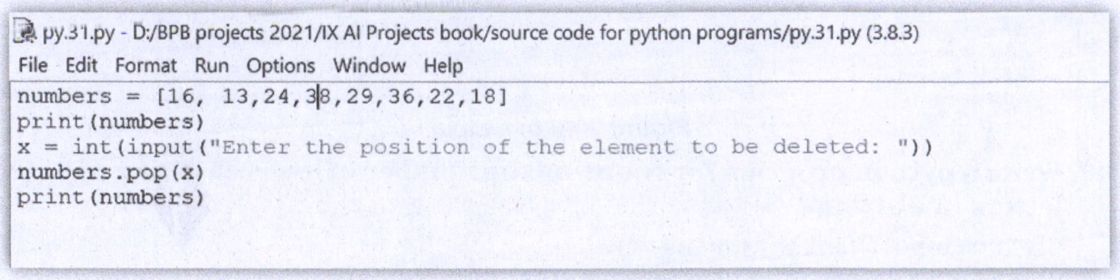

```
py.31.py - D:/BPB projects 2021/IX AI Projects book/source code for python programs/py.31.py (3.8.3)
File Edit Format Run Options Window Help
numbers = [16, 13,24,38,29,36,22,18]
print(numbers)
x = int(input("Enter the position of the element to be deleted: "))
numbers.pop(x)
print(numbers)
```

Figure 3.41 a: *Code*

```
Python 3.8.3 Shell
File Edit Shell Debug Options Window Help
Python 3.8.3 (tags/v3.8.3:6f8c832, May 13 2020, 22:20:19) [MSC v.1925 32 bit (Intel)] on win32
Type "help", "copyright", "credits" or "license()" for more information.
>>>
= RESTART: D:/BPB projects 2021/IX AI Projects book/source code for python programs/py.31.py
[16, 13, 24, 38, 29, 36, 22, 18]
Enter the position of the element to be deleted: 4
[16, 13, 24, 38, 36, 22, 18]
>>>
```

Figure 3.41 b: *Output*

42. Write a python program that can compute the factorial of a given number.

```
def fact(x):
    if x == 0:
        return 1
    return x * fact(x - 1)
x=int(input("Enter the number:"))
print(fact(x))
```

```
py.31.py - D:/BPB projects 2021/IX AI Projects book/source code for python programs/py.31.py (3.8.3)
File Edit Format Run Options Window Help
def fact(x):
    if x == 0:
        return 1
    return x * fact(x - 1)
x=int(input("Enter the number:"))
print(fact(x))
```

Figure 3.42 a: *Code*

```
Python 3.8.3 Shell
File Edit Shell Debug Options Window Help
Python 3.8.3 (tags/v3.8.3:6f8c832, May 13 2020, 22:20:19) [MSC v.1925 32 bit (Intel)] on win32
Type "help", "copyright", "credits" or "license()" for more information.
>>>
= RESTART: D:/BPB projects 2021/IX AI Projects book/source code for python programs/py.31.py
Enter the number:7
5040
>>> |
```

Figure 3.42 b: *Output*

43. Write a python program for counting the number of lowercase and uppercase letters in a string.

```
string=input("Enter string:")
count1=0
```

```
count2=0
for i in string:
    if(i.islower()):
        count1=count1+1
    elif(i.isupper()):
        count2=count2+1
print("The number of lowercase characters is:")
print(count1)
print("The number of uppercase characters is:")
print(count2)
```

```
py.31.py - D:/BPB projects 2021/IX AI Projects book/source code for python programs/py.31.py (3.8.3)
File Edit Format Run Options Window Help
string=input("Enter string:")
count1=0
count2=0
for i in string:
    if(i.islower()):
        count1=count1+1
    elif(i.isupper()):
        count2=count2+1
print("The number of lowercase characters is:")
print(count1)
print("The number of uppercase characters is:")
print(count2)
```

Figure 3.43 a: Code

```
Python 3.8.3 Shell
File Edit Shell Debug Options Window Help
Python 3.8.3 (tags/v3.8.3:6f8c832, May 13 2020, 22:20:19) [MSC v.1925 32 bit (Intel)] on win32
Type "help", "copyright", "credits" or "license()" for more information.
>>>
= RESTART: D:/BPB projects 2021/IX AI Projects book/source code for python programs/py.31.py
Enter string:I love my India and its Culure.
The number of lowercase characters is:
21
The number of uppercase characters is:
3
>>>
```

Figure 3.43 b: Output

44. Write a python program that can accept two strings and print the larger string.

```
string1 = input("Enter first string: ")
string2 = input("Enter second string: ")
```

```
count1 = 0
count2 = 0
for i in string1:
    count1 = count1 + 1

for j in string2:
    count2 = count2 + 1

if (count1 < count2):
    print ("Larger string is:")
    print (string2)

elif (count1 == count2):
    print ("Both strings are equal.")
else:
    print ("Larger string is:")
    print (string1)
```

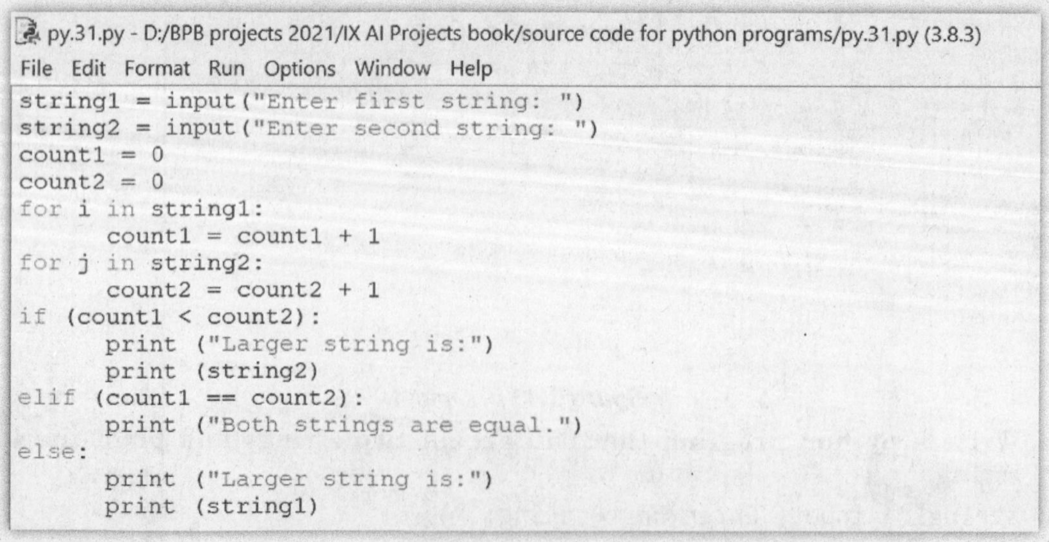

```
py.31.py - D:/BPB projects 2021/IX AI Projects book/source code for python programs/py.31.py (3.8.3)
File Edit Format Run Options Window Help
string1 = input("Enter first string: ")
string2 = input("Enter second string: ")
count1 = 0
count2 = 0
for i in string1:
    count1 = count1 + 1
for j in string2:
    count2 = count2 + 1
if (count1 < count2):
    print ("Larger string is:")
    print (string2)
elif (count1 == count2):
    print ("Both strings are equal.")
else:
    print ("Larger string is:")
    print (string1)
```

***Figure 3.44 a:** Code*

```
Python 3.8.3 Shell
File Edit Shell Debug Options Window Help
Python 3.8.3 (tags/v3.8.3:6f8c832, May 13 2020, 22:20:19) [MSC v.1925 32 bit (Intel)] on win
Type "help", "copyright", "credits" or "license()" for more information.
>>>
= RESTART: D:/BPB projects 2021/IX AI Projects book/source code for python programs/py.31.py
Enter first string: Beautiful ladies are roaming here and there.
Enter second string: Boys are playing football.
Larger string is:
Beautiful ladies are roaming here and there.
>>> |
```

Figure 3.44 b: *Output*

45. Write a python program for counting the number of 'l' letters in a string.

```
count = 0
for letter in 'structural engineering is used here.':
    if(letter == 'e'):
        count += 1
print(count,'letters found')
```

```
py.31.py - D:/BPB projects 2021/IX AI Projects book/source code for python programs/py.31.py (3.8.3)
File Edit Format Run Options Window Help
count = 0
for letter in 'structural enginnering is used here.':
    if(letter == 'e'):
        count += 1
print(count,'letters found')
```

Figure 3.45 a: *Code*

```
Python 3.8.3 Shell
File Edit Shell Debug Options Window Help
Python 3.8.3 (tags/v3.8.3:6f8c832, May 13 2020, 22:20:19) [MSC v.1925 32 bit (Intel)] on win32
Type "help", "copyright", "credits" or "license()" for more information.
>>>
= RESTART: D:/BPB projects 2021/IX AI Projects book/source code for python programs/py.31.py
5 letters found
>>> |
```

Figure 3.45 b: *Output*

46. Write a python program to interchange the first and last element in a list.

```
def swapList(newList):
    size = len(List)
```

```
        temp = List[0]
        List[0] = List[size - 1]
        List[size - 1] = temp
        return List
    List = [10, 12, 35, 39,23, 56, 24,67,89]
    print(swapList(List))
```

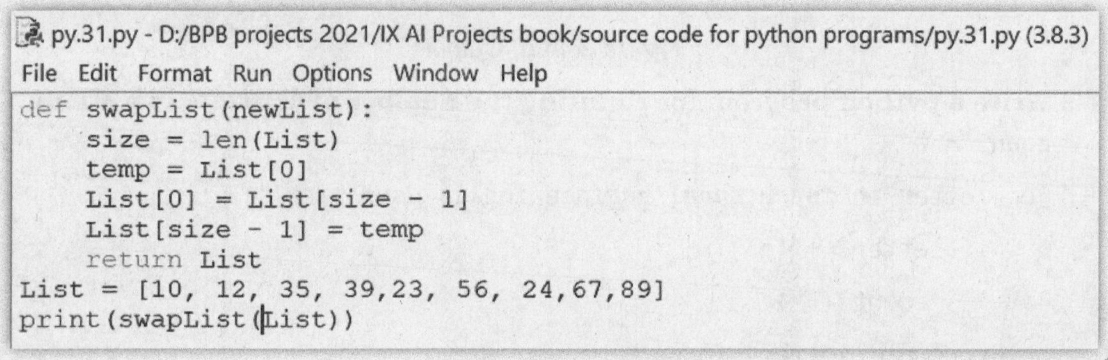

```
py.31.py - D:/BPB projects 2021/IX AI Projects book/source code for python programs/py.31.py (3.8.3)
File Edit Format Run Options Window Help
def swapList(newList):
    size = len(List)
    temp = List[0]
    List[0] = List[size - 1]
    List[size - 1] = temp
    return List
List = [10, 12, 35, 39,23, 56, 24,67,89]
print(swapList(List))
```

***Figure 3.46 a:** Code*

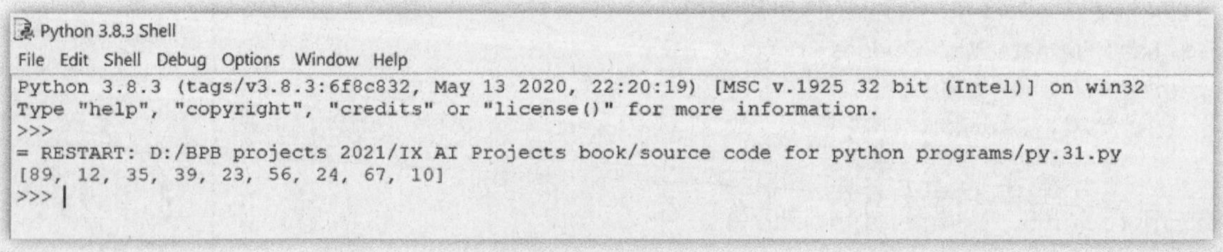

```
Python 3.8.3 Shell
File Edit Shell Debug Options Window Help
Python 3.8.3 (tags/v3.8.3:6f8c832, May 13 2020, 22:20:19) [MSC v.1925 32 bit (Intel)] on win32
Type "help", "copyright", "credits" or "license()" for more information.
>>>
= RESTART: D:/BPB projects 2021/IX AI Projects book/source code for python programs/py.31.py
[89, 12, 35, 39, 23, 56, 24, 67, 10]
>>> |
```

***Figure 3.46 b:** Output*

47. Write a python program to create a histogram from a given list of integers.

```
    def histogram( items ):
        for n in items:
            output = ‘’
            times = n
            while( times > 0 ):
              output += ‘$’
              times = times - 1
```

```
        print(output)
    histogram([1,2, 3, 4,5,6])
```

```
py.31.py - D:/BPB projects 2021/IX AI Projects book/source code for python programs/py.31.py (3.8.3)
File Edit Format Run Options Window Help
def histogram( items ):
    for n in items:
        output = ''
        times = n
        while( times > 0 ):
          output += '$'
          times = times - 1
        print(output)
histogram([1,2, 3, 4,5,6])
```

Figure 3.47 a: *Code*

```
Python 3.8.3 Shell
File Edit Shell Debug Options Window Help
Python 3.8.3 (tags/v3.8.3:6f8c832, May 13 2020, 22:20:19) [MSC v.1925 32 bit (Intel)] on win32
Type "help", "copyright", "credits" or "license()" for more information.
>>>
= RESTART: D:/BPB projects 2021/IX AI Projects book/source code for python programs/py.31.py
$
$$
$$$
$$$$
$$$$$
$$$$$$
>>> |
```

Figure 3.47 b: *Output*

48. Write a python program to check whether the specific value is contained in a group of values.

```
def is_group_member(group_data, n):
    for value in group_data:
        if n == value:
            return True
    return False
print(is_group_member([1, 5, 8, 3], 3))
print(is_group_member([5, 8, 3], -1))
```

```
py.48.py - D:/BPB projects 2021/IX AI Projects book/source code for python programs/py.48.py (3.8.3)
File  Edit  Format  Run  Options  Window  Help
def is_group_member(group_data, n):
    for value in group_data:
        if n == value:
            return True
    return False
print(is_group_member([1, 5, 8, 3], 3))
print(is_group_member([5, 8, 3], -1))
```

Figure 3.48 a: *Code*

```
Python 3.8.3 Shell
File  Edit  Shell  Debug  Options  Window  Help
Python 3.8.3 (tags/v3.8.3:6f8c832, May 13 2020, 22:20:19) [MSC v.1925 32 bit (Intel)] on win32
Type "help", "copyright", "credits" or "license()" for more information.
>>>
= RESTART: D:/BPB projects 2021/IX AI Projects book/source code for python programs/py.48.py
True
False
>>>
```

Figure 3.48 b: *Output*

49. Write a python program to the solution of (x + y) * (x + y) for the values of x, y as 5,6 respectively.

```
x, y = 5,6
result = x * x + 2 * x * y + y * y
print("({} + {}) ^ 2) = {}".format(x, y, result))
```

```
py.48.py - D:/BPB projects 2021/IX AI Projects book/source code for python programs/py.48.py (3.8.3)
File  Edit  Format  Run  Options  Window  Help
x,y=5,6
result = x * x + 2 * x * y + y * y
print("({} + {}) ^ 2) = {}".format(x, y, result))
```

Figure 3.49 a: *Code*

```
Python 3.8.3 Shell
File  Edit  Shell  Debug  Options  Window  Help
Python 3.8.3 (tags/v3.8.3:6f8c832, May 13 2020, 22:20:19) [MSC v.1925 32 bit (Intel)] on win32
Type "help", "copyright", "credits" or "license()" for more information.
>>>
= RESTART: D:/BPB projects 2021/IX AI Projects book/source code for python programs/py.48.py
(5 + 6) ^ 2) = 121
>>>
```

Figure 3.49 b: *Output*

50. Write a python program for the calculation of the hypotenuse of a right-angled triangle.

```
print("Input lengths of shorter triangle sides:")
a = float(input("a: "))
b = float(input("b: "))
c = ((a**2) + (b**2))**0.5
print("The length of the hypotenuse is", c )
```

```
py.48.py - D:/BPB projects 2021/IX AI Projects book/source code for python programs/py.48.py (3.8.3)
File Edit Format Run Options Window Help
print("Input lengths of shorter triangle sides:")
a = float(input("a: "))
b = float(input("b: "))
c = ((a**2) + (b**2))**0.5
print("The length of the hypotenuse is", c )
```

Figure 3.50 a: *Code*

```
Python 3.8.3 Shell
File Edit Shell Debug Options Window Help
Python 3.8.3 (tags/v3.8.3:6f8c832, May 13 2020, 22:20:19) [MSC v.1925 32 bit (Intel)] on win32
Type "help", "copyright", "credits" or "license()" for more information.
>>>
= RESTART: D:/BPB projects 2021/IX AI Projects book/source code for python programs/py.48.py
Input lengths of shorter triangle sides:
a: 5
b: 7
The length of the hypotenuse is 8.602325267042627
>>>
```

Figure 3.50 b: *Output*

51. Write a python program to generate the prime numbers from 1 to n.

```
num =int(input("Enter the range: "))
for n in range(1,num):
    for i in range(2,n):
        if(n%i==0):
            break
    else:
        print(n)
```

py.48.py - D:/BPB projects 2021/IX AI Projects book/source code for python programs/py.48.py (3.8.3)

File Edit Format Run Options Window Help

```
num =int(input("Enter the range: "))
for n in range(1,num):
    for i in range(2,n):
        if(n%i==0):
            break
    else:
        print(n)
```

***Figure 3.51 a:** Code*

Python 3.8.3 Shell

File Edit Shell Debug Options Window Help

```
Python 3.8.3 (tags/v3.8.3:6f8c832, May 13 2020, 22:20:19) [MSC v.1925 32 bit (Intel)] on win32
Type "help", "copyright", "credits" or "license()" for more information.
>>>
= RESTART: D:/BPB projects 2021/IX AI Projects book/source code for python programs/py.48.py
Enter the range: 7
1
2
3
5
>>> |
```

***Figure 3.51 b:** Output*

52. Write a python program for matrix multiplication.

```
X = [[8,5,1],
[9 ,3,2],
[4 ,6,3]]
Y = [[8,5,3],
[9,5,7],
[9,4,1]]
result = [[0,0,0],
[0,0,0],
[0,0,0]]
for i in range(len(X)):
    for j in range(len(Y[0])):
            result[i][j] = X[i][j] * Y[i][j]
for x in result:
    print(x)
```

py.48.py - D:/BPB projects 2021/IX AI Projects book/source code for python programs/py.48.py (3.8.3)

File Edit Format Run Options Window Help

```
X = [[8,5,1],
[9 ,3,2],
[4 ,6,3]]
Y = [[8,5,3],
[9,5,7],
[9,4,1]]
result = [[0,0,0],
[0,0,0],
[0,0,0]]
for i in range(len(X)):
    for j in range(len(Y[0])):
        result[i][j] = X[i][j] * Y[i][j]
for X in result:
    print(X)
```

Figure 3.52 a: *Code*

Python 3.8.3 Shell

File Edit Shell Debug Options Window Help

```
Python 3.8.3 (tags/v3.8.3:6f8c832, May 13 2020, 22:20:19) [MSC v.1925 32 bit (Intel)] on win32
Type "help", "copyright", "credits" or "license()" for more information.
>>>
= RESTART: D:/BPB projects 2021/IX AI Projects book/source code for python programs/py.48.py
[64, 25, 3]
[81, 15, 14]
[36, 24, 3]
>>>
```

Figure 3.52 b: *Output*

53. Write a python program to print the half diamond.

```
def halfDiamondStar(N):
    for i in range(N):
        for j in range(0, i + 1):
            print("*", end = "")
        print()
    for i in range(1, N):
        for j in range(i, N):
            print("*", end = "")
        print()
N = 5;
halfDiamondStar(N);
```

```
py.48.py - D:/BPB projects 2021/IX AI Projects book/source code for python programs/py.48.py (3.8.3)
File Edit Format Run Options Window Help
def halfDiamondStar(N):
    for i in range(N):
        for j in range(0, i + 1):
            print("*", end = "")
        print()
    for i in range(1, N):
        for j in range(i, N):
            print("*", end = "")
        print()
N = 5;
halfDiamondStar(N);
```

Figure 3.53 a: *Code*

```
Python 3.8.3 Shell
File Edit Shell Debug Options Window Help
Python 3.8.3 (tags/v3.8.3:6f8c832, May 13 2020, 22:20:19) [MSC v.1925 32 bit (Intel)] on win32
Type "help", "copyright", "credits" or "license()" for more information.
>>>
= RESTART: D:/BPB projects 2021/IX AI Projects book/source code for python programs/py.48.py
*
**
***
****
*****
****
***
**
*
>>>
```

Figure 3.53 b: *Output*

54. Write a python program to find the sum of the series 2+22+222+2222+22222.

```
number_of_terms = 5

start = 2

sum = 0

for i in range(0, number_of_terms):

    print(start, end=" ")

    sum += start

    start = (start * 10) + 2

print("\nSum of above series is:", sum)
```

```
py.53.py - D:/BPB projects 2021/IX AI Projects book/source code for python programs/py.53.py (3.8.3)
File Edit Format Run Options Window Help
number_of_terms = 5
start = 2
sum = 0
for i in range(0, number_of_terms):
    print(start, end=" ")
    sum += start
    start = (start * 10) + 2
print("\nSum of above series is:", sum)
```

Figure 3.54 a: *Code*

```
Python 3.8.3 Shell
File Edit Shell Debug Options Window Help
Python 3.8.3 (tags/v3.8.3:6f8c832, May 13 2020, 22:20:19) [MSC v.1925 32 bit (Intel)] on win32
Type "help", "copyright", "credits" or "license()" for more information.
>>>
= RESTART: D:/BPB projects 2021/IX AI Projects book/source code for python programs/py.53.py
2 22 222 2222 22222
Sum of above series is: 24690
>>>
```

Figure 3.54 b: *Output*

55. Write a python program to multiply all values in a list using traversal.

```
def multiplyList(myList) :
    result = 1
    for x in myList:
        result = result * x
    return result
list1 = [1, 2, 3]
list2 = [3, 2, 4]
print(multiplyList(list1))
print(multiplyList(list2))
```

```
py.53.py - D:/BPB projects 2021/IX AI Projects book/source code for python programs/py.53.py (3.8.3)
File Edit Format Run Options Window Help
def multiplyList(myList) :
    result = 1
    for x in myList:
         result = result * x
    return result
list1 = [1, 2, 3]
list2 = [3, 2, 4]
print(multiplyList(list1))
print(multiplyList(list2))
```

***Figure 3.55 a:** Code*

```
Python 3.8.3 Shell
File Edit Shell Debug Options Window Help
Python 3.8.3 (tags/v3.8.3:6f8c832, May 13 2020, 22:20:19) [MSC v.1925 32 bit (Intel)] on win32
Type "help", "copyright", "credits" or "license()" for more information.
>>>
= RESTART: D:/BPB projects 2021/IX AI Projects book/source code for python programs/py.53.py
6
24
>>> |
```

***Figure 3.55 b:** Output*

56. Write a python program to check if a substring is present in a given string.

```
def check(string, sub_str):
    if (string.find(sub_str) == -1):
        print("NO")
    else:
        print("YES")
string = "satya writes satya"
sub_str ="satya"
check(string, sub_str)
```

```
py.53.py - D:/BPB projects 2021/IX AI Projects book/source code for python programs/py.53.py (3.8.3)
File Edit Format Run Options Window Help
def check(string, sub_str):
    if (string.find(sub_str) == -1):
        print("NO")
    else:
        print("YES")
string = "satya reads satya"
sub_str ="satya"
check(string, sub_str)
```

***Figure 3.56 a:** Code*

```
Python 3.8.3 Shell
File Edit Shell Debug Options Window Help
Python 3.8.3 (tags/v3.8.3:6f8c832, May 13 2020, 22:20:19) [MSC v.1925 32 bit (Intel)] on win32
Type "help", "copyright", "credits" or "license()" for more information.
>>>
= RESTART: D:/BPB projects 2021/IX AI Projects book/source code for python programs/py.53.py
YES
>>>
```

Figure 3.56 b: *Output*

57. Write a python program for counting the number of words in a string.

```
str1 = input("Enter your own string :")
total = 1
for i in range(len(str1)):
    if(str1[i] == ' ' or str1 == '\n' or str1 == '\t'):
        total = total + 1
print("Total Number of Words in this String = ", total)
```

```
py.53.py - D:/BPB projects 2021/IX AI Projects book/source code for python programs/py.53.py (3.8.3)
File Edit Format Run Options Window Help
str1 = input("Please Enter your Own String :")
total = 1
for i in range(len(str1)):
    if(str1[i] == ' ' or str1 == '\n' or str1 == '\t'):
        total = total + 1
print("Total Number of Words in this String = ", total)
```

Figure 3.57 a: *Code*

```
Python 3.8.3 Shell
File Edit Shell Debug Options Window Help
Python 3.8.3 (tags/v3.8.3:6f8c832, May 13 2020, 22:20:19) [MSC v.1925 32 bit (Intel)] on win32
Type "help", "copyright", "credits" or "license()" for more information.
>>>
= RESTART: D:/BPB projects 2021/IX AI Projects book/source code for python programs/py.53.py
Please Enter your Own String :Hell Friends! This is my new innovation.
Total Number of Words in this String =  7
>>>
= RESTART: D:/BPB projects 2021/IX AI Projects book/source code for python programs/py.53.py
Please Enter your Own String :This beautiful animal is not fit for a zoo.
Total Number of Words in this String =  9
>>>
```

Figure 3.57 b: *Output*

58. Write a python program to check whether the number is perfect square or not.

```
number = int(input("Enter the Number:"))
root = (number)**0.5
```

```
if int(root + 0.5) ** 2 == number:
    print("Entered number is a perfect square")
else:
    print("Entered number is not a perfect square")
```

```
py.53.py - D:/BPB projects 2021/IX AI Projects book/source code for python programs/py.53.py (3.8.3)
File Edit Format Run Options Window Help
number = int(input("Enter the Number:"))
root = (number)**0.5
if int(root + 0.5) ** 2 == number:
    print("Entered number is a perfect square")
else:
    print("Entered number is not a perfect square")
```

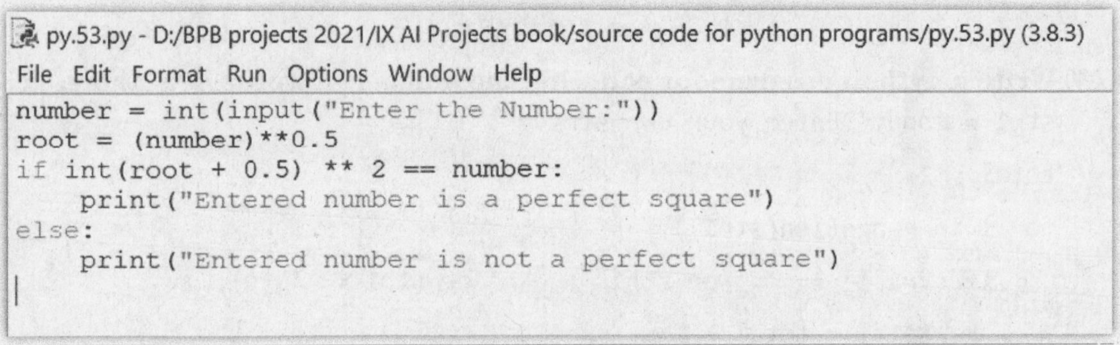

Figure 3.58 a: *Code*

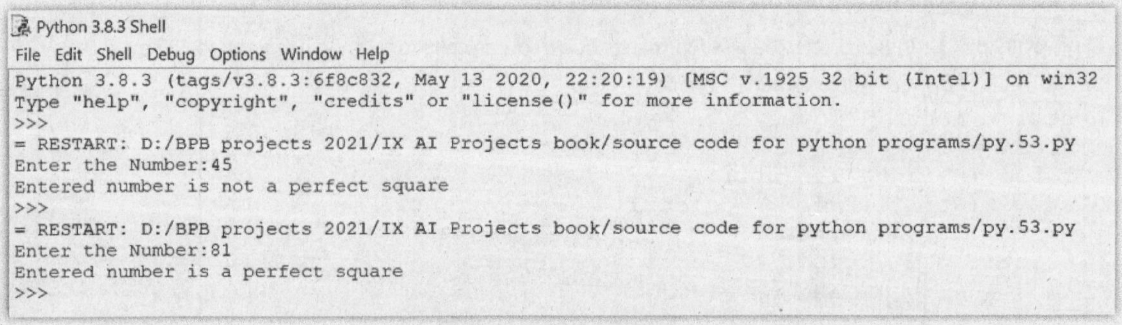

```
Python 3.8.3 Shell
File Edit Shell Debug Options Window Help
Python 3.8.3 (tags/v3.8.3:6f8c832, May 13 2020, 22:20:19) [MSC v.1925 32 bit (Intel)] on win32
Type "help", "copyright", "credits" or "license()" for more information.
>>>
= RESTART: D:/BPB projects 2021/IX AI Projects book/source code for python programs/py.53.py
Enter the Number:45
Entered number is not a perfect square
>>>
= RESTART: D:/BPB projects 2021/IX AI Projects book/source code for python programs/py.53.py
Enter the Number:81
Entered number is a perfect square
>>>
```

Figure 3.58 b: *Output*

59. Write a python program to print all the odd numbers from 12 to 28.

```
print("Odd numbers are")
for i in range(12,28):
    if(i%2!=0):
        print(i)
```

```
py.53.py - D:/BPB projects 2021/IX AI Projects book/source code for python programs/py.53.py (3.8.3)
File Edit Format Run Options Window Help
print("Odd numbers are")
for i in range(12,28):
    if(i%2!=0):
        print(i)
```

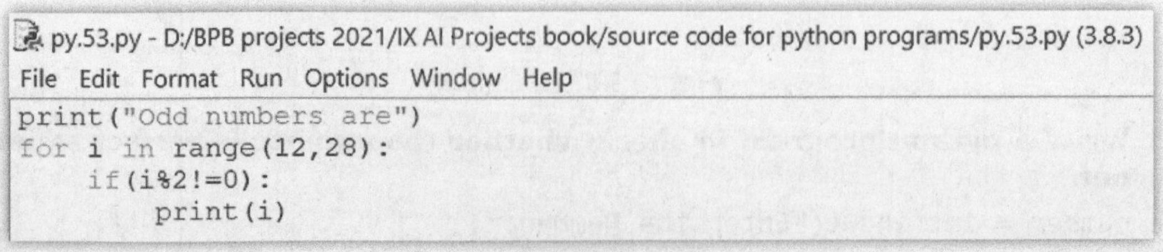

Figure 3.59 a: *Code*

```
Python 3.8.3 Shell
File Edit Shell Debug Options Window Help
Python 3.8.3 (tags/v3.8.3:6f8c832, May 13 2020, 22:20:19) [MSC v.1925 32 bit (Intel)] on win32
Type "help", "copyright", "credits" or "license()" for more information.
>>>
= RESTART: D:/BPB projects 2021/IX AI Projects book/source code for python programs/py.53.py
Enter the Number:45
Entered number is not a perfect square
>>>
= RESTART: D:/BPB projects 2021/IX AI Projects book/source code for python programs/py.53.py
Enter the Number:81
Entered number is a perfect square
>>>
```

Figure 3.59 b: *Output*

60. Write a python program for the salary slip of an employee by entering the basic salary from the user and calculating the net salary as per the data given below:

```
HRA=15%of basic salary,
TA = 23% of basic salary,
DA= 38% of basic salary,
Gross income= Basic salary +HRA+TA+DA,
Income Tax = 5.5% of gross income.
Net salary =Gross income-Income Tax
sal=int(input("Enter the salary of an employee:"))
hra=0.15*sal
ta=0.23*sal
da=0.38*sal
gi=sal+hra+ta+da
itax=0.055*gi
netsal=gi-itax
print("Salary Slip")
print("Salary=",sal)
print("TA =",ta)
print("DA =", da)
print("HRA =",hra)
print("Gross Income =",gi)
```

```
print("Income Tax =",itax)
print("Net Salary =",netsal)
```

py.59.py - D:/BPB projects 2021/IX AI Projects book/source code for python programs/py.59.py (3.8.3)

File Edit Format Run Options Window Help

```
sal=int(input("Enter the salary of an employee:"))
hra=0.15*sal
ta=0.23*sal
da=0.38*sal
gi=sal+hra+ta+da
itax=0.055*gi
netsal=gi-itax
print("Salary Slip")
print("Salary=",sal)
print("TA =",ta)
print("DA =", da)
print("HRA =",hra)
print("Gross Income =",gi)
print("Income Tax =",itax)
print("Net Salary =",netsal)
```

Figure 3.60 a: *Code*

Python 3.8.3 Shell

File Edit Shell Debug Options Window Help

```
Python 3.8.3 (tags/v3.8.3:6f8c832, May 13 2020, 22:20:19) [MSC v.1925 32 bit (Intel)] on win32
Type "help", "copyright", "credits" or "license()" for more information.
>>>
= RESTART: D:/BPB projects 2021/IX AI Projects book/source code for python programs/py.59.py
Enter the salary of an employee:50000
Salary Slip
Salary= 50000
TA = 11500.0
DA = 19000.0
HRA = 7500.0
Gross Income = 88000.0
Income Tax = 4840.0
Net Salary = 83160.0
>>> |
```

Figure 3.60 b: *Output*

3.1.2 Unsolved python problems

1. Write a python program to accept three distinct digits and print all possible combinations from the digits.
2. Write a python program to search the power of a number using the exponential operator.
3. Write a python program to check if a number entered by the user is divisible by 3 and 8 or not.

4. Write a python program that shows the use of a floor division operator.
5. Write a python program to check whether an entered number is greater than 30 or not.
6. Write a python program to calculate the product of three numbers input by the user and display their product.
7. Write a python program to display all odd numbers in a list.
8. Write a python program to find the factorial of a number entered.
9. Write a python program to find the area and circumference of a circle.
10. Write a python program to find and display even and odd numbers in a list.

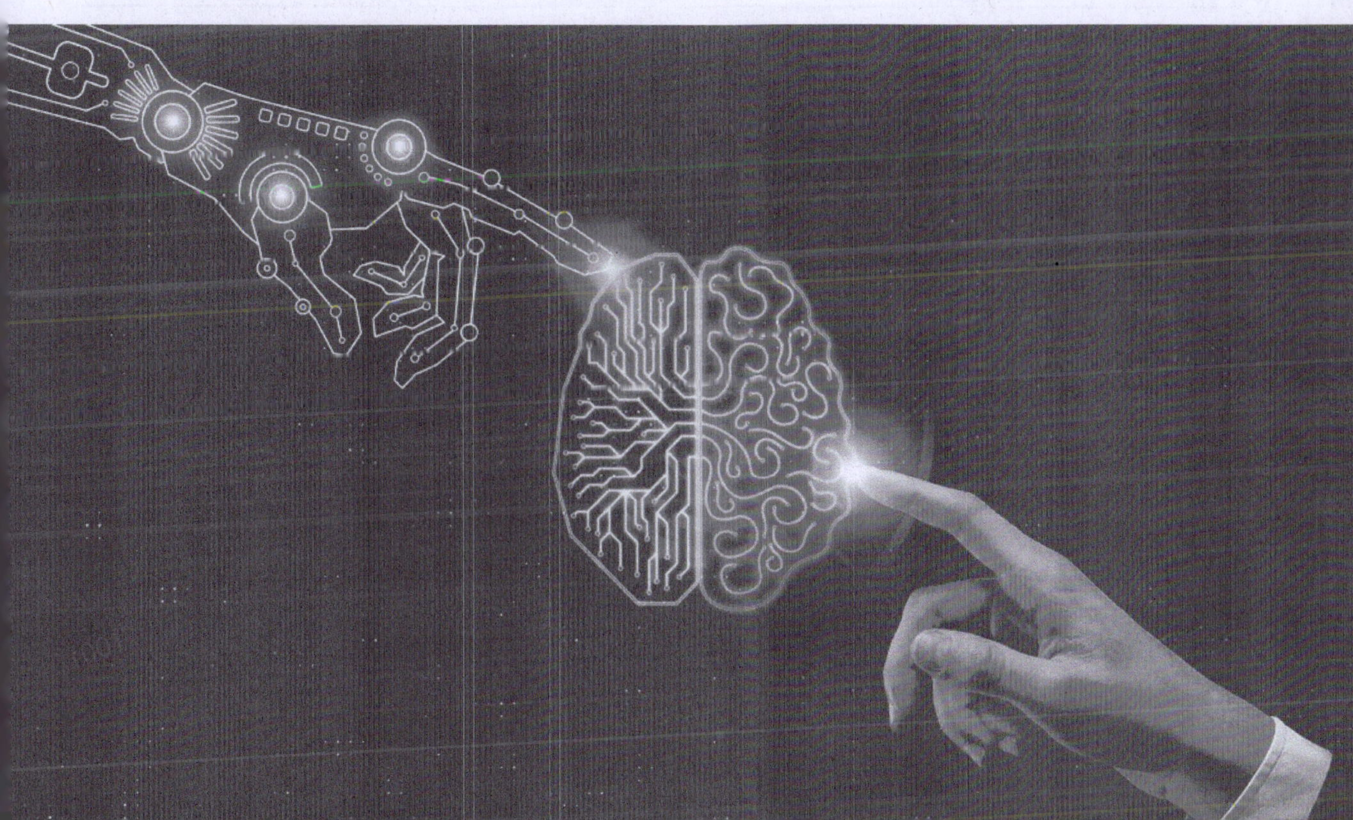

Notes

4 Activities, Projects, and Practical (Chapterwise)

1. Introduction to AI

1. Understanding AI through gaming: individual activity

All the learners shall play the following three games based on different AI domains by using the link given:

(i) **Rock, Paper, and Scissors** (based on data) (http://bit.ly/iai4yrps) (this game explains the basic principles of an adaptive AI technology. The computer learns to identify patterns of a person's behaviour by analyzing his/her decision making and improves on its score accordingly.)

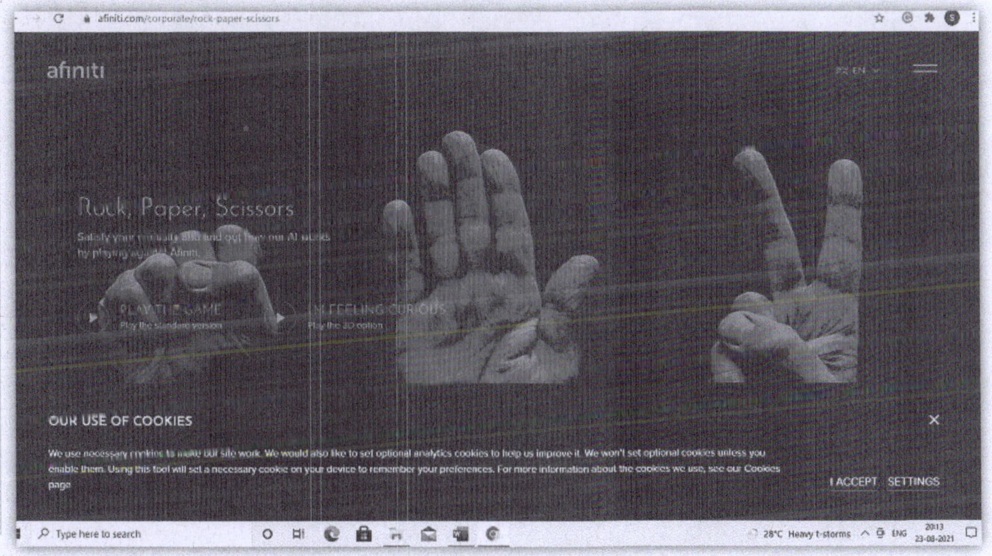

Figure 4.1

(ii) **Mystery Animal** (based on Natural Language Processing-NLP) (http://bit.ly/iai4yma) (It is a 20 questions game to identify the mystery animal. The learners will ask the questions, and the computer answers the mystery animal within 20 turns.)

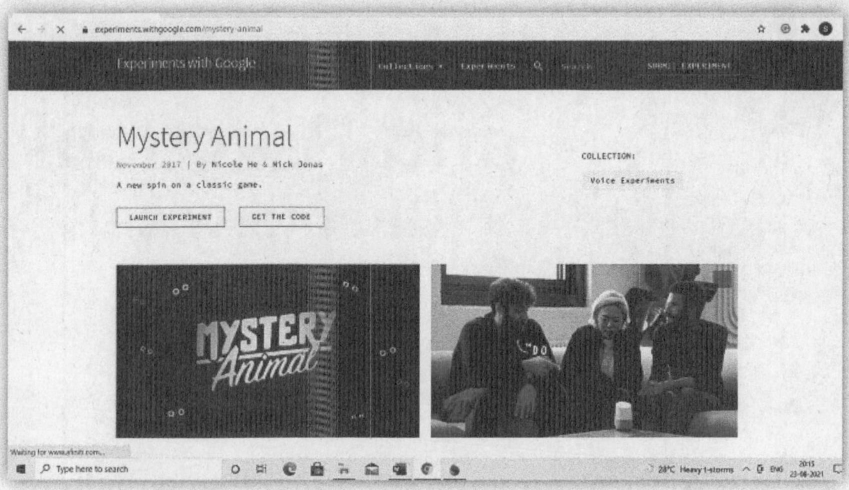

Figure 4.2

(iii) **Emoji Scavenger Hunt** (based on Computer Vision (This game explains the use of computer vision using the AI concept in our lives and uses the Neural Network based image recognition feature of AI.) (https://emojiscavengerhunt.withgoogle.com)

Figure 4.3

2. Group discussion after video session: class activity

Some videos on the Smart City concept, like those that are mentioned below, will be screened by the teacher. All learners will watch the video analytically and will participate in the class discussion after viewing videos on the topics related to the concept of Smart Cities, Smart Schools, Smart Homes, etc. All learners will be provided the opportunity to express his/her views.

Figure 4.4

The teacher may screen any of the following videos, followed by class discussion:

(i) Top 5 Future Smartest City In India | Smart City In India 2019
https://www.youtube.com/watch?v=4F8GWmwhtdM

(ii) Home automation in Ahmedabad - SMART HOME
https://www.youtube.com/watch?v=kGKyUFTgbJU

(iii) What is a smart city? | CNBC Explains
https://www.youtube.com/watch?v=bANfnYDTzxE

3. Writing an interactive story: individual activity

Imagine that you are an author. You have to imagine the future home fitted with AI devices and then write an interactive story by using the Story Speaker extension in Google docs

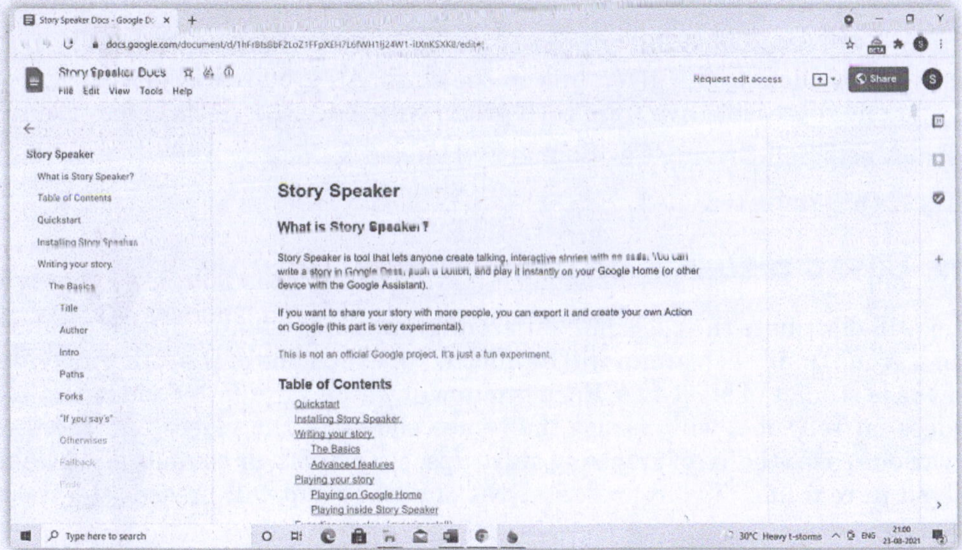

Figure 4.5

4. Playing an online game: individual activity

All the learners shall play the game "Go" available free online by clicking the following link: https://www.flyordie.com/go/

Figure 4.6

5. Reflection on a video on 'interaction of two AI Devices': group activity

All the learners will be divided into groups of 4-6 learners without any bias. The teacher will screen the video by clicking the given link in the class. All groups will discuss the content of the video, and one representative from each group will share the views before the full class.

(i) Robot Meets Self Driving Car-Sophia by Hanson & Jack by Audi
https://www.youtube.com/watch?v=vtX-qVUfCKI

6. Theme-based research on case studies: group work

The teacher will distribute the class into different groups of students without gender bias (4-6 students in a group), and each group will be allotted to watch one of the following videos based on different case studies of start-ups. Each group will watch the allotted video and some other related videos on YouTube, will discuss the issues shown in the videos and then, prepare a report on various case studies of inspiring start-ups, companies, or communities where AI has been involved in real life. Two representatives of each group will present the report before the full class.

Figure 4.7

(i) Top Artificial Intelligence Start-ups in 2018
https://www.youtube.com/watch?v=HkVZ9UjRqdc

(ii) 10 Artificial Intelligence (AI) startups in India (you should Know) 2019
https://www.youtube.com/watch?v=yoO2xGBHjJI

(iii) 13 of the smartest Artificial Intelligence companies, according to MIT
https://www.youtube.com/watch?v=I4qM33A2OH8

7. Creating a job ad: pair activity

The class will be distributed into pairs without any bias and randomly. Each pair will have to create a job advertisement for a firm by describing the nature of the job available and the skill-set required for the job in 2035. The pairs shall have to figure out how AI is going to transform the nature of jobs and create the Ad accordingly.

Figure 4.8

8. Watching videos: group discussion

The teacher will arrange the screening of the following videos in the class, and it will be followed by a group discussion on the future of AI. Each learner will be given the opportunity to share his/her views.

(i) AI VS AI – CHATBOTS TALKING TO EACH OTHER IS CREEPY
https://www.youtube.com/watch?v=2QKzqCBfKMI

(ii) THE ROBOT KILLER ANKI VECTOR VS MANTIS! ARTIFICIAL INTELLIGENCE AGAINST MANTIS
https://www.youtube.com/watch?v=gOSZzSA2m74

(iii) Artificial Intelligence & the Future - Rise of AI (Elon Musk, Bill Gates, Sundar Pichai) | Simplilearn
https://www.youtube.com/watch?v=wTbrk0suwbg

Figure 4.9: *Pair presentation*

9. Class discussion on the video show on AI Ethics

The following videos will be screened in the class on AI Ethics, followed by a class discussion under the guidance of the teacher. All the learners will participate in the class discussion to put their views on AI Ethics.

(i) AI FOR GOOD - Ethics in AI
https://www.youtube.com/watch?v=vgUWKXVvO9Q

(ii) Sophia answers the Trolley Problem
https://www.youtube.com/watch?v=8MjIU4eq_A

10.Role play on AI ethics awareness: group activity

Learners will participate in the Roleplay where they have to play the roles of major stakeholders, and they have to decide what is correct ethically and what is not for a given scenario.

Situation: A company named SahilAjay AI Research and Service Solutions Pvt Ltd is engaged in doing research work by collecting data from mobiles. Sometimes the company does not take consent from the users to collect data. In each group, learners will play the roles of stakeholders like company management personnel (CEO, CTO, Managers, Developers, etc.), mobile users, users of the data provided by the company, etc. the stakeholders will discuss and share their views in dramatization on AI Ethics in the processes used by the company.

Figure 4.10: *Dramatisation*

11. Debate: individual activity

All the learners shall participate in the debate on the topic **'Use of AI technology is affecting the lives positively'** and present their views either in affirmation or against the topic. They will have to deliberate with their points as to why AI is beneficial/ harmful to society. Each learner will be given two minutes to speak.

12. Research on the future of AI: group activity

Learners will work in groups of 4-6 and will be allotted a theme (transportation /entertainment/ industry/education/training, etc.) around which they have to search for present AI trends and need to visualize the future of the AI in and around the respective theme allotted to them. Group Report is to be presented before the full class.

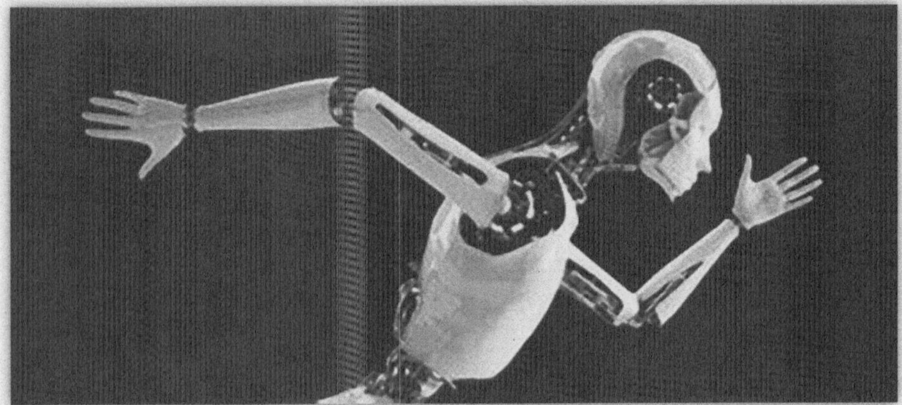

Figure 4.11

13. Letter writing: individual activity

Imagine that you are residing in a super City of the future called "**FC201**," having all facilities and devices using AI, say in 2045. Write a Letter to yourself in the future. It means that you have to write a letter to self-keeping the future in context. You will describe what you have learned so far or what you would like to learn someday.

Figure 4.12

14. Reflection on viewing the videos: larger group activity

(i) Cute Robots You Can BUY - Robots are Your Ultimate Life Hack
https://www.youtube.com/watch?v=-OTd-S7rY98

(ii) Tonight Showbotics: Jimmy Meets Sophia the Human-Like Robot
https://www.youtube.com/watch?v=Bg_tJvCA8zw

(iii) Robot Sophia, a social humanoid robot developed by Hanson Robotics, at the IAA World Congress
https://www.youtube.com/watch?v=nyjGBph9YjE

2. Project cycle

1. Poster making: individual activity

Each learner will prepare a poster on the theme **"AI Project Life Cycle"**.

All the posters prepared by learners will be displayed in the class.

2. Problem statement: group work

All the learners will be divided into small groups (4-6 learners) without bias. Each group will discuss and prepare the statement of an AI problem related to their surroundings.

3. Powerpoint presentation on project cycle stages: group work

All the learners will be divided into five groups without bias. Each group will be allotted a stage related to AI Project Cycle. Each group will research the allotted topic, deliberate it in the group discussion and prepare a presentation using PowerPoint. Two representatives of each group will present the topic in the class.

4. Theme based research on data visualization tools: group work

All the learners will be divided into seven groups without bias. Each group will be allotted a data visualization tool for research by using the library and internet and making a report. Two representatives from each group will present the oral report on the allotted theme.

Figure 4.13: *Group work*

5. Brainstorming session on AI selection: group work

The teacher will initiate the brainstorming session in the class on the topic "Tools and Techniques for Selection of an AI Project." All the learners will discuss various themes and prepare a list of AI projects.

6. Group discussion on data and analysis: group work

All the learners will participate in the class discussion to find out the answers to the questions related to data and analysis, like:

a. From where can you get the data?
b. What features of data are required?
c. What is the frequency of collecting the data for the selected project?
d. What happens when you don't find enough data?
e. What type of data analysis is needed to be done?
f. How will you validate data?
g. What actions are informed from the data analysis?

After group discussion, the class will list down some conclusions drawn.

7. Collage making on decision tree: pair activity

All the learners in the class will be divided into pairs without gender bias. After doing research in the library and on the internet, each pair will prepare a collage on a **"Decision Tree"**.

8. Group activity on design an AI project cycle

The teacher will divide the class into small groups of 4-6 learners randomly. Each group will identify a problem statement in their neighbouring area and design the AI Project Cycle steps learned so far to depict predicted trends and strategies required. The report prepared by each group will have the following points:

- Problem statement
- Brief description
- Data sources (newspapers, magazines, articles, journals, internet, etc.)
- Tabulated data
- Graphs/ Charts
- Suggested Solution (s) of the problem

3. Neural network

1. Playing a game on the working of the neural network: group activity

Divide the whole class into four groups A, B, C, and D without any bias. During the game, all learners will keep silent and will not discuss anything. Each group will represent one layer of the neural network.

The X learners of group A represent layer 1, i.e., the input layer. The second group B of Y learners acts as the hidden layer 1. The third group C of Z students acts as hidden layer 2. The fourth group D of one student acts as the output layer.

The input layer takes in some data, which is passed on to hidden layers for some processing. The output layer finally gets all information from the hidden layer and gives meaningful information as the final result.

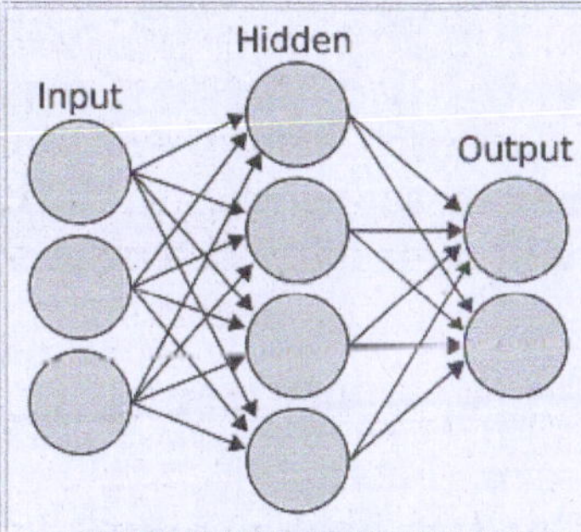

Figure 4.14: ANN

2. Learning neural networks through gaming: group discussion

The teacher will screen the following videos in the class, which shall be viewed by the learners carefully to understand Neural Networks. It will be followed by a group discussion.

(i) Neural network racing cars around a track
https://www.youtube.com/watch?v=wL7tSgUpy8w

(ii) Multi-Agent Hide and Seek
https://www.youtube.com/watch?v-kopoLzvh5jY

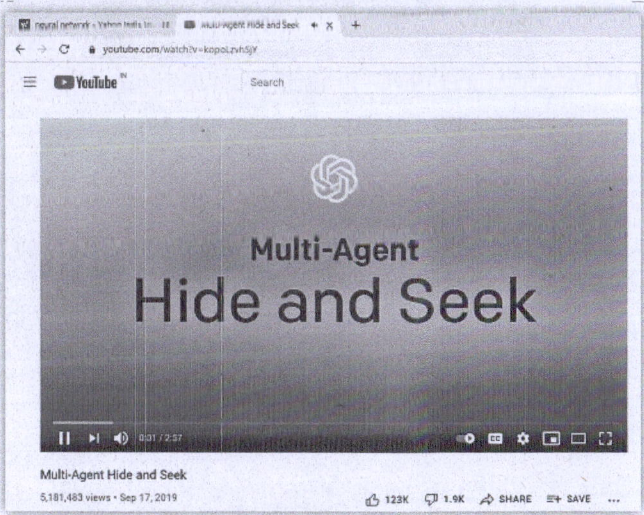

Figure 4.15

3. Creating a poster on neural network: pair activity

All the learners will be divided into pairs without any bias. Each pair will prepare a poster on any one of the topics mentioned as below:

'Neural Network'/'Decision Tree'/'Visualization Tools'.

All the posters thus prepared will be displayed in the class.

4. Class reflection after watching videos on ML: group work

The following videos will be screened by the teacher in the class, and they will be followed by a reflection activity. The learners will be sensitized towards Machine learning.

(i) How Machines Learn
https://www.youtube.com/watch?v=R9OHn5ZF4Uo

(ii) How Machines *Really* Learn. [Footnote]
https://www.youtube.com/watch?v=wvWpdrfoEv0

5. Report making on handwriting: individual activity

All the learners will open the following link to understand the handwriting with a Neural Network and Play with a Neural Network that generates the handwriting based on your style. Write your experiences in the form of a report.

https://experiments.withgoogle.com/handwriting-with-a-neural-net

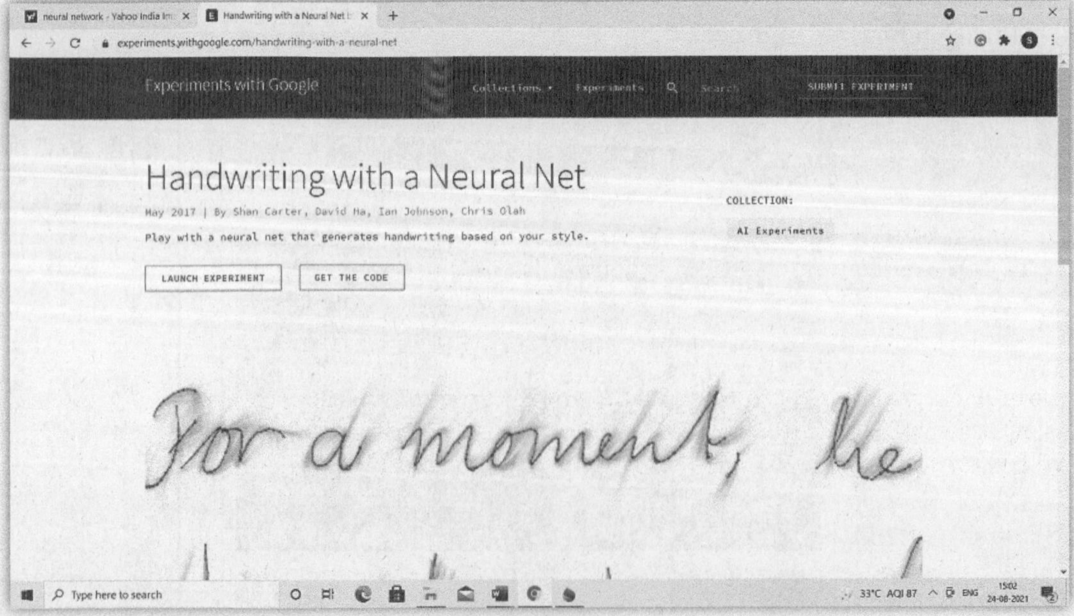

Figure 4.16

6. Quiz on NN: individual activity

All the learners will open the following link to play and understand the quiz with a Neural Network. Canvas quiz is regarded as a starter kit for developers to make custom, voice-enabled question-answer games for the Google Assistant.

https://experiments.withgoogle.com/collection/canvasquiz

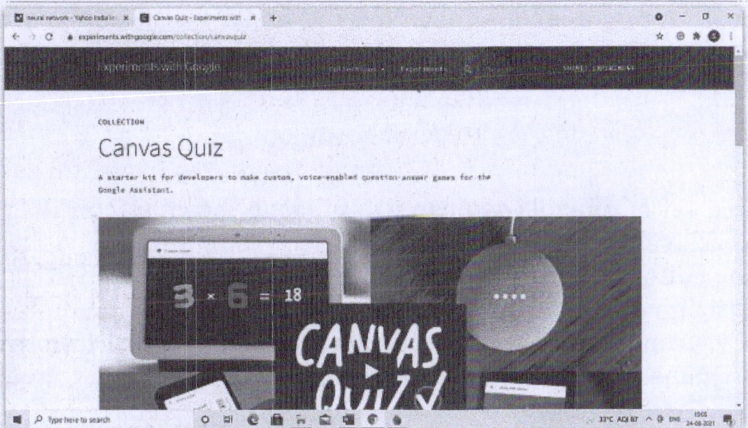

Figure 4.17

4. Python basics

1. Learning programming through gaming: individual activity

Introduction to programming using Online Gaming portals like Code Combat. Students will go through the following link and will play few games online to understand the Code Combat games:

https://www.game-accessibility.com/game/

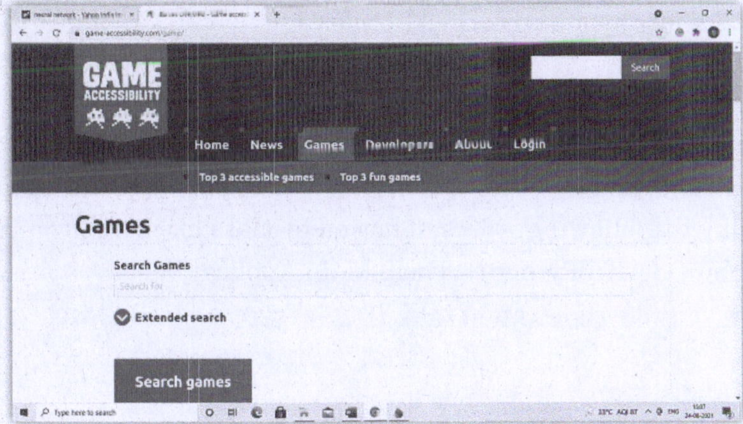

Figure 4.18

The game **Code Combat** is about learning programming language while playing a game. It is an RPG kind of game with cartoon fantasy graphics. You can play this game in your web browser. It is free for a while, but after that, you need to buy a subscription.

The screen is split into two sections. The left section is a labyrinth where you can see where your character has to go, and the right section of the screen is a code editor where you can type your commands for the character. By typing the commands correctly and in the correct order, you can solve a level. During a level, you get a set of tasks you need to perform. Tasks can be like killing enemies and finding gems. With the collected gems, you can buy new equipment like weapons and armor.

How to play?

There is a restricted set of controls you can use to move the character (e.g. self.move (), self. moveLeft(), self.attack(self.findNearestEnemy()), etc.). You need to type the commands in the correct order on the editor screen. When you run the program you created, you will see your character move through the level in the order you typed the commands. When there is a program error, or you made a wrong order of commands, you will lose lives or die. During the progress of the game, you will learn new ways to type commands, create loops and logic operators.

Unfortunately, this game cannot be played with a visual/physical/auditory disability. You need to see where the character has to go in order to solve a level.

This game can be hard to play if you have a learning disability. But the whole idea of this game is to learn a programming language in a fun way. Everything you need to do in this game is explained well, and you can try commands with a trial-and-error method to see if your code is correct.

2. Debate on future of python: individual activity

All the learners will participate in the debate on the topic 'Future of Python is not certain' and present their views either in affirmation of the topic or against it. They have to deliberate with their points about the future of Python in AI projects.

3. Class discussion on video screening: group work

The teacher will arrange the screening of a video on the following topics and have a class discussion after viewing videos on the topics related to Python applications.

The teacher will play the following videos, followed by class discussion:

(i) What Can You Do with Python? - The 3 Main Applications
https://www.youtube.com/watch?v=kLZuut1fYzQ

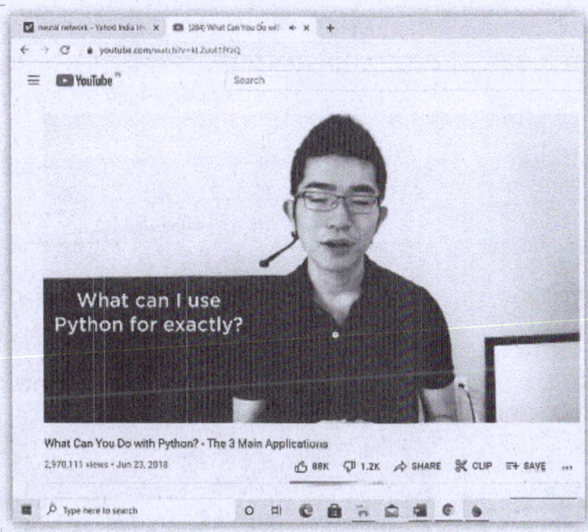

Figure 4.19

4. Creating codes/programs by using python IDLE

Create the following codes/programs:

a. Take a Boolean value "True" and a float number "6,9" and perform the AND operation on both.

b. Take a string " Zero" and a Boolean value " False" and try adding both by using the Bool() function.

c. Take a string "Shweta " and the float value "17.3" and try and add both of them by using the float() function.

d. Write a program to exhibit the use of relational operators.

e. For accepting an integer from the user and checking when this integer is greater than 10.

f. Write a program to calculate the cost of cuboid volume-wise.

g. Write a program to display the quotient and remainder.

5. Group work

The teacher will divide the class into small groups of 4-6 learners without gender bias. Each group will discuss the situation and share their experiences in the class.

(a) Situation: The group has to prepare the final result of class X A having 42 students after discussion. What should be the steps to prepare the result and the following details?

Average score of the class:

- The average percentage of the class performance:
- The number of students who passed:

- The number of students who failed:
- The success percentage of the class:
- Top 5 students of the class.

Figure 4.20

(b) Group Discussion: Each group will study the following for discussion:

A group of students in Satya International School has prepared the result by following the steps given below:

Step 1: To collect the exam scores for Mathematics, Science, Social Science, Hindi, and English for all the students.

Step 2: To prepare a database (List) of students and their marks in each subject out of 100 marks, that might look like as follows:

Roll No	Name	Marks in Hindi	Marks in English	Marks in Science	Marks in Mathematics	Marks in Social science	Total Marks	Marks %
1	Amita	77	98	89	95	87	446	89.2
2	Ananya	72	81	89	77	88	407	81.4
3	Bhanu	76	89	69	94	91	419	83.8
4	Chaitanya	67	56	54	76	71	324	64.8
5								
42	Zaved	84	68	78	75	78	383	76.6

Step 3: Use the formula for the calculation of percentage in the above table.

Step 4: Analysis of the database created to calculate the following details:

- Average Score of the class:
- The average percentage of the class performance:
- Number of students who passed:
- Number of students who failed:
- Success percentage of the class:
- Top 5 students of the class:

Discuss in the class whether the above steps are correct or need improvement.

(c) **Conclusion:** After going through this process, the students will conclude that preparing the exam result manually is a tedious and time-consuming process. Hence, it should be automated by creating a python script!

Each group will create a python script of result creation.

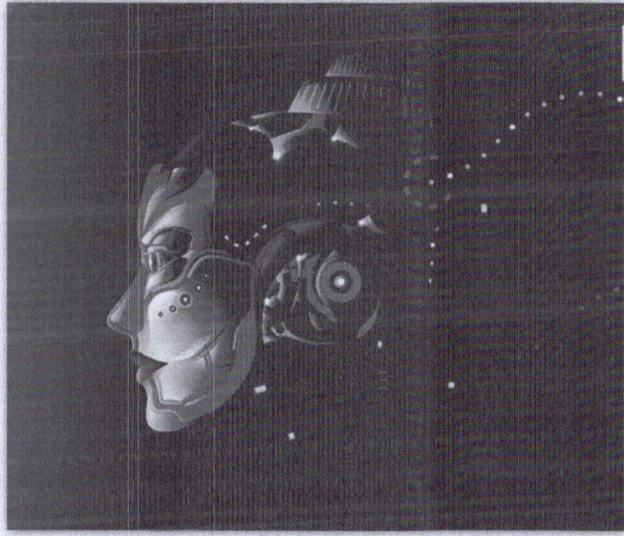

Figure 4.21

Notes

5 Viva Questions (Chapter wise)

1. Introduction to AI

1. **Define artificial intelligence.**

Ans. An ability of a computer or computer-controlled robot to perform tasks generally associated with intelligent human beings is called AI.

2. **What are the three sub-categories of Artificial Intelligence?**

Ans. Artificial Intelligence can be sub-divided into three categories: Artificial Intelligence, Machine Learning, and Deep Learning.

3. **What are the three domains of AI?**

Ans. The main three domains of AI are Data, Computer Vision (CV), and Natural Language Processing (NLP).

4. **Who was the first person to define the goal of artificial intelligence?**

Ans. John McCarthy (1955)

Figure 5.1: *John McCarthy*

5. **What is the primary goal of AI?**

Ans. 'The goal of AI is to develop machines that behave as though they were intelligent.'

6. **Define intelligence?**

Ans. Intelligence is the ability to understand, apply knowledge, and improve skills that have played a significant role in our evolution and in establishing human civilization.

7. **Who gave the following definition of AI?**
"The science of making machines for doing things that would require intelligence if done by man is termed as Artificial Intelligence."

Ans. Alan Turing.

8. **Who created NetTalk, which learned to pronounce words in 1985?**

Ans. Terry Sejnowski.

9. Which system in 1997 defeated World Chess Champion?

Ans. IBM's Deep Blue system.

10. Who used the term "artificial intelligence" in 1955?

Ans. John McCarthy.

11. Who, in1952, prepared the first computer learning application?

Ans. Arthur Samuel.

12. What is deep learning?

Ans. In deep learning, the machine uses different layers to learn from the data.

13. Define machine learning.

Ans. Machine Learning is the art of the study of algorithms that learn from examples and experience.

14. Which automobile company became the first one to launch a self-driving vehicle in 2018?

Ans. Tesla

15. What is the full form of SDGs?

Ans. Sustainable Development Goals.

16. What is the full form of NLP?

Ans. Natural Language Processing.

17. What is the foundational element that makes AI so powerful?

Ans. Data

18. What is the full form of AGI?

Ans. Artificial General Intelligence.

19. Which robot is a social humanoid robot developed by Hanson Robotics, Hong Kong, in 2016?

Ans. Robot Sophia

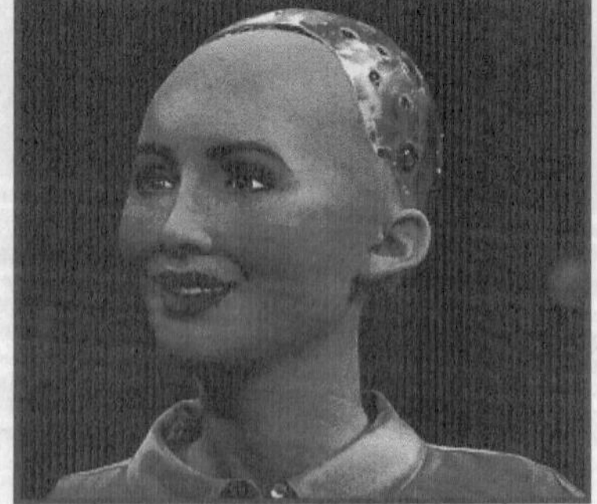

Figure 5.2: *Sophia Robot*

20. What is genome sequencing?

Ans. Genome sequencing is the analysis to identify the order of nucleotides.

21. Define collaborative filtering.

Ans. Collaborative filtering focuses on identifying similar users and recommend items preferred by related other users.

22. What are content-based recommendations?

Ans. It understands users' interest based on the ratings/feedback provided for a few items and suggesting similar items to them.

23. What do you mean by IoT?

Ans. The network of interconnected things or devices having sensors, software, network connectivity, and necessary electronics; that are used to collect and exchange data, making them responsive, is called the Internet of Things (IoT).

24. Define artificial general intelligence.

Ans. AGI is the intelligence that can be as intelligent as human beings and perform intellectual tasks as humans can do.

25. What is PathNet?

Ans. PathNet is defined as a neural network algorithm that uses agents embedded in the neural network to discover what parts of the network are to be re-used for new tasks.

26. What is artificial super intelligence?

Ans. Artificial Superintelligence has the ability to surpass or outperform the most intelligent human beings in every intellectual factor and by an extreme margin.

27. What is a smart city?

Ans. A Smart city is a city or urban area that uses different types of electronic gadgets, sensors , and the Internet of Things (IoT) for collecting data and then using the insights gained from the collected data to manage assets, resources, and services efficiently.

Figure 5.3: Smart city

28. What is park adelaide?

Ans. This is a mobile app installed by The city of Adelaide as a smart parking system in February 2018 that provides the user with accurate and real-time parking information.

29. Which chatbot was created by Microsoft that was forced to close in less than one day, on March 23, 2016?

Ans. Tay chatbot

30. Define data mining.

Ans. Data mining is all about extracting meaningful knowledge from data.

31. What is HMI?

Ans. Human-machine interaction (HMI) is the communication and interaction between a human and a machine via a user interface.

32. What are the other terms used for HMI?

Ans. The man-machine interface (MMI), computer-human interface, or human-computer interface.

33. What is a chatbot?

Ans. A Chabot is a computer program designed to simulate conversation with human users, especially over the Internet.

34. Give two examples of chatbots.

Ans. Alexia, Slush, Vainu, Dominos, etc.

35. What is the full form of PCA?

Ans. Principal Component Analysis

36. Define feature extraction.

Ans. Feature extraction is the process of identifying a minimal set of informative features or attributes from the provided dataset.

37. What is CAA?

Ans. Crossbar Adaptive Array (CAA) is a neural network capable of self-learning.

38. Define a neural network.

Ans. A Neural Network is comprised of interconnections between the set of computing nodes at consecutive layers.

39. What do you mean by CNN?

Ans. Convolutional Neural Networks (CNN) rolls the received input with the learned spatial filters/patterns to identify features at the convolution layer, and these signals are feed-forwarded to the next layers for performing recognition tasks.

40. What is the full form of RNN?

Ans. Recurrent Neural Networks.

41. How does deep learning perform?

Ans. The deep learning framework performs automatic feature extraction along with classification learning in a better way.

42. What is ANN?

Ans. An artificial neural network comprises a collection of simulated neurons.

43. Define node.

Ans. Each neuron in ANN is called a node that is connected to other nodes via links that correspond to biological axon-synapse-dendrite connections.

44. Define vector machines.

Ans. Vector machines or support vectors are capable of solving classification problems.

45. What are SDGs?

Ans. The Sustainable Development Goals (SDGs) or the Global Goals were adopted by all United Nations Member States as a universal call to take action to end poverty, protecting the planet, and ensuring peace and prosperity by 2030.

46. How many SDGs were adopted by the UNO?

Ans. 17 SDGs.

47. What do you mean by roboethics?

Ans. The term "robot ethics" or "robotics" refers to the morality of how humans design, construct, use, and treat robots, and it considers both how artificially intelligent devices may be used to harm or benefit humans and how they may be used to benefit humans.

48. What is the main cause of AI bias?

Ans. Bias in AI systems occurs due to the data used or fault in the algorithmic model.

49. Define AI bias.

Ans. AI bias is also known as Machine learning bias or Algorithm bias. it is a phenomenon that occurs when an algorithm produces incorrect results due to erroneous theories in the machine learning process.

50. Which chatbot has been produced by Amazon?

Ans. Alexa

51. Define Computer Vision (CV).

Ans. Computer Vision is defined as the ability of a machine to extract information from an image that is necessary to solve a task.

Figure 5.4: Alexa

52. What is the purpose of machine learning?

Ans. Its main purpose is to enable machines to learn by themselves using the provided data for making accurate Predictions/ Decisions.

53. What is the most common source of data collection by many companies?

Ans. Smartphones

54. What is the full form of IoT?

Ans. Internet of Things

55. What do you mean by AI ethics?

Ans. The ethics of AI lies in the ethical quality of its Prediction, the ethical quality of the end outcomes drawn out of that, and the ethical quality of the impact it has on human beings.

56. What is deep learning?

Ans. Deep Learning deals with a large amount of data which enables software to train itself to perform tasks dealing.

57. A robo can speak 9 indian and 37 foreign languages. it is developed by a teacher in kendriya vidyalaya, mumbai- mr. dinesh patel. what is its name?

Ans. Robo Shalu.

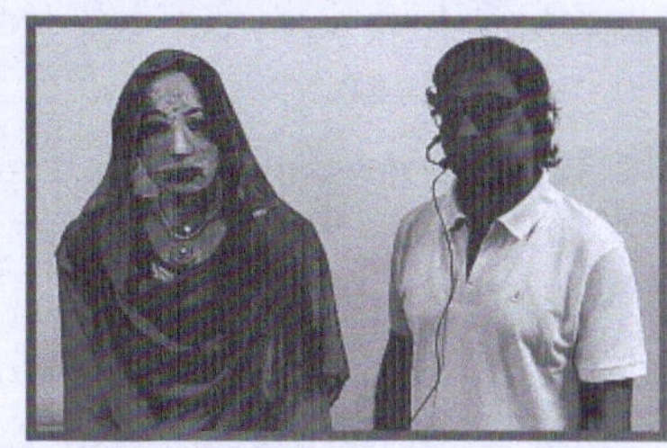

Figure 5.5: *Robot Shalu*

58. Name two common machine learning applications.

Ans. Targeted marketing, recommendation engine, Customer churn prevention, Sentiment analysis, Risk Management, Anti-money laundering, Fraud detection (any two).

59. Define NLP.

Ans. Natural Language Processing inputs machines the ability to read and understand human language.

60. What is the goal of CV?

Ans. The goal of Computer vision is not only to see but also to process and provide useful results based on the observations.

61. Give two examples in which CV is used.

Ans. Self-driven car, facial recognition device, face filter techniques, medical imaging, etc

62. What do you mean by espionage?

Ans. Espionage (spying) involves the disclosure or theft of many types of information, especially secrets, political, military, business, or industrial information.

63. What is identity theft?

Ans. Identity theft is the use of an individual's personally identifying information by someone else (often a stranger) without individual's permission or knowledge.

64. What do you mean by data retrieval?

Ans. This is the process of identifying and extracting data from a database as per the query provided by the users.

65. What is copyright infringement?

Ans. Copyright infringement is the use or reproduction of copyright-protected material without the permission of the copyright holder.

66. What are the sources to collect data?

Ans. Data is collected from various sources, like Surveys, Sensors, Observations, Web scrapping (Internet), Interviews, Documents and records, Oral histories, etc.

67. Which form of AI is the most advanced form of Artificial Intelligence?

Ans. Deep Learning (DL)

68. Define data privacy?

Ans. Data privacy is defined as a branch of data security concerned with the proper handling of data -consent, notice, and regulatory obligations.

69. What are the different forms in which data is collected?

Ans. Numeric, text, audio, video, or image.

70. An AI domain is used by search engines like Google, Yahoo, Bing, Ask, and AOL. Name it.

Ans. Data

71. What is web scraping?

Ans. Web Scraping is the collection of Web data from websites on the Internet using a web browser.

72. What is the main function of sensors?

Ans. Sensors or Transducers convert real-world phenomena like temperature, force, and movement to voltage or current signals that can be used as inputs.

73. What is a spreadsheet?

Ans. A spreadsheet is a computer program used for accounting and recording data using rows and columns to enter information.

74. What is the full form of SQL?

Ans. Structured Query Language.

75. What is a chatbot?

Ans. Any computer program designed to simulate human conversation through voice commands or text chats, or both is called a chatbot.

76. What is a corpus?

Ans. A structured but large set of texts that can be read by machines and have been produced in a natural communicative setting is called a corpus.

77. What is the full form of NLTK?

Ans. Natural Language Toolkit.

78. What is natural language toolkit?

Ans. NLTK is one of the platforms for building Python programs that can work with human language data.

2. AI Project Cycle

1. Define data.

Ans. Data is defined as the raw fact, which is organized together to form information that needs to be processed further for analysis and data visualization.

2. How many stages are there in an AI-project cycle?

Ans. Five stages

3. What is the name of the initial phase of the project cycle?

Ans. Problem scoping

4. Name the second stage of the project cycle.

Ans. Data collection / Data acquisition

5. What is the last stage of the project cycle?

Ans. Evaluation

6. Name the third stage of the project cycle.

Ans. Data exploration

7. What is feature engineering?

Ans. The process of repeating rapidly and testing new data points that can be derived from the data source and is called feature engineering.

8. Define the main purpose of data analysis.

Ans. The main purpose of Data Analysis (DA) is to extract useful information from huge data and to make decisions.

9. Define data scraping.

Ans. A technique/method in which a computer program extracts data from a human-readable output from another program is called data scraping.

Figure 5.6

10. What is text data?

Ans. The Text data type stores any kind of text data that can contain both single-byte and multibyte characters that the locale supports.

11. What are open-sourced websites?

Ans. Open-sourced websites are the government portals from where the information can be used and referred to.

12. Define numerical data.

Ans. The data where data points are exact numbers is called numerical data.

13. What is categorical data?

Ans. Categorical data represents characteristics, such as gender, a cricket player's position, team, hometown, etc.

14. Define LOOPY.

Ans. LOOPY is defined as an interactive tool that can be used to play with simulations in real-time without using any coding.

15. What is sisense?

Ans. Sisense provides a full-stack analytics platform where its visualization capabilities provide a simple-to-use drag and drop interface which creates charts and more complex graphics with a minimum of hassle.

16. What is data analysis?

Ans. The process of cleaning, transforming, and modeling data to discover useful information for making business decisions is defined as data analysis.

17. Which tool is regarded as 'the grandmaster of data visualization software?

Ans. Tableau

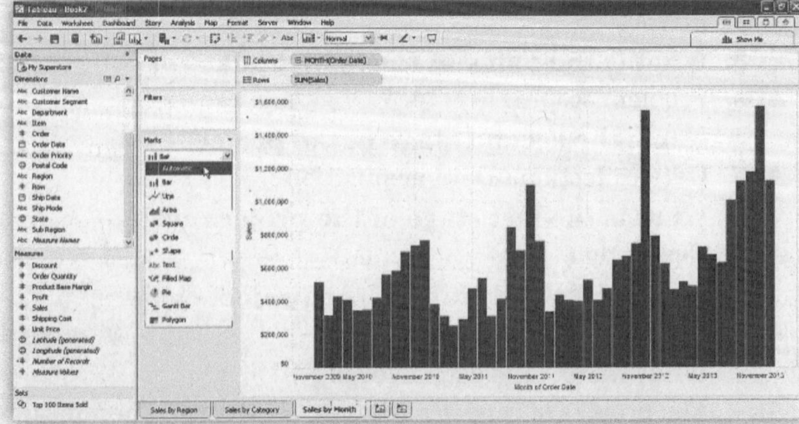

***Figure 5.7:** Tableau*

18. What do you mean by time-series data?

Ans. The time-series data is a sequence of numbers collected at regular intervals over some time.

19. Define descriptive analysis.

Ans. Descriptive analysis is an analysis of complete data or a sample of summarised numerical data to show the mean and deviation for continuous data.

20. What do you mean by text analysis?

Ans. Text Analysis or Data Mining is a method to discover a pattern in large data sets by using databases or data mining tools to extract and examine data.

21. What is a decision tree?

Ans. A Decision tree is a flowchart that is like a tree structure, in which each internal node denotes a test on an attribute, while each branch represents an outcome of the test, and each leaf node (terminal node) represents a class label.

22. What is statistical analysis?

Ans. Statistical analysis

23. Define data visualization.

Ans. Data visualization is defined as the graphic representation of data that involves producing images for communicating relationships among the represented data to viewers/users.

24. What do you mean by 'fusion chart'?

Ans. Fusion chart is a widely-used and JavaScript-based charting and data visualization package.

25. What does a decision tree display?

Ans. Decision trees display a sequence of steps and give people an effective and easy way to visualize the potential options of a decision and its range of possible outcomes.

26. What do you mean by datawrapper?

Ans. Datawrapper is a tool for data visualization and has a simple and clear interface that makes it very easy to upload data and create straightforward charts and also maps.

27. Define categorical variable decision tree.

Ans. A categorical variable decision tree includes categorical target variables that are divided into categories.

28. Name all the components of the AI project cycle.

Ans. Five components of the AI Project Cycle are Problem scoping, Data acquisition, Data exploration, Modelling, and Evaluation.

29. What do you mean by a problem statement?

Ans. The problem statement gives a clear idea about the basic framework required to achieve the goal.

30. What is the full form of API?

Ans. Application Programming Interface.

31. What are the main qualities of training data?

Ans. The training data needs to be reliable, authentic, and accurate for the AI machine to work efficiently.

32. For which purpose is testing data used?

Ans. Testing data is used to assess the AI machine for its efficiency and performance too.

33. What are the main qualities of an open-sourced data website (Govt portal)?

Ans. Open-sourced websites or government portals are authentic, accurate, and reliable.

34. What do you mean by loop?

Ans. The concept of a 'Loop' is used to define a chain of events in the system and relationships between them.

35. What is data acquisition?

Ans. Data Acquisition is a process to collect data for the problem scoped, which has to be correct, authentic, and reliable.

36. Define testing dataset.

Ans. A testing dataset is a dataset provided to the model ML algorithm after training the algorithm.

37. What do you mean by Evaluation in an AI-based project?

Ans. Evaluation is a testing technique where the model is installed in the real world, and it is tested in as many ways as possible.

38. What is the objective of the evaluation stage?

Ans. The evaluation stage is to evaluate whether the ML algorithm is able to predict with high accuracy or not before deployment.

39. What is a decision tree?

Ans. A decision tree is a simple graphical representation for classifying examples.

40. Which stage is data modeling in the AI project cycle?

Ans. Fourth stage

41. What do you mean by data exploration?

Ans. Data exploration is a method to collect data that has to be authentic and reliable.

42. What are the types of data analysis?

Ans. Text, Statistical, Diagnostic, Predictive, and Prescriptive Analysis

43. What are the other names given for web scraping?

Ans. Web data extraction, web harvesting, and Screen Scraping.

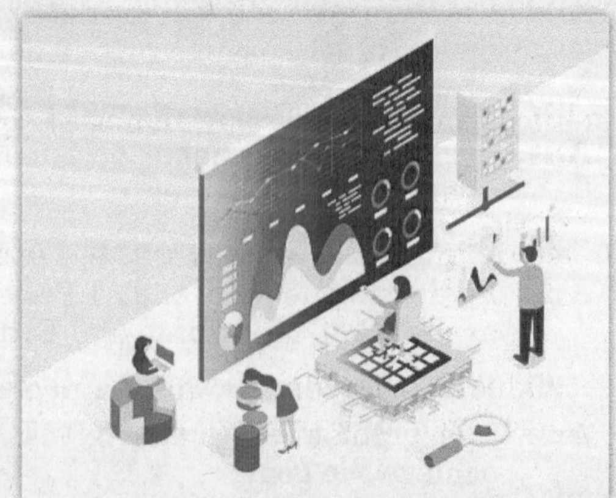

Figure 5.8

44. Define web scraping.

Ans. Web scraping is defined as a technique used for extracting huge amounts of data from websites on the Internet by using a web browser.

45. What is an API?

Ans. Application Programming Interfaces (API) is the piece of code that helps to connect one application to another to collect data from it.

46. When is a system map used in the project cycle?

Ans. System Map is used to find relationships between different elements of the problem that is scoped.

47. What do you mean by data modeling?

Ans. Data Modeling is defined as a process in which Al-Enabled algorithms are being designed as per the requirements of the system, and later, the model is implemented.

48. What do you mean by data visualization in an AI project?

Ans. Data visualization is defined as a form of visual art that grabs users' interest and keeps their eyes on the message.

49. What are the two parameters that are considered for the evaluation of an AI model?

Ans. Prediction and Reality.

50. What do you mean by 'Reality'?

Ans. The "Reality" is the real scenario for which the Prediction has been made.

3. Neural Networks

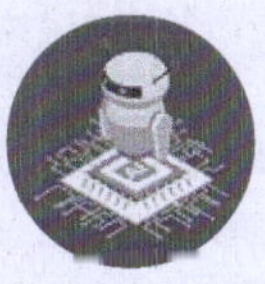

1. Define a neural network.

Ans. A neural network is a computational data model that is capable of capturing and representing complex input/output relationships.

2. Mention two uses of ANN.

Ans. Computer vision, speech recognition, machine translation, social network filtering, playing board and video games, and medical diagnosis (any two).

3. What is a feedforward ANN?

Ans. A Feedforward Artificial Neural Network consisting of several layers of processing units wherein each layer is providing feeding input to the next layer in a feedthrough manner.

4. What are the three basic layers of ANN?

Ans. Three layers are: An input layer, hidden layer, and output layer.

5. What is the full form of BNN?

Ans. Biological Neural Network.

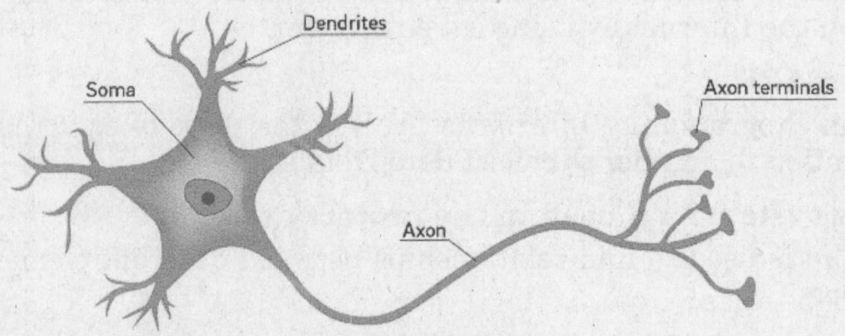

Figure 5.9: BNN

6. **Define machine learning.**

Ans. Machine learning is a component of Artificial Intelligence that learns from the previous dataset.

7. **What is supervised learning (SL)?**

Ans. In Supervised Learning, all data is labeled, and the algorithms learn to predict the output from the input data.

8. **What is done by supervised learning models?**

Ans. Supervised learning models can make predictions based on labeled datasets.

9. **What are the two important features of 'unsupervised learning'?**

Ans. In Unsupervised Learning, all data is unlabelled, and the algorithms learn to inherent structure from the input data.

10. **Define reinforcement learning.**

Ans. Reinforcement Learning (RL) is defined as a Machine Learning method that helps to discover which action gives the highest reward over a longer period.

11. **What is classification in ML?**

Ans. Classification is defined as a systematic grouping of observations into different categories.

12. **Mention two applications of classification.**

Ans. Applications of classification include speech recognition, biometric identification, handwriting recognition, etc.

13. **Which type of dataset is used in classification and clustering?**

Ans. Classification and clustering work on discrete datasets.

14. **Which type of data regression works?**

Ans. Regression works with continuous data.

15. **What is the main characteristic of RL?**

Ans. The biggest characteristic of RL is that there is no supervisor, only a real number or reward signal.

16. What is the main difference between RL and SL?

Ans. The Reinforcement Learning method works on interacting with the environment, whereas the supervised learning method works on given sample data or examples.

17. What is the main challenge of the RL method?

Ans. The biggest challenge of the RL method is that parameters may affect the speed of learning.

18. Which type of learning is used in gaming by the computer?

Ans. Reinforcement Learning.

19. What are the features of a NN?

Ans. The variables or attributes in the data set are termed as features in a NN.

20. What is the activation value?

Ans. The nodes take input data to perform simple operations on the data, and the result of these operations is passed to other neurons. The output at each node is called activation or node value.

21. What is the main similarity between nodes of ANN and neurons in BNN?

Ans. ANNs are composed of multiple nodes, which are similar in action to biological neurons.

22. For which purpose is testing data used?

Ans. Testing data is used to check the efficiency of the model.

23. What do you mean by QuickDraw?

Ans. QuickDraw is a game by Google where neural net tries to guess what the users are redrawing.

24. What is SketchCode?

Ans. SketchCode is an app that is used to convert handmade drawings into HTML code.

25. How does deep learning (DL) occur?

Ans. Deep learning learns by using a neural network that acts like a human brain and then analyses the data as humans do.

26. Give two examples of deep learning.

Ans. Chatbots, automatic translation of the text, adding colours to mono colour images, autonomous vehicles, computer vision, text generation (use of punctuation and grammar), etc.

27. What is the function of an axon in a neuron?

Ans. The function of an axon in a neuron is to transmit information to different neurons, muscles, and glands.

28. Who invented the first neurocomputer?

Ans. Dr. Robert Hecht-Nielsen.

29. What does positive and negative weight value exhibit in ANN?

Ans. A positive weight exhibits an excitatory connection, and negative values mean inhibitory connections.

30. What is the usual acceptable range of output in ANN?

Ans. Between –1 and 1.

31. What is the function of a dendrite in a neuron of a human neuron cell?

Ans. The function of a dendrite in a neuron is to send messages to the neuron cell body for the cell to function.

32. What is the other name for the cell body of a neuron?

Ans. The cell body is also called soma.

33. What is the main function of 'soma'?

Ans. Soma connects to the dendrites so as to bring information to the neuron and the axon.

34. What do you mean by AutoDraw?

Ans. AutoDraw is a fast drawing tool that acts like a magic wand for everyone to create anything visual and quick.

35. Who has developed the Auto Draw tool?

Ans. AutoDraw is a tool developed by Google Creative Lab.

36. What is 'topology'?

Ans. The organization or arrangement of the processing elements in ANN, their interconnections, inputs, and outputs are simply known as Topology.

37. Define classification in SL.

Ans. Classification is defined as the process of learning a model that identifies different predetermined classes of data and is a two-step process comprised of a learning step and a classification step.

38. What do you mean by regression?

Ans. A regression problem is one in which the output variable is a real value, like dollars, weight, etc.

39. Define CNN.

Ans. A Convolutional Neural Network (CNN) is a specific type of artificial neural network that uses perceptrons, a machine learning unit algorithm, for supervised learning to analyze data.

40. What do you mean by perceptrons?

Ans. In Machine Learning (ML), the Perceptron is an algorithm for supervised learning of binary classifiers.

41. Give one example of the unsupervised learning algorithm.

Ans. k-means for clustering problems, or Apriori algorithm for association rule learning problems.

42. What are the types of unsupervised learning?

Ans. Clustering and Association.

43. When is unsupervised learning required?

Ans. Unsupervised learning is required when there is no example data set available with known answers.

44. What is bayou?

Ans. Bayou is a software-coding application that uses Neural Sketch learning. It is helpful for human programmers to write many codes/programs in response to keywords.

4. Python Basics

1. What do you mean by 'algorithm'?

Ans. An algorithm means a procedure or a technique. An algorithm is a sequence of steps used to solve a particular problem.

2. What is a 'flowchart'?

Ans. A flowchart is a programming tool that uses different symbols to design a solution to a problem.

3. Who designed the first flow chart in 1945?

Ans. John Von Neumann.

4. What is often considered as a blueprint of a design used for solving a specific problem?

Ans. Flowchart

5. Which geometrical shape is used to indicate page connector in a flow chart?

Ans. Circle

6. Which geometrical shape is used to represent the start and end of the flowchart?

Ans. Oval

7. Which symbol is used to show the flow of logic by connecting symbols in a flow chart?

Ans. Arrow or Flowline.

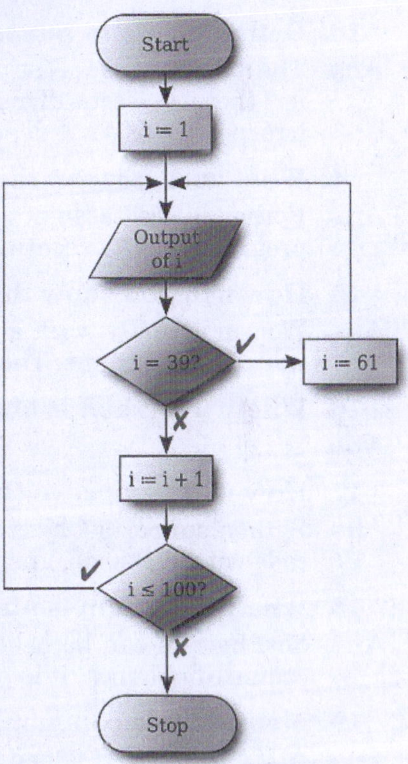

Figure 5.10: Flowchart

8. Which shape is used for arithmetic operations and data manipulations in the flowchart?

Ans. Rectangle

9. Which geometrical shape is used for input and output operation in a flowchart?

Ans. Parallelogram

10. Which shape in a flowchart is used to represent the operation in which there are two/three alternatives, true and false, etc.?

Ans. Diamond

11. What is the meaning of Sequence in programming?

Ans. In programming, Sequence means to place statements one after the other, and the execution takes place starting from top to bottom.

12. Define 'branching.'

Ans. In branch control, there is some condition, and according to the condition, a decision of either TRUE or FALSE is evaluated. In case it is TRUE, one of the two options is mentioned, whereas, in the case of the FALSE condition, the other alternative is taken.

13. Define the main purpose of the python virtual environment.

Ans. The main purpose of the python virtual environment is to create an isolated environment for these projects. This means that each project can have its own dependencies irrespective of what dependencies every other project has.

14. What does it mean that python is interpreted?

Ans. Python is processed at runtime by the interpreter, and we do not need to compile our program before executing it. This is called the interpretation of Python.

15. How will you show that python is interactive?

Ans. We can actually work at Python prompt and interact with the interpreter directly to write our programs. That's why Python is interactive.

16. Whether python is object-oriented program (OOP)?

Ans. Yes.

17. How will you prove that python is an OOP?

Ans. Python supports Object-Oriented style or technique programming that encapsulates code within objects, and hence, it is an object-oriented program.

18. Whether python is platform-independent?

Ans. Yes. Python can be used across different platforms and technologies with the basic coding, and hence, it is platform-independent.

19. Mention two commonly used python AI libraries.

Ans. AIMA, Simple AI, Open CV, Easy AI, etc.

20. Which website is used for free installation of Python?

Ans. https://www.python.org

21. Which website is used to download python documentation?

Ans. https://www.python.org/doc

22. Define a python identifier.

Ans. A Python identifier is a name that is used to identify a variable, function, class, module, or another object.

23. What may be the value of a python identifier?

Ans. An identifier may start with a letter A to Z or a to z or an underscore (followed by zero or more letters), and underscore and digits (0 to 9).

24. Define strings in python.

Ans. Strings in Python are defined as a continuous set of characters represented in the quotation marks.

25. What are comparison operators?

Ans. Comparison Operators (Relational Operator) compare the values on either side of them and decide the relation among them.

26. Define membership operators.

Ans. Membership operators in Python test for membership in a sequence, such as strings, lists, or tuples.

27. What are identify operators?

Ans. Identity operators compare the memory locations of two objects.

28. What is type conversion?

Ans. Type conversion is defined as the process of converting the value of one data type (integer, string, float, etc.) to another data type.

29. What is explicit type conversion?

Ans. In Explicit Type Conversion, users can convert the data type of an object to the required data type.

30. What is 'type casting'?

Ans. Explicit type conversion in Python is also called 'Type Casting.'

31. What is a package in python?

Ans. A package is defined as a collection of Python modules. In other words, a package is a directory of Python modules containing an additional application environment.

32. Define NumPy.

Ans. NumPy is a Python library that will allow the user to handle multi-dimensional arrays and matrices. It also offers multiple high-level mathematical functions to operate on these.

33. What is the other name for loops?

Ans. Iteration or iterative statements.

Figure 5.11

34. What is the role of a python interpreter?

Ans. Python program is processed at runtime by the interpreter, and we do not need to compile our program before executing it.

35. How is python interactive?

Ans. We can actually work at Python prompt and interact with the interpreter directly to write our programs. That's why Python is interactive.

36. What is the use of matplotlib?

Ans. Matplotlib is a package that is used to plot 2D figures like lines, bar, histogram, pie charts, etc.

37. What are strings in python?

Ans. Strings in Python are defined as a continuous set of characters represented in the quotation marks.

38. What do you mean by identity operators?

Ans. Identity operators compare the memory locations of two objects.

39. Define type conversion.

Ans. The conversion of the value of one data type (integer, float, string, etc.) to another data type is called type conversion.

40. What is explicit type conversion?

Ans. In Explicit Type Conversion, users can convert the data type of an object to the required data type.

41. Which type of conversion in python is called 'type casting'?

Ans. Explicit type conversion.

42. What is the full form of OOPs?

Ans. Object-Oriented Programs.

6 Multiple Choice Questions (MCQs) (Chapter wise)

1. Introduction to AI

1. Which feature is not related to Artificial Intelligence?

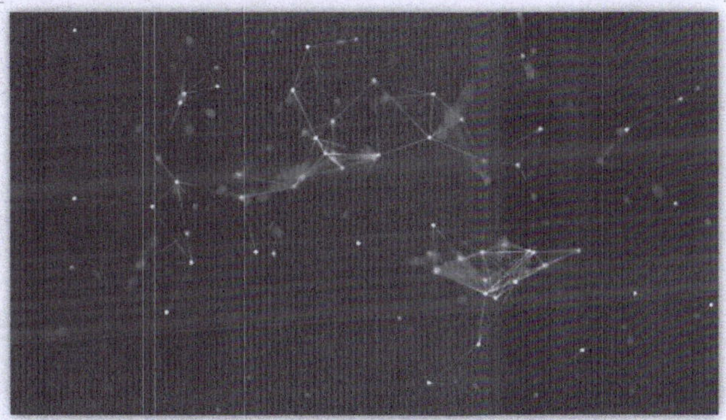

Figuro 6.1

   a. Creativity ☐ b. Preciseness ☐
   c. Consistency ☐ d. Multitasking ☐

2. Which properties are not related to Natural Intelligence?
   a. Non-Precise ☐ b. Non-creative ☐
   c. Non-consistent ☐ d. Not easy to handle ☐

3. This is the ability of machines to perform cognitive tasks, which a human brain can do, like thinking, perceiving, learning, problem-solving, decision making, etc. It is called:
   a. Artificial Intelligence ☐ b. Supervised Learning ☐
   c. ANN ☐ d. CNN ☐

4. Rock-Paper-Scissors game is based upon:
   a. NLP ☐ b. Data ☐

c. Computer Vision ☐ d. All of these ☐

5. Which game is based on computer vision?
   a. Rock-Paper Scissors ☐ b. Identify the Mystery Animal ☐
   c. Emoji Scavenger Hunt Game ☐ d. None of these ☐
6. Which is not regarded as a domain of AI?
   a. NLP ☐ b. CNN ☐
   c. Data ☐ d. Computer Vision ☐
7. Which of the following is not a sub-category of Machine Learning?
   a. Project-Based Learning ☐ b. Supervised Learning ☐
   c. Unsupervised Learning ☐ d. Reinforcement Learning ☐
8. How many do UN Sustainable Development Goals (SDGs) give?
   a. 08 ☐ b. 10 ☐
   c. 17 ☐ d. 23 ☐
9. What is the full form of BNN?

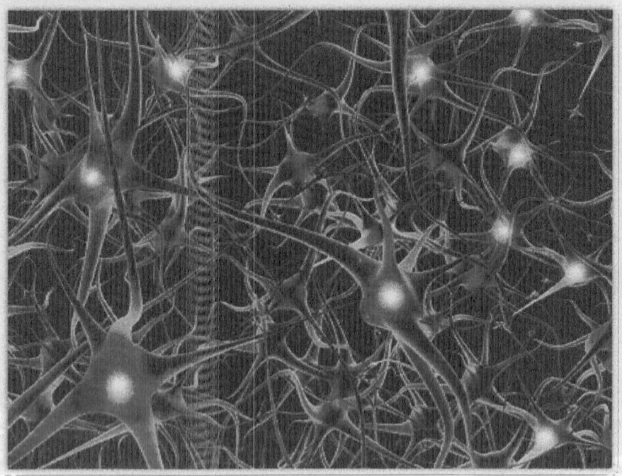

   Figure 6.2

   a. Biological Neural Network ☐ b. Bio Neural Network ☐
   c. Biological Network of Neurons ☐ d. Biology of Neural Networking ☐
10. Which part is not a framework part of Smart city?
    a. Smart Environment ☐ b. Smart Governance ☐
    c. Smart Economy ☐ d. Smart Transport ☐
11. Which of the following dimension is a core element of sustainable development?
    a. Economic growth ☐ b. Social inclusion ☐
    c. Environmental protection ☐ d. All of these ☐

12. Which of the following SDGs is related to end hunger?
    a. No Poverty ☐ b. Zero hunger ☐
    c. Life under Sea ☐ d. Reduced inequalities ☐
13. Which subjects are not covered in the field of study of AI?
    a. Human behaviour, biology ☐
    b. Psychology, language, and linguistics ☐
    c. Statistics, computer science ☐ d. None of the above ☐
14. Which of the following pairs of subject and domain are incorrect?
    i. **Computer Science:** Building computers
    ii. **Mathematics:** Algorithms, computability, proof, methods of representation, tractability and decidability
    iii. **Neuro-Science:** How the basic information processing units, i.e., neurons Process Information
    iv. **Linguistics:** Grammar, syntax, knowledge representations
    v. **Statistics:** Learning from data, uncertainty/ certainty of modeling
    vi. **Economics:** Rational economic agents, the usefulness of data & models, decision Theory
    vii. **Cognitive Sciences:** Processes and things in nature, interpretation of different Phenomena and their impact

    a. (i) (ii) (iii) ☐ b. (iv) (v) ☐
    c. (vi) (vii) ☐ d. All of the above ☐
15. Who gave 'Three Laws of Robotics' in 1950?
    a. Arthur Samuel ☐
    b. Isaac Asimov ☐
    c. Alan Turing ☐
    d. William Stanford ☐

Figure 6.3

16. Who created NetTalk, which learned to pronounce words?
    a. Terry Sejnowski ☐ b. Alan Turing ☐
    c. Asimov ☐ d. Gerald Dejong ☐
17. Who created the Turing Test to determine the intelligence of a computer?
    a. Isaac Asimov ☐ b. Alan Turing ☐
    c. James Turing ☐ d. Alan Samuel ☐

18. Which of the following systems defeated the World Chess Champion in 1997?
    a. IBM's Deep Blue system ☐ b. Google's DeepMind system ☐
    c. IBM's Watson ☐ d. AlphaGo ☐
19. Who was the first computer scientist to coin the term "artificial intelligence" in 1955?
    a. Arthur Samuel ☐ b. Alan Turing ☐
    c. John McCarthy ☐ d. Frank Rosenblatt ☐
20. Who prepared the first computer learning application in1952?
    a. Alan Turing ☐
    b. Asimov ☐
    c. Arthur Samuel ☐
    d. John McCarthy ☐

Figure 6.4

21. When was Deep Learning introduced?
    a. 1985 ☐ b. 2003 ☐
    c. 2010 ☐ d. 2015 ☐
22. In 2018, which company became the first automaker to launch a self-driving vehicle?
    a. Audi ☐ b. Tesla ☐
    c. Mercedes ☐ d. Suzuki ☐
23. What is the art of the study of algorithms that learn from examples and experience known as?
    a. Deep Learning ☐ b. Machine Learning ☐
    c. Supervised Learning ☐ d. PBL ☐
24. Which of the following companies is considered a giant player in the field of data?
    a. Google ☐ b. Facebook ☐
    c. Amazon ☐ d. All the above ☐
25. Which robot became a Saudi Arabian citizen, the first robot to become a citizen of any country in the world?
    a. Robot Shalu ☐ b. Robot Sophia ☐
    c. Robot Manav ☐ d. Robot George ☐
26. Which Indian robot was created by a teacher of Kendriya Vidyalaya, IIT Mumbai, and that can speak 9 Indian and 37 foreign languages?
    a. Robot Shalu ☐ b. Robot Sophia ☐
    c. Robot Manav ☐ d. Robot George ☐

27. Which of the following products is used in a smart home?
    a. Cameras
    b. Thermostat (controlling the temperature of AC or fridge)
    c. Motion sensors
    d. All the above
28. Which of the following products is not a part of Smart home?
    a. LED lights are controlled by using the smartphone.
    b. Turning lights and appliances at home on or off from the mobile device.
    c. Door locks and garage doors are controlled by using a smartphone.
    d. None of the above
29. Which of the following will possess more cognitive capabilities than gifted human beings?
    a. AGI
    b. ASI
    c. ANN
    d. None of the above
30. Which statements are part of AI Ethics?
    i. Financial investments in AI should be accompanied by funding for research on ensuring its beneficial use.
    ii. If an AI system causes harm, it should be possible to determine why.
    iii. A culture of cooperation, trust, and transparency must be raised among researchers and developers of AI.
    iv. Teams developing AI systems should actively cooperate to avoid money saving on safety standards.
    v. AI systems should be safe and secure throughout their operational lifetime.
    vi. The designers and makers of advanced AI systems are considered as the stakeholders in the moral implications of the use, misuse, and actions of these systems/devices, with a responsibility and opportunity to shape those implications.
    vii. Highly autonomous AI systems should be designed so that their goals and behaviours can be assured to align with human values throughout the operation.

    a. (ii) (iii) (iii)
    b. (iv) (v) (vii)
    c. (vi) (ii) (i)
    d. All of the above
31. Which of the following has the potential to resolve the key challenges posed by excessive urban population?
    a. Artificial Intelligence (AI)
    b. IoT
    c. Genome Sequencing
    d. Both (a) and (b)

32. Which Chatbot was created by Microsoft that was forced to close in less than one day?
    a. Tay chatbot ☐ b. Tina chatbot ☐
    c. Jay chatbot ☐ d. Toy chatbot ☐
33. What is the name of an assistant that is enabled to communicates with humans through text messages?
    a. Chatterpatter ☐ b. Chatbot ☐
    c. Airbot ☐ d. Voicebot ☐
34. Which of the following is NOT a part of Data Science?
    a. Machine Learning ☐ b. Artificial Intelligence ☐
    c. Deep Learning ☐ d. Nano-science ☐
35. Which of the following statements is INCORRECT?
    a. Al systems should be designed and operated so that it is compatible with ideals of human dignity, freedoms, rights, and cultural diversity. ☐
    b. The usage of AI to personal data must not unreasonably limit people's real or alleged liberty. ☐
    c. Al technologies should benefit and empower high-powered people. ☐
    d. People should be given the right to access, manage, and control the data they generate, given Al systems' power to analyze and utilize that data. ☐
36. Which of the following robots is India's first 3D printed humanoid robot that was developed in 2014 by Diwakar Vaish in Noida, UP?
    a. Manavi ☐
    b. Shama ☐
    c. Manav ☐
    d. Rashmi ☐

Figure 6.5: Diwakar Vaish

37. Which of the following statements is **correct?**
    a. The economic prosperity created by AI can be shared among all countries for the benefit of the world. ☐
    b. The power granted by control of highly advanced AI systems should respect and improve, rather than disrupt, the social and civic processes on which the health of society depends. ☐
    c. The arms race, particularly in lethal autonomous weapons, should be minimized and ultimately avoided by the governments. ☐
    d. All the above ☐

38. Which application is not considered an application of AI?
    a. Remote-controlled Car ☐ b. Google search ☐
    c. Robot drones ☐ d. Self-Driving Car ☐
39. Which of the following about the drawbacks of AI is correct?
    a. Unlimited Ability ☐ b. Can't Handle Emergency Situation ☐
    c. Easy code ☐ d. Low cost ☐
40. The full form of NLP in relation to AI is:
    a. Neural Learning Process ☐ b. Neuro-Linguistic Processing ☐
    c. Natural Language Processing ☐ d. Natural Logic Processing ☐
41. Which of the following is associated with the study of computer algorithms that improve their efficiency automatically through experience?
    a. Data science ☐ b. Machine Learning (ML) ☐
    c. Deep Learning (DL) ☐ d. None of the above ☐
42. An Indian Robot Shalu can speak 9 Indian and 37 foreign languages and is developed by a teacher in Kendriya Vidyalaya, Mumbai. Who is he?
    a. Diwakar Vaish ☐ b. Dinesh Patel ☐
    c. Satya Rekha ☐ d. Ranjit S. ☐
43. Which SDG is not proposed by UNO?
    a. No Poverty ☐ b. Zero illiteracy ☐
    c. Zero hunger ☐ d. Low Quality Education ☐
44. Which of the following is capable of solving classification problems?
    a. M ☐ b. A ☐
    c. D ☐ d. N ☐
45. Rashmi is an Indian realistic lip-syncing multilingual humanoid robot that can speak four languages (English, Hindi, Bhojpuri, and Marathi). Who was its developer in 2019?
    a. Ranjit Srivastava ☐
    b. Rashmi Ahuja ☐
    c. Divakar Vaish ☐
    d. Dinesh Patel ☐

Figure 6.6: Ranjit Srivastava

2. Project Cycle

1. What is Data?
   a. A raw fact
   b. A piece of information
   c. A fact and/ visual
   d. Any meaningful information
2. Which tool is used to convert the information more meaningful for making decisions?
   a. Python
   b. Excel
   c. QlikView
   d. All of the above

Figure 6.7

3. For what purpose is training Data used in the AI machine?
   a. Testing the model
   b. Making predictions
   c. Giving input to the machine
   d. Processing
4. Which quality of the training data is necessary for using it for AI machines?
   a. Authentic
   b. Accurate
   c. Reliable
   d. All of the above
5. Which of the following type of problems are solved by using a decision tree?
   a. Classification problems
   b. Regression problems
   c. Both (a) and (b)
   d. None of the above
6. The AI model is evaluated for its efficiency on the basis of the results while comparing with the results we already have. Name the process.
   a. Problem scoping
   b. Data Visualisation
   c. Data Mining
   d. Evaluation
7. Which quality is NOT necessary for the training data used for the AI machine?
   a. Authentic
   b. Discrete
   c. Reliable
   d. Accurate

8. Which approach is used in AI models?
   a. Rule-based approach ☐ b. Project-based approach ☐
   c. Learning-based approach ☐ d. both (a) and (c) ☐
9. For which purpose the visualization technique is used?
   a. For using order, layout, and hierarchy to prioritize ☐
   b. For handling and understanding big data ☐
   c. For enabling to make comparisons easily ☐
   d. All of the above ☐
10. Which tool has a tree-like structure of decisions and their possible outcomes?
   a. Decision tree ☐ b. Neural network ☐
   c. Fusion Chart ☐ d. Bar Graph ☐

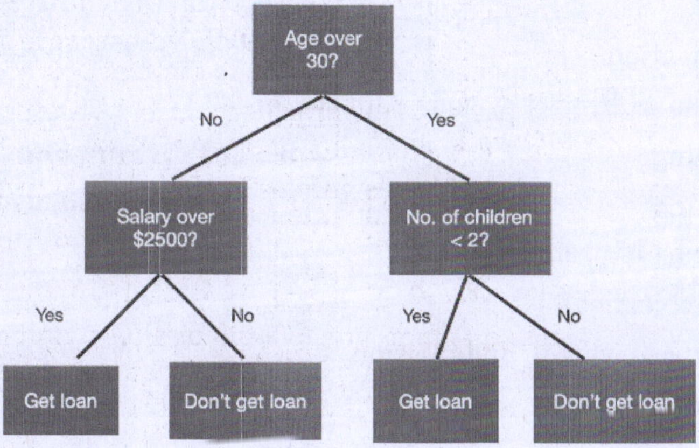

Figure 6.8

11. Which of the following is NOT related to data visualization?
   a. Vector mechanics ☐ b. System Mapping ☐
   c. Histogram ☐ d. Sketchy graphs ☐
12. Which one of the following is used as a Data Visualisation tool?
   a. Fusion chart ☐ b. Pie chart ☐
   c. Bar diagram ☐ d. All of the above ☐

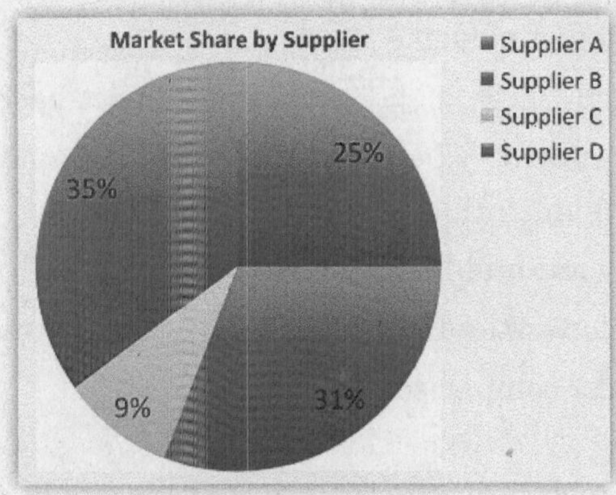

Figure 6.9: *Pie Chart*

13. Which of the following components of the AI project cycle does select the best model by checking their advantages, disadvantages, and efficiency?
    a. Data Mining ☐ b. Data Modelling ☐
    c. Data Visualisation ☐ d. None of the above ☐
14. In which step of the AI Project cycle is data collected?
    a. Data Modelling ☐ b. Data Evaluation ☐
    c. Project Scoping ☐ d. Data Acquisition ☐
15. Which is **NOT** a part of problem scoping?
    a. Measurable objectives ☐
    b. Project's purpose, vision, and mission ☐
    c. Concerned stakeholders ☐
    d. None of the above ☐
16. Which of the following is **NOT** a component of the decision tree?
    a. Leaf ☐ b. Nodes ☐
    c. Branches ☐ d. Flowers ☐
17. Which of the following approach is used in a Decision Tree?
    a. Bottom-up ☐ b. Top-down ☐
    c. Both (a) and (b) ☐ d. None of the above ☐
18. Which stage is the first stage of the AI project cycle?
    a. Problem Scoping ☐ b. Data mining ☐
    c. Data Acquisition ☐ d. Evaluation ☐
19. Which of the following is **NOT** an open-sourced data website?
    a. https://www.india.gov.in/data-portal-india ☐

b. https://data.gov.in/
c. https://dbie.rbi.org.in/DBIE/dbie.rbi?site=home
d. None of the above

20. Which of the following is included in sustainable development.
    a. Recycling and reuse of waste products/materials,
    b. Scientific management of renewable resources, especially bio-resources,
    c. Promoting afforestation
    d. All of the above
21. Which of the following sources is not used for data acquisition?
    a. SPI
    b. API
    c. Survey
    d. System map
22. Which of the following features is NOT associated with ANN?
    a. The neural network system is modeled on the human brain.
    b. Every artificial neural network (ANN) is controlled by the human brain.
    c. Every neural network node is essentially a machine learning algorithm.
    d. Neural networks are able to automatically extract features without input from the coder/programmer.
23. Which word is not a part of the 4Ws Problem Canvas?
    a. Where
    b. What
    c. Who
    d. Why
24. Which step of the AI Project is associated with data collection from different sources?
    a. Project Scoping
    b. Data Modelling
    c. Data Exploration
    d. Data Evaluation
25. Which of the following sources is an authentic one for data acquisition?
    a. APIs
    b. Sensors
    c. Web Scraping
    d. All of the above
26. Which of the following is **NOT** the SDGs as adopted by UNO?
    a. Quality Education
    b. No Poverty
    c. Zero Hunger
    d. Gender Discrimination
27. For which purpose is the visualization technique used?
    a. Handling and understanding big data
    b. Enabling to make comparisons easily

c. Using order, layout, and hierarchy to prioritize
d. All of the above

28. A process of cleaning, transforming, and modeling data to discover useful information for making business decisions is known as:
    a. Data analysis
    b. Data scraping
    c. Data mining
    d. Data acquisition
29. Which of the following is a part of the project charter?
    a. Project's purpose, vision, and mission
    b. Measurable objectives and success criteria
    c. Elaborated project description, conditions, and risks
    d. All the above
30. Which statement is correct?
    a. The training data needs to be reliable, authentic, and accurate for the AI machine to work efficiently.
    b. Testing data is used to assess the AI machine for its efficiency and performance too.
    c. Data features can be collected from various sources like newspapers, cameras, observations, surveys, questionnaires, etc.
    d. All of the above
31. Which of the following is not categorical data?
    a. Gender of students
    b. List of hometowns of employees
    c. Record of the temperature of patients in a hospital
    d. Player's position in a cricket team
32. Which technique is used in which a computer program extracts data from a human-readable output from another program?
    a. Data scraping
    b. Data acquisition
    c. Data modeling
    d. Vector mechanics
33. Which of the following statements is **INCORRECT**?
    a. The time-series data is a sequence of numbers collected at regular intervals over some time.
    b. The numerical data is the data where data points are exact numbers.
    c. A technique in which a computer program extracts data from a human-readable output from another program is termed data modeling.

d. Data is the foundational element that makes AI so powerful.

34. What is the foundational element that makes AI so powerful?

a. Data
b. Facts
c. Neural Networks
d. None of the above

35. Which of the following is **NOT** a data type?

a. Numerical data
b. Classical data
c. Categorical data
d. Time series data

36. How many basic types of data are known from a machine learning perspective?

a. 3
b. 4
c. 5
d. 6

37. A company has the following data. Identify the time series data out of it.

i. Server metrics,
ii. Application performance monitoring,
iii. Network data, Sensor data,
iv. Economic indicators
v. Clicks on social sites

a. (i) (ii) (iii)
b. (iii) (v)
c. (iv) (v)
d. (i) (ii) (iii) (iv) (v)

38. Which of the following is **NOT** time-series data?

a. Weather records
b. Economic indicators
c. Patient health evolution metrics
d. None of the above

39. Which of the following statements is **NOT** correct?

a. The initiation phase aims to define the project.
b. The Project Charter documents the primary requirements for the project.
c. The structured data is not easy to use.
d. The Text data type stores any kind of text data that can contain both single-byte and multibyte characters.

40. Which of the following is **NOT** a type of data analysis?

a. Statical Analysis
b. Diagnostic Analysis
c. Predictive Analysis
d. Prescriptive Analysis

41. Which of the following statements is **INCORRECT**?

a. Tableau is regarded as *'the grandmaster of data visualization software.'*

b. Open-sourced websites are the government portals from where the information can be purchased. ☐

c. Fusion charts are a widely-used and JavaScript-based charting and visualization package. ☐

d. Data visualization is the graphic representation of data. ☐

42. Which of the following is a type of statistical analysis?

a. Narrative analysis ☐ b. Descriptive Analysis ☐

c. Inferential Analysis ☐ d. Both (b) and (c) ☐

43. For which purpose is the diagnostic analysis performed?

a. To identify the behavioural patterns. ☐

b. To predict some decision. ☐

c. To get refined data ☐

d. None of the above ☐

44. Which of the following phases are included in the data analysis process?

i. Data Requirement Gathering

ii. Data Collection

iii. Data Cleaning

iv. Data Analysis

v. Data Interpretation

vi. Data Visualisation

a. (i)(ii)(iii) ☐ b. (ii)(iii)(v) (vi) ☐

c. (vi)(v)(iv) (iii) ☐ d. (i)(ii)(iii) (iv) (v) (vi) ☐

45. In data visualization, data is presented as:

a. Pictorial/Graphs/ Charts ☐ b. Texts ☐

c. Maps ☐ d. None of the above ☐

46. Which of the following statements are related to Data visualization?

i. It clarifies which factors influence customer behaviour.

ii. It identifies areas that need attention or improvement.

iii. It predicts sales volumes.

iv. It helps human beings understand which products to place where.

v. It helps to manipulate data.

a. (i) (ii) (iii) ☐ b. (iii) (v) ☐

c. (ii) (iii) (iv) ☐ d. (i) (ii) (iii) (v) ☐

47. Which of the following tools is regarded as 'the grandmaster of data visualization software?

    a. Tableau ☐ b. QlikView ☐

    c. Fusion charts ☐ d. High charts ☐

48. Which of the following is an advantage of the decision tree?

    a. Easy to use and interpret. ☐

    b. Easy to prepare, and simple to explain. ☐

    c. Can handle both categorical and numerical data. ☐

    d. All of the above ☐

49. Which language/script is used in creating Fusion charts?

    a. Java ☐ b. C++ ☐

    c. Python ☐ d. All of the above ☐

50. Which of the following is **NOT** a data visualization tool?

    a. Datawrapper ☐ b. Fusion chart ☐

    c. Low charts ☐ d. QlikView ☐

51. Which of the following data visualization tool is mostly used by media organizations to create charts and statistics for media coverage?

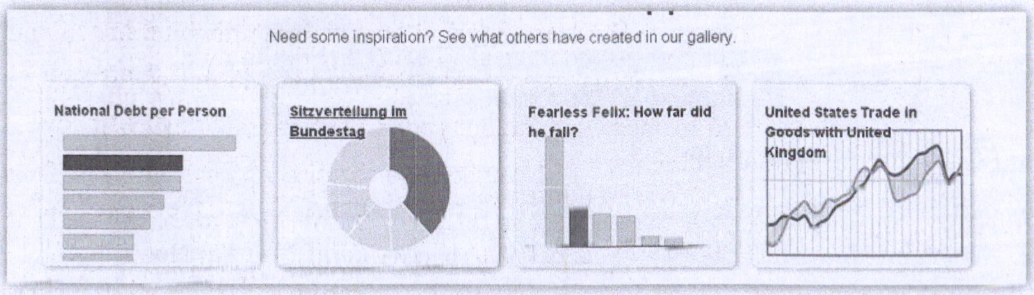

Figure 6.10

    a. Plotly ☐ b. Datawrapper ☐

    c. High charts ☐ d. QlikView ☐

52. Which of the following data visualization tools does use integration with analytics-oriented programming languages, like Python, R, Matlab, etc.?

    a. QlikView ☐ b. Plotly ☐

    c. Datawrapper ☐ d. Fusion charts ☐

53. What does a branch of the decision tree represent?

    a. Input ☐

    b. A possible decision, outcome, or reaction ☐

c. End results

d. Classification of attributes

54. What is represented by a node in a decision tree?

a. A place where an attribute is picked and ask a question

b. The answers to the question

c. The actual output

d. None of the above

55. What is the number of types of decision trees based on the target variables?

a. 2 b. 3

c. 4 d. 6

56. Which of the following is NOT an advantage of decision trees?

a. They are resistant to outliers.

b. Adding new features is easy.

c. They can handle only one type of data.

d. They provide strategic answers to uncertain situations.

3. Neural Networks

1. What is the full form of ANN?

a. Artificial Neural Node b. Artificial Neural Network

c. Artificial Neural Network d. Artificial Neutral Node

2. What is the meaning of SL in AI?

a. Slow Learner b. Slow Learning

c. Supervised Learning d. Slightly Learnt

3. Which of the following terms is NOT related to Neural networks?

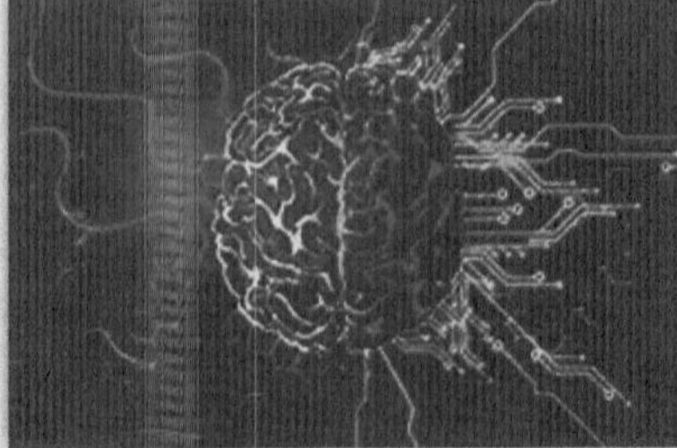

Figure 6.11: *NN*

a. ANN ☐ b. BNN ☐

c. PNN ☐ d. RL ☐

4. Which sub-category is related to supervised learning?

a. Clustering ☐ b. Classification ☐

c. Regression ☐ d. Both (b) and (c) ☐

5. Artificial neuron is also known as:

a. Cluster ☐ b. Perceptron ☐

c. Regression ☐ d. ANN ☐

6. Which one of the following layers in ANN is used to take the input from the user?

a. Input Layer ☐ b. Hidden Layer ☐

c. Output Layer ☐ d. None of the above ☐

7. Which one of the following is the function of the Hidden Layer?

a. Receive data from the Input Layer ☐

b. Process the data ☐

c. Give the data to the Output Layer ☐

d. All of the above ☐

8. Which of the following is NOT a part of a neuron in BNN?

a. Axon ☐ b. Dendrite ☐

c. Loaf ☐ d. Cell body ☐

9. Which body part is used to send signals away from neurons in the human nervous system?

a. Nucleus ☐ b. Axons ☐

c. Dendrites ☐ d. Cell body ☐

10. Who has developed the AutoDraw tool?

a. Microsoft AI Learning ☐ b. Intel AI Models ☐

c. Google Creative Lab ☐ d. SatyaNadela Labs ☐

11. Which of the following is not a type of reinforcement learning?

a. Positive Reinforcement ☐ b. Negative Reinforcement ☐

c. Neutral Reinforcement ☐ d. None of the above ☐

12. Which one of the following statements is **INCORRECT**?

a. Machine learning is a component of AI. ☐

b. Classification and clustering work on discrete data. ☐

c. Classification is defined as a systematic grouping of observations into different categories. ☐

d. In supervised learning, the algorithm learns from a dataset that is not labeled.

13. Which of the following statements is NOT correct?
    a. Reinforcement Learning (RL) is used in gaming.
    b. Testing data is used to check the efficiency of the model.
    c. QuickDraw is a game by Microsoft where neural network tries to guess what you are redrawing.
    d. SketchCode app is used to convert the handmade drawing into HTML code.
14. Which app is used to convert the handmade drawing into HTML code?
    a. SketchCode b. QuickDraw
    c. LearnDraw d. Vinci code
15. Which of the following is an application of Artificial Neural Network (ANN)?
    i. Optimization of logistics for transportation networks,
    ii. Medical and disease diagnosis,
    iii. Character and voice recognition (Natural Language Processing),
    iv. Targeted marketing,
    v. Robotic control systems.
    vi. For financial predictions for stock prices, currency, futures options, bankruptcy, bond ratings, etc.
    viii. Drones
    a. (ii) (iii) (iv) b. (iv) (v) (vii)
    c. (vii) (vi) (v) (iv) (iii) d. (i) (ii) (iii) (iv) (v) (vi)
16. Which of the following is **NOT** an application of ANN?
    a. Ecosystem evaluation, medical imaging
    b. Forecasting of Electrical load and energy demand, identification of compounds
    c. Outdoor games for children, wood cutting industries
    d. Process and quality control in industries, facial recognition
17. How many types of ANN are there?
    a. 2 b. 3
    c. 4 d. 5
18. Which of the following is **NOT** a type of ANN?
    a. FeedForward ANN b. Feedback ANN
    c. Neutral ANN d. None of the above

19. Which of the following examples is **NOT** related to Supervised Learning?
    a. Linear regression for regression problems.
    b. Random forest for classification and regression problems.
    c. Support vector machines for classification problems.
    d. None of the above
20. Which one of the following examples is not related to SL?
    a. Classifying the patients whether a patient is suffering from a particular disease or not.
    b. Predicting weather.
    c. Classifying the received emails whether an email is a spam or not.
    d. Predicting house/property price or stock market price.

4. Python Basics

1. Which of the following statements is correct?
   a. Python is case-sensitive when dealing with identifiers.
   b. Python is not case-sensitive when dealing with identifiers.
   c. Python is machine-dependent when dealing with identifiers.
   d. None of these
2. Which geometrical symbol is used to indicate the flow of logic by connecting symbols in a flow chart?
   a. Single arrow
   b. Double arrow
   c. Diamond
   d. Triangle
3. The function range(6) will return a sequence:
   a. 1, 2, 3, 4,5,6
   b. 0, 1, 2, 3,4,5
   c. 1, 2, 3,4,5
   d. 0, 1, 2, 3,4
4. The appropriate reason to make Python the most suitable coding language for AI Projects is:
   a. Flexibility, Readability, Good visualization options
   b. A low entry barrier, Platform dependence

c. A great library ecosystem, No Community support ☐

d. None of the above ☐

5. Which geometrical shape is used to show page connector in a flow chart?

a. Triangle ☐ b. Square ☐

c. Rectangle ☐ d. Circle ☐

6. Which symbol is used while ending all control flow statements in Python?

a. Full Stop (.) ☐ b. Colon (:) ☐

c. Semicolon (;) ☐ d. Hash sign (#) ☐

7. Which statement is INCORRECT regarding the rules for a variable name?

a. A statement may begin with a lowercase alphabet. ☐

b. Special characters like @, *, % are allowed in a statement. ☐

c. Spaces are allowed in a statement. ☐

d. Letters, numbers, and underscore (_) characters are allowed in a statement. ☐

8. Which of the following statements will check if 'x' is less than or equal to 'y'?

a. if x is less than equal to y: ☐ b. if x <= y: ☐

c. if x >= y: ☐ d. if x < == y: ☐

9. What is the output of max(mylist), if mylist%=[7457, 7413, 1303, 3567, 7416]?

a. 5 ☐ b. 7416 ☐

c. 7457 ☐ d. 1303 ☐

10. What is the reason for gaining maximum popularity by Python as a programming language?

a. Easy in writing and Less execution of codes ☐

b. Availability of prebuilt libraries ☐

c. Flexibility in providing an API from an existing language ☐

d. All the above ☐

11. Which statement about the flowchart is NOT TRUE?

a. The flowchart shows the logic of a program in a simple way. ☐

b. The flowchart is an easy and efficient tool to analyze a problem. ☐

c. It is difficult to convert the flow chart into any programming language code. ☐

d. The flowchart makes program or system maintenance easier. ☐

12. What is a graphical representation of a sequence of steps to solve a problem known as?

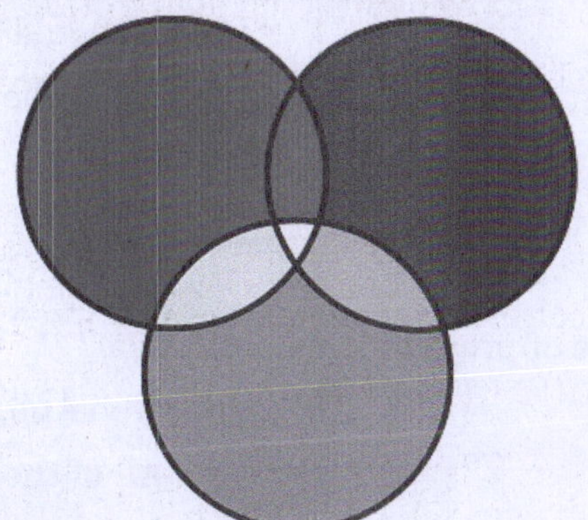

Figure 6.12

a. Vector analysis ☐ b. Venn diagram ☐
c. Flowchart ☐ d. Pie chart ☐

13. Which geometrical shape is used to represent the start and the end in a flowchart?

a. Triangle ☐ b. Square ☐
c. Oval ☐ d. Diamond ☐

14. Which geometric shape is used for arithmetic operations and data manipulations in a flowchart?

a. Rectangle ☐ b. Square ☐
c. Triangle ☐ d. Diamond ☐

15. Which geometrical shape is used in a flowchart to represent the operations having two/three alternatives, true and false, etc.?

a. Square ☐ b. Triangle ☐
c. Diamond ☐ d. Rectangle ☐

16. What is the number of type conversions used in Python?

a. 1 ☐ b. 2 ☐
c. 3 ☐ d. 4 ☐

17. Due to which property is Python one of the fastest-growing programming languages?

a. Ease of Learning ☐ b. Scalability ☐
c. Adaptability ☐ d. All the above ☐

18. What is the other name for 'Iterative statements' in Python?

a. Lists ☐ b. Loops ☐
c. Operators ☐ d. Tuples ☐

19. Which of the following applications does use Python?
    a. Database Access
    b. Web and Internet Development
    c. Desktop GUI Applications
    d. All of the above
20. What is represented by a parallelogram in a flowchart?
    a. Beginning and end of flowchart
    b. Input and output operation
    c. Arithmetic operation
    d. All the above
21. Which of the following type of projects is using Python?
    a. Data Science,
    b. Web App, IoT
    c. Mobile App, AI
    d. All of the above
22. Which one of the following is used to create Strings by enclosing characters inside it?
    a. Single quotes (' ')
    b. Double Quotes (" ")
    c. Triple quotes (""" """)
    d. Any of them
23. The file extension for a Python program is
    a. .python
    b. .py
    c. .pyt
    d. .pt
24. Which function is used to convert a string of digits into an integer?
    a. conv()
    b. string()
    c. int()
    d. str()
25. All control flow statements in Python start with:
    a. Semicolon (;)
    b. Hash sign (#)
    c. Colon (:)
    d. Full Stop (.)
26. Which of the following is used to add a new element to the end of the list?
    a. append()
    b. insert()
    c. add()
    d. push()
27. Which of the following is used to add an element '15' at index 5 in my list?
    a. mylist.insert(15, 5)
    b. mylist.insert(5, 15)
    c. mylist.add(4,15)
    d. mylist.append(15,5)
28. Which statement is CORRECT for a variable name?
    a. Spaces are not allowed.
    b. Letters, numbers, and () underscore characters are allowed.
    c. Special characters like @, *, % are allowed.
    d. All the above

29. Which of the following statements does check if a is greater than or equal to b?

    a. if a is less than equal to b: ☐ b. if a >= b: ☐
    c. if a < == b: ☐ d. if a < = b: ☐

30. Which command is used to create a list having four elements (1,3,6,9)?

    a. Mylist = list(1,3,6,9) ☐ b. Mylist = [1,3,6,9] ☐
    c. Mylist = list([1,3,6,9) ☐ d. All of the above ☐

31. What is the number of white spaces used for indentation?

    a. 2 ☐ b. 3 ☐
    c. 4 ☐ d. 5 ☐

32. What is the output of sum(mylist), if mylist= [1,3,6,9]?

    a. 4 ☐ b. 19 ☐
    c. 21 ☐ d. Displays an error ☐

33. What is the output of min(mylist), if mylist%=[313, 4313, 363, 3313, 414]?

    a. 3313 ☐ b. 4313 ☐
    c. 313 ☐ d. 414 ☐

34. The process where a set of instructions are repeated in a sequence a number of times until and unless a condition is met, is known as:

    a. Sequential ☐ b. Looping ☐
    c. Iteration ☐ d. Idealization ☐

ANSWERS

(Chapter 1)

1. (a)	2. (b)	3. (a)	4. (b)	5. (c)	6. (b)	7. (a)	8. (c)	9. (a)	10. (d)
11. (c)	12. (d)	13. (d)	14. (b)	15.(a)	16. (b)	17. (a)	18. (c)	19. (c)	20. (b)
21. (b)	22. (b)	23. (d)	24. (b)	25. (a)	26. (d)	27. (d)	28. (b)	29. (d)	30. (d)
31. (a)	32. (b)	33. (d)	34. (c)	35. (c)	36. (d)	37. (a)	38. (b)	39. (c)	40. (b)
41. (b)	42. (b)	43. (b)	44. (d)	45 (a)					

(Chapter 2)

1.(a)	2.(d)	3.(c)	4.(d)	5.(c)	6.(d)	7.(b)	8.(d)	9.(d)	10.(a)
11.(a)	12.(d)	13.(c)	14.(d)	15.(d)	16.(d)	17.(b)	18.(a)	19.(d)	20.(d)
21.(a)	22.(b)	23.(a)	24.(c)	25.(d)	26.(a)	27.(d)	28.(a)	29.(d)	30.(d)
31.(c)	32.(a)	33.(c)	34.(a)	35.(b)	36.(b)	37.(d)	38.(d)	39.(c)	40. (a)
41.(b)	42.(d)	43.(a)	44.(d)	45.(a)	46.(c)	47.(a)	48.(d)	49.(a)	50.(c)
51.(b)	52.(b)	53.(b)	54.(a)	55.(a)	56 (c)				

(Chapter 3)

1.(c)	2.(c)	3.(c)	4.(d)	5.(b)	6.(a)	7.(a)	8.(c)	9.(b)	10.(c)
11.(c)	12.(d)	13.(c)	14.(a)	15.(d)	16.(c)	17.(a)	18.(c)	19.(d)	20.(b).

(Chapter 4)

1.(a)	2.(a)	3.(b)	4.(a)	5.(d)	6.(b)	7.(c)	8.(b)	9.(c)	10.(d)
11.(d)	12.(c)	13.(c)	14.(a)	15.(c)	16.(b)	17.(d)	18.(b)	19.(d)	20.(b).
21.(d)	22.(d)	23.(b)	24.(c)	25.(b)	26.(a)	27.(b)	28.(d)	29.(b)	30.(d)
31.(c)	32.(b)	33.(c)	34.(c)						

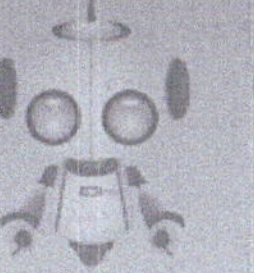
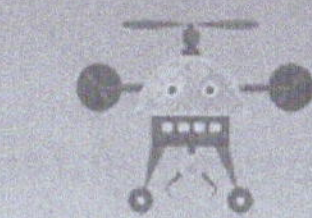

7 Python Codes for Bright Learners

Solve the following python problems:

1. Write a python program to enter a number n and print an identity matrix of the desired size.
2. Write a python program for merging more than one string.
3. Write a python program to check the number is an armstrong or not.
4. Write a python program to get a string where all occurrences of its first character to be changed to '$,' except the first character itself.
5. Write a python program to check a number is a strong number.
6. Write a python program to reverse a string.
7. Write a python program to calculate the number of words in a string.
8. Write a python program to reverse each word of a string entered by the user.
9. Write a python program to identify whether the number is a perfect square or not.
10. Write a python program to print all the odd numbers from 11 to 30.
11. Write a python program to sum all odd numbers from 1 to n (a given number).
12. Write a python program to check the number is a perfect number or not.

Solutions

1. **Write a python program to read a number n and print an identity matrix of the desired size.**

```
n=int(input("Enter a number: "))
for i in range(0,n):
    for j in range(0,n):
        if(i==j):
            print("1",sep=" ",end=" ")
        else:
            print("0",sep=" ",end=" ")
print()
```

```
py.21.py - D:/BPB projects 2021/IX AI Projects book/source code for python programs/py.21.py (3.8.3)
File Edit Format Run Options Window Help
n=int(input("Enter a number: "))
for i in range(0,n):
    for j in range(0,n):
        if(i==j):
            print("1",sep=" ",end=" ")
        else:
            print("0",sep=" ",end=" ")
print()
```

Figure 7.1 a: *Code*

```
Python 3.8.3 Shell
File Edit Shell Debug Options Window Help
Python 3.8.3 (tags/v3.8.3:6f8c832, May 13 2020, 22:20:19) [MSC v.1925 32 bit (Intel)] on win32
Type "help", "copyright", "credits" or "license()" for more information.
>>>
= RESTART: D:/BPB projects 2021/IX AI Projects book/source code for python programs/py.21.py
Enter a number: 3
1 0 0 0 1 0 0 0 1
>>>
= RESTART: D:/BPB projects 2021/IX AI Projects book/source code for python programs/py.21.py
Enter a number: 5
1 0 0 0 0 0 1 0 0 0 0 0 1 0 0 0 0 0 1 0 0 0 0 0 1
>>>
```

Figure 7.1 b: *Output*

2. **Write a python program for merging more than one string.**

```
s1="Hello friends!"
s2="I am SP Verma, a Career Counsellor."
s3="I would like to share with you the career options available after XII."
s=s1+s2+s3
print(s)
```

```
py.5.py - D:/BPB projects 2021/IX AI Projects book/source code for python programs/py.5.py (3.8.3)
File Edit Format Run Options Window Help
s1="Hello Friends!"
s2="I am SP Verma, a career counsellor."
s3="I would like to share with you the career options available after XII."
s=s1+s2+s3
print(s)
```

Figure 7.2 a: *Code*

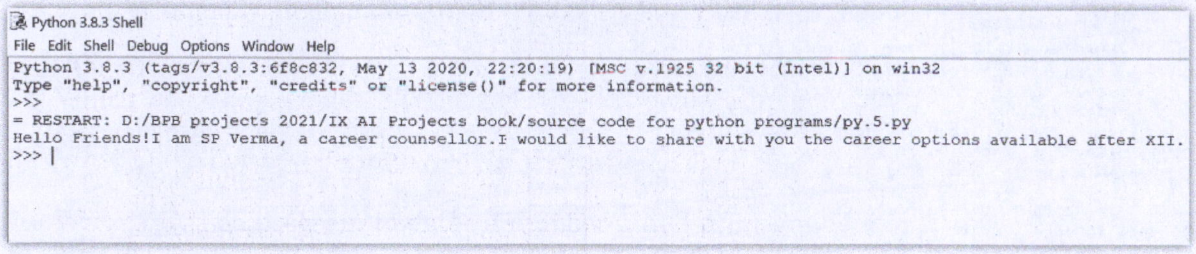

```
Python 3.8.3 Shell
File Edit Shell Debug Options Window Help
Python 3.8.3 (tags/v3.8.3:6f8c832, May 13 2020, 22:20:19) [MSC v.1925 32 bit (Intel)] on win32
Type "help", "copyright", "credits" or "license()" for more information.
>>>
= RESTART: D:/BPB projects 2021/IX AI Projects book/source code for python programs/py.5.py
Hello Friends!I am SP Verma, a career counsellor.I would like to share with you the career options available after XII.
>>> |
```

Figure 7.2 b: *Output*

3. **Write a python program to check the number is an armstrong or not.**

   (An armstrong is a number that is equal to the sum of cubes its digits. Examples: 1,153,370,371,407,etc.)

```
num = int(input("Enter a number: "))
sum = 0
temp = num
while temp > 0:
   digit = temp % 10
   sum += digit ** 3
   temp //= 10
if num == sum:
   print(num,"is an Armstrong number")
else:
   print(num,"is not an Armstrong number")
```

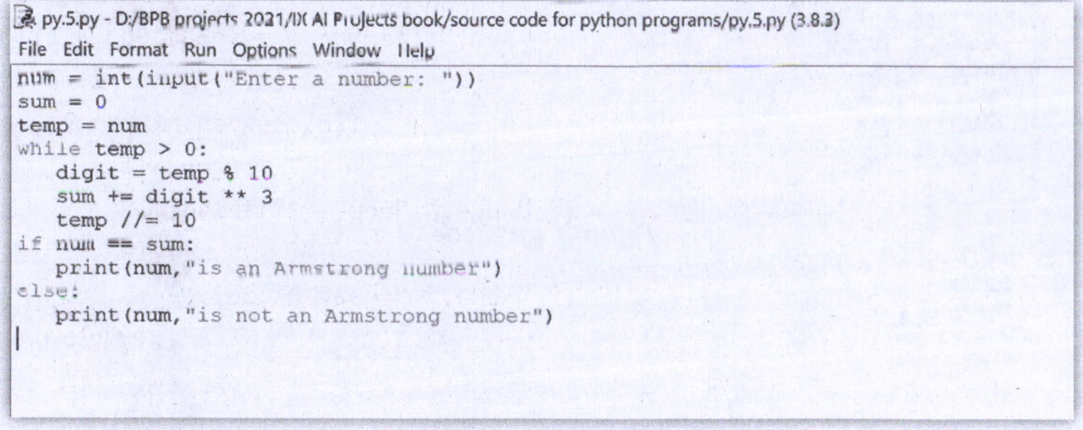

```
py.5.py - D:/BPB projects 2021/IX AI Projects book/source code for python programs/py.5.py (3.8.3)
File Edit Format Run Options Window Help
num = int(input("Enter a number: "))
sum = 0
temp = num
while temp > 0:
   digit = temp % 10
   sum += digit ** 3
   temp //= 10
if num == sum:
   print(num,"is an Armstrong number")
else:
   print(num,"is not an Armstrong number")
|
```

Figure 7.3 a: *Code*

```
Python 3.8.3 Shell
File Edit Shell Debug Options Window Help
Python 3.8.3 (tags/v3.8.3:6f8c832, May 13 2020, 22:20:19) [MSC v.1925 32 bit (Intel)] on win32
Type "help", "copyright", "credits" or "license()" for more information.
>>>
= RESTART: D:/BPB projects 2021/IX AI Projects book/source code for python programs/py.5.py
Enter a number: 6
6 is not an Armstrong number
>>>
= RESTART: D:/BPB projects 2021/IX AI Projects book/source code for python programs/py.5.py
Enter a number: 1
1 is an Armstrong number
>>>
= RESTART: D:/BPB projects 2021/IX AI Projects book/source code for python programs/py.5.py
Enter a number: 141
141 is not an Armstrong number
>>>
= RESTART: D:/BPB projects 2021/IX AI Projects book/source code for python programs/py.5.py
Enter a number: 407
407 is an Armstrong number
>>> |
```

***Figure 7.3 b:** Output*

4. **Write a python program to get a string where all occurrences of its first characters are to be changed to '$', except the first character itself.**

```
def change_char(str1):
  char = str1[0]
  str1 = str1.replace(char, '$')
  str1 = char + str1[1:]
  return str1
print(change_char('restart'))
```

```
py.5.py - D:/BPB projects 2021/IX AI Projects book/source code for python programs/py.5.py (3.8.3)
File Edit Format Run Options Window Help
def change_char(str1):
  char = str1[0]
  str1 = str1.replace(char, '$')
  str1 = char + str1[1:]
  return str1
print(change_char('restart'))
```

***Figure 7.4 a:** Code*

```
Python 3.8.3 Shell
File Edit Shell Debug Options Window Help
Python 3.8.3 (tags/v3.8.3:6f8c832, May 13 2020, 22:20:19) [MSC v.1925 32 bit (Intel)] on win32
Type "help", "copyright", "credits" or "license()" for more information.
>>>
= RESTART: D:/BPB projects 2021/IX AI Projects book/source code for python programs/py.5.py
resta$t
>>>
```

***Figure 7.4 b:** Output*

5. **Write a python program to check the number is a strong number.**

```
sum1=0
num=int(input("Enter a number:"))
temp=num
while(num):
    i=1
    f=1
    r=num%10
    while(i<=r):
        f=f*i
        i=i+1
    sum1=sum1+f
    num=num//10
if(sum1==temp):
    print("The number is a strong number")
else:
    print("The number is not a strong number")
```

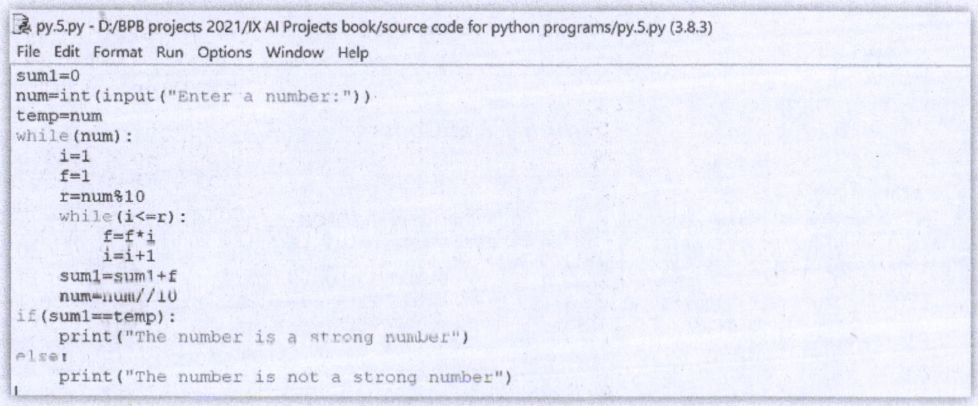

```
py.5.py - D:/BPB projects 2021/IX AI Projects book/source code for python programs/py.5.py (3.8.3)
File Edit Format Run Options Window Help
sum1=0
num=int(input("Enter a number:"))
temp=num
while(num):
    i=1
    f=1
    r=num%10
    while(i<=r):
        f=f*i
        i=i+1
    sum1=sum1+f
    num=num//10
if(sum1==temp):
    print("The number is a strong number")
else:
    print("The number is not a strong number")
```

Figure 7.5 a: *Code*

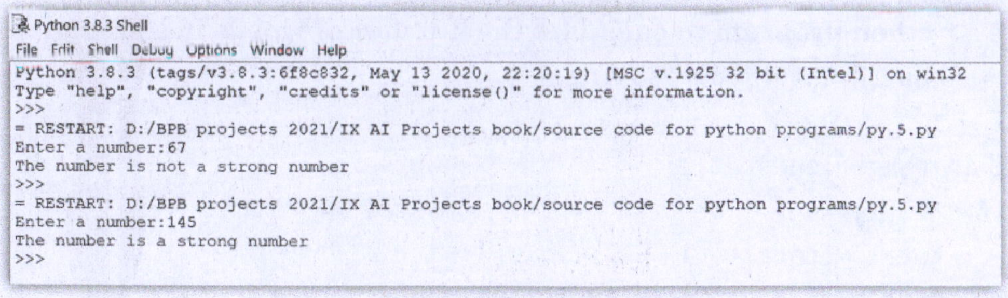

```
Python 3.8.3 Shell
File Edit Shell Debug Options Window Help
Python 3.8.3 (tags/v3.8.3:6f8c832, May 13 2020, 22:20:19) [MSC v.1925 32 bit (Intel)] on win32
Type "help", "copyright", "credits" or "license()" for more information.
>>>
= RESTART: D:/BPB projects 2021/IX AI Projects book/source code for python programs/py.5.py
Enter a number:67
The number is not a strong number
>>>
= RESTART: D:/BPB projects 2021/IX AI Projects book/source code for python programs/py.5.py
Enter a number:145
The number is a strong number
>>>
```

Figure 7.5 b: *Output*

6. **Write a python program to reverse a string.**

```
def reverse(s):
  str = ""
  for i in s:
    str = i + str
  return str
s = "SATYA LIKES REKHA"
print("The original string  is : ",end="")
print(s)
print("The reversed string(using loops) is : ",end="")
print(reverse(s))
```

```
py.5.py - D:/BPB projects 2021/IX AI Projects book/source code for python programs/py.5.py (3.8.3)
File Edit Format Run Options Window Help
def reverse(s):
  str = ""
  for i in s:
    str = i + str
  return str
s = "SATYA LIKES REKHA"
print("The original string  is : ",end="")
print(s)
print("The reversed string(using loops) is : ",end="")
print(reverse(s))
```

Figure 7.6 a: *Code*

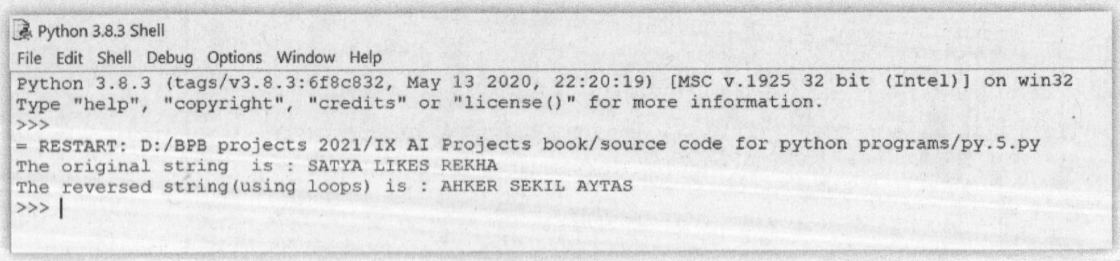

```
Python 3.8.3 Shell
File Edit Shell Debug Options Window Help
Python 3.8.3 (tags/v3.8.3:6f8c832, May 13 2020, 22:20:19) [MSC v.1925 32 bit (Intel)] on win32
Type "help", "copyright", "credits" or "license()" for more information.
>>>
= RESTART: D:/BPB projects 2021/IX AI Projects book/source code for python programs/py.5.py
The original string  is : SATYA LIKES REKHA
The reversed string(using loops) is : AHKER SEKIL AYTAS
>>> |
```

Figure 7.6 b: *Output*

7. **Write a python program to calculate the number of words in a string.**

```
str1 = input(" Enter your string: ")
total = 1
for i in range(len(str1)):
    if(str1[i] == ' ' or str1 == '\n' or str1 == '\t'):
        total = total + 1
print("Total number of words in the string = ", total)
```

```
py.5.py - D:/BPB projects 2021/IX AI Projects book/source code for python programs/py.5.py (3.8.3)
File Edit Format Run Options Window Help
str1 = input(" Enter your Own String : ")
total = 1
for i in range(len(str1)):
    if(str1[i] == ' ' or str1 == '\n' or str1 == '\t'):
        total = total + 1
print("Total Number of Words in this String = ", total)
```

Figure 7.7 a: *Code*

```
Python 3.8.3 Shell
File Edit Shell Debug Options Window Help
Python 3.8.3 (tags/v3.8.3:6f8c832, May 13 2020, 22:20:19) [MSC v.1925 32 bit (Intel)] on win32
Type "help", "copyright", "credits" or "license()" for more information.
>>>
= RESTART: D:/BPB projects 2021/IX AI Projects book/source code for python programs/py.5.py
 Enter your Own String : I like my country very much.
Total Number of Words in this String =  6
>>>
= RESTART: D:/BPB projects 2021/IX AI Projects book/source code for python programs/py.5.py
 Enter your Own String : I and Ramesh went to zoo to see wild animals.
Total Number of Words in this String =  10
>>> |
```

Figure 7.7 b: *Output*

8. **Write a python program to reverse each word of a string entered by the user.**

```
def rev_sentence(sentence):
    words = sentence.split(' ')
    reverse_sentence = ' '.join(reversed(words))
    return reverse_sentence
if __name__ == "__main__":
    input = 'Satya likes Rekha'
    print (rev_sentence(input))
```

```
py.5.py - D:/BPB projects 2021/IX AI Projects book/source code for python programs/py.5.py (3.8.3)
File Edit Format Run Options Window Help
def rev_sentence(sentence):
    words = sentence.split(' ')
    reverse_sentence = ' '.join(reversed(words))
    return reverse_sentence
if __name__ == "__main__":
    input = 'Satya likes Rekha'
    print (rev_sentence(input))
|
```

Figure 7.8 a: *Code*

```
Python 3.8.3 Shell
File  Edit  Shell  Debug  Options  Window  Help
Python 3.8.3 (tags/v3.8.3:6f8c832, May 13 2020, 22:20:19) [MSC v.1925 32 bit (Intel)] on win32
Type "help", "copyright", "credits" or "license()" for more information.
>>>
= RESTART: D:/BPB projects 2021/IX AI Projects book/source code for python programs/py.5.py
Rekha likes Satya
>>> |
```

***Figure 7.8 b:** Output*

9. Write a python program to identify whether the number is perfect square or not.

```
number = int(input("Enter the Number:"))
root = (number)** (0.5)
if int(root + 0.5) ** 2 == number:
    print("Entered number is a perfect square")
else:
    print("Entered number is not a perfect square")
```

```
*py.5.py - D:/BPB projects 2021/IX AI Projects book/source code for python programs/py.5.py (3.8.3)*
File  Edit  Format  Run  Options  Window  Help
number = int(input("Enter the Number:"))
root = (number)** (0.5)
if int(root + 0.5) ** 2 == number:
    print("Entered number is a perfect square")
else:
    print("Entered number is not a perfect square")
```

***Figure 7.9 a:** Code*

```
*Python 3.8.3 Shell*
File  Edit  Shell  Debug  Options  Window  Help
Python 3.8.3 (tags/v3.8.3:6f8c832, May 13 2020, 22:20:19) [MSC v.1925 32 bit (Intel)] on win32
Type "help", "copyright", "credits" or "license()" for more information.
>>>
= RESTART: D:/BPB projects 2021/IX AI Projects book/source code for python programs/py.5.py
Enter the Number:16
Entered number is a perfect square
>>>
= RESTART: D:/BPB projects 2021/IX AI Projects book/source code for python programs/py.5.py
Enter the Number:67
Entered number is not a perfect square
>>>
= RESTART: D:/BPB projects 2021/IX AI Projects book/source code for python programs/py.5.py
Enter the Number:81
Entered number is a perfect square
>>> |
```

***Figure 7.9 b:** Output*

10. Write a python program to print all the odd numbers from 11 to 30.

```
print("Odd numbers are")
for i in range(11,30):
    if(i%2!=0):
        print(i)
```

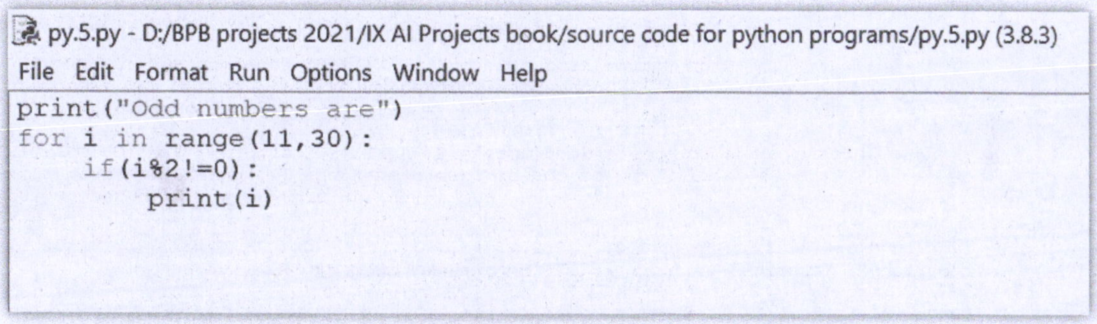

```
py.5.py - D:/BPB projects 2021/IX AI Projects book/source code for python programs/py.5.py (3.8.3)
File Edit Format Run Options Window Help
print("Odd numbers are")
for i in range(11,30):
    if(i%2!=0):
        print(i)
```

Figure 7.10 a: Code

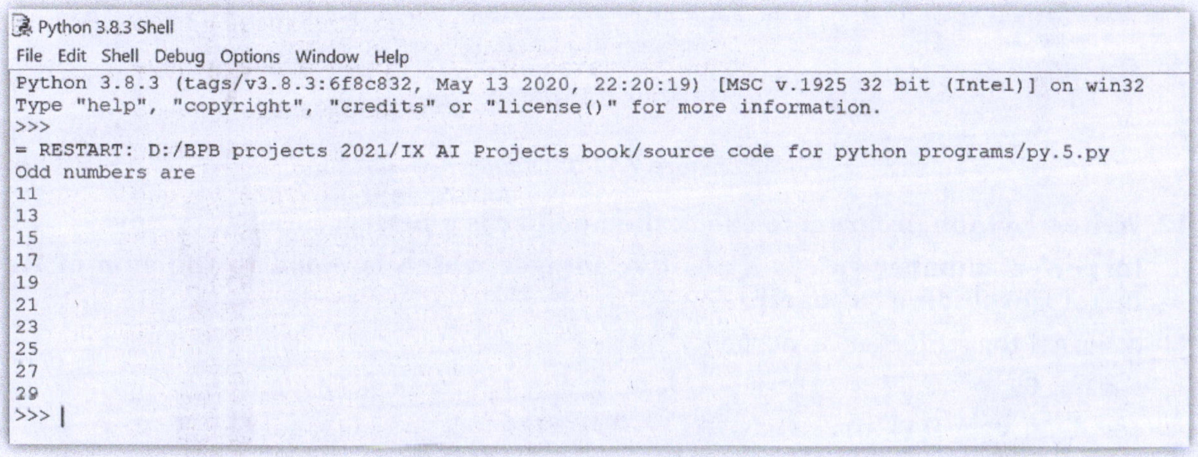

```
Python 3.8.3 Shell
File Edit Shell Debug Options Window Help
Python 3.8.3 (tags/v3.8.3:6f8c832, May 13 2020, 22:20:19) [MSC v.1925 32 bit (Intel)] on win32
Type "help", "copyright", "credits" or "license()" for more information.
>>>
= RESTART: D:/BPB projects 2021/IX AI Projects book/source code for python programs/py.5.py
Odd numbers are
11
13
15
17
19
21
23
25
27
29
>>> |
```

Figure 7.10 b: Output

11. Write a python program to sum of all odd numbers from 1 to n (a given number).

```
n=int(input("Enter n value:"))
sum=0
for i in range(9,n+1,20):
sum+=i
print(sum)
```

```
py.5.py - D:/BPB projects 2021/IX AI Projects book/source code for python programs/py.5.py (3.8.3)
File Edit Format Run Options Window Help
n=int(input("Enter n value:"))
sum=0
for i in range(1,n+1,2):
    sum+=i
print(sum)
```

Figure 7.11 a: Code

```
Python 3.8.3 Shell
File Edit Shell Debug Options Window Help
Python 3.8.3 (tags/v3.8.3:6f8c832, May 13 2020, 22:20:19) [MSC v.1925 32 bit (Intel)] on win32
Type "help", "copyright", "credits" or "license()" for more information.
>>>
= RESTART: D:/BPB projects 2021/IX AI Projects book/source code for python programs/py.5.py
Enter n value:10
25
>>>
= RESTART: D:/BPB projects 2021/IX AI Projects book/source code for python programs/py.5.py
Enter n value:18
81
>>>
```

Figure 7.11 b: Output

12. Write a python program to check the number is a perfect number or not.

(A perfect number “n”, is a positive integer which is equal to the sum of its factors, excluding “n” itself.)

```
n = int(input("Enter a number: "))
sum1 = 0
for i in range(1, n):
    if(n % i == 0):
        sum1 = sum1 + i
if (sum1 == n):
    print("The number is a Perfect number.")
else:
    print("The number is not a Perfect number.")
```

```
py.5.py - D:/BPB projects 2021/IX AI Projects book/source code for python programs/py.5.py (3.8.3)
File Edit Format Run Options Window Help
n = int(input("Enter any number: "))
sum1 = 0
for i in range(1, n):
    if(n % i == 0):
        sum1 = sum1 + i
if (sum1 == n):
    print("The number is a Perfect number!")
else:
    print("The number is not a Perfect number!")
```

Figure 7.12 a: Code

```
Python 3.8.3 Shell
File Edit Shell Debug Options Window Help
Python 3.8.3 (tags/v3.8.3:6f8c832, May 13 2020, 22:20:19) [MSC v.1925 32 bit (Intel)] on win32
Type "help", "copyright", "credits" or "license()" for more information.
>>>
= RESTART: D:/BPB projects 2021/IX AI Projects book/source code for python programs/py.5.py
Enter any number: 1
The number is not a Perfect number!
>>>
= RESTART: D:/BPB projects 2021/IX AI Projects book/source code for python programs/py.5.py
Enter any number: 22
The number is not a Perfect number!
>>>
= RESTART: D:/BPB projects 2021/IX AI Projects book/source code for python programs/py.5.py
Enter any number: 6
The number is a Perfect number!
>>>
= RESTART: D:/BPB projects 2021/IX AI Projects book/source code for python programs/py.5.py
Enter any number: 28
The number is a Perfect number!
>>>
```

Figure 7.12 b: Output

For more practice:

1. Write a python program to count the number of vowels in a string.
2. Write a python program to check the number is perfect cube.
3. Write a python program to find the LCM of two numbers.
4. Write a program to find numbers that are divisible by five and multiple of 3 between 100 and 200.
5. Write a program to display the quotient and remainder.

Notes

Annexure 1
Guidelines for Making Project File

While participating in the class activities, practical, and projects, each learner has to keep a record of participating in these actions date-wise, and learning experiences gained. So, prepare three files -one for each of Activities, Practical, and Project(s). Learners may be asked to participate in either of the types of the Project by their teachers:

- Individual Project,
- Pair Project,
- Group Project

A project file will contain the following items:

(i) **Synopsis**: It is a summary of your idea and should include the purpose of the Project, the procedure used, data, and conclusion.

(ii) **Research paper**: The research paper should be prepared along with the Project with relevant written material. It helps organize data as well as thoughts. A good research paper includes the following topics:

- **Title page**: Write the project title in the centre of the first page, and put your name, name of your Guide teacher, name and address of your school.
- **Aim / Objective**: The aim includes the hypothesis, an explanation of what prompted the research, and what may be achieved.
- **Scientific Principle Involved**: Describe the principles involved.
- **Material Used**: List all the items used during the Project.
- **Method:** This topic describes how you carried the Project. Describe in detail the methodology used during the project to collect the data or make the observations. The report should be detailed enough for someone to be able to repeat the Project.
- **Discussion**: The results and conclusions drawn based on the data collected should have a smooth flow. Put your ideas and thoughts, observations and results logically.
- **Conclusion**: This describes the findings and conclusion(s) of the Project. Summarize the results. Be specific, and never introduce anything in the conclusion that has not been discussed earlier.
- **Scope of the Project:** Describe here the future scope of the project, if any extension of the project is possible.
- **Acknowledgment:** Give credit to those who assisted you; they may be individuals, educational institutes, etc.

- **References:** List all the documents (books/ journal articles/magazines/specific internet URLs) that are used to consult during project preparation.

(iii) Documents as Proofs: These may include pictures, photographs, press coverage, etc.

General rules:

The following points are to be taken care of while maintaining a project file:

- While working on a project, each student/team is requested to follow the guidelines.
- Select a Topic/ sub-topic carefully after consulting your teacher.
- After Choosing the topic carefully, start working on it as early as possible.
- Search for source information for your Project by attending the library, accessing the Internet, and visiting various search engines available to find information.
- Plan your project by including the following points:
    - The purpose, aim of your Project;
    - The different variable or the things that you are going to change during the Project to evolve a new concept;
    - The outcome of the Project;
    - Detailed procedure outlining how you will execute the Project;
    - The material you will require at each stage of the Project.
- Prepare a Time frame to allow sufficient time for all stages. Distribute the work among members if it is a group project. Prepare a flowchart for preparing the complete Project, allocate work, and fix responsibilities within the team.
- Also, ensure that time allotted is realistic, and deadlines are strictly adhered to.
- Make and test the hypothesis because, in any research-based Project, it is most important to think, identify and determine the different variables that may be involved, think about ways to change one at a time.
- Record your data and observations carefully, including all experiments where success was not achieved as per the set criteria. Collect it as raw data in tabular form.
- Observations may be written descriptions of what you have noticed during the execution of the Project. These observations are valuable for drawing conclusions and, therefore, these should be carefully noted in a log book.
- Consult your guide/teacher to ensure that you are working in the right direction and the methodology being used is correct. Be inquisitive!
- Use raw data to draw conclusions.
- Summarize results and derive conclusions in a paragraph. It can be in the form of a table of processed numerical data or graphs. It may be in the form of the output of the Python code after running on the computer, whose printout may be taken.

- Define utility and further scope of Project and also determine cost viability if it has a futuristic value.
- Find out Cost feasibility in preparing the Project.
- Maintain discipline during all activities.
- Maintain neatness in presenting the reports in writing.
- Involve yourself fully in the activities by active participation and sharing your thoughts and experience.
- Stick to the time frame for your activities, practical, and Project.
- Don't use unfair means while presenting the Project. Credit the source of information and provide the list of references at the end of the Project.
- As languages are an important means of communication, and hence, present your Project using good language. Watch your grammar, spelling, and wording.
- Take photographs, and make videos of the supporting activities undertaken by you while working on the Project.

Oral presentation:

During the oral presentation of the project, keep the following points in your mind:

- Ensure that you are audible and clear.
- Speak in clear language.
- Prepare to explain in the language in which you and teachers/judges are most comfortable.
- Speak with confidence!
- Answer politely all questions asked during cross-questioning.
- Try to understand the concepts related to your Project so that you may answer all related questions.
- Explain with a cheerful smile and good body language to have a good gesture.
- Do show respect to all judges and/visitors.
- Listening to others' viewpoints, suggestions, and ideas is a good option. A scientist should be open to ideas.
- Rehearse explanation to share the details within a stipulated time limit. An explanation should be to the point.
- Do not argue with the judges/the visitors in case the Project is presented in public.

Annexure 2
History of AI

- **1949:** Edmund Berkeley published the book "Giant Brains: Or Machines That Think", in which he assumed a machine that can think.
- **1950:** Alan Turing published the research paper "Computing Machinery and Intelligence," in which he created the 'Turing Test' to determine the intelligence of a computer.
- **1950:** Isaac Asimov published his famous 'Three Laws of Robotics'.
- **1951:** Marvin Minsky and Dean Edmunds built SNARC (Stochastic Neural Analog Reinforcement Calculator), the first artificial neural network which used 3000 vacuum tubes to simulate a network of 40 neurons.
- **1952:** Arthur Samuel prepared the 'first computer learning application'.
- **1955:** John McCarthy, the computer scientist, coined the term "artificial intelligence."
- **1957:** Frank Rosenblatt designed the 'first artificial neural network'.
- **1967:** Computer-based pattern recognition began with the nearest neighbour algorithm.
- **1979:** Stanford University students invent the self-navigating Stanford Cart.
- **1981:** Explanation Based Learning (EBL) was introduced by Gerald Dejong, allowing a computer to create aa set of rules based on training data.
- **1985:** Terry Sejnowski created 'NetTalk', which learned to pronounce words.
- **1993:** Vernor Vinge published "The Coming Technological Singularity," in which he predicted that within the next thirty years, humans would have the technological means to create superhuman intelligence and then, the human era will be ended.'
- **1997:** IBM's Deep Blue system defeated the World Chess Champion.
- **2003:** Deep Learning introduced.
- **2006:** Geoffrey Hinton coined the term "deep learning" to explain new algorithms that empower computers to distinguish objects and images, and video.
- **2010:** Microsoft's Kinect was released, tracking 20 human features to allow people to interact with the computer through movements and gestures.
- **2011:** Nevada in the USA became the first jurisdiction in the world where autonomous vehicles can be legally operated on public roads.
- **2012:** A convolutional neural network was designed by researchers at the University of Toronto, which achieved an error rate of only 16% in the ImageNet Large Scale Visual

Recognition Challenge, a significant improvement over the 25% error rate achieved by the best entry the year before.

- **2014:** Generative Adversarial Networks (GANs) introduced.
- **2015:** Google DeepMind's AlphaGo (version Fan) defeated three-time European Go champion two dan professional Fan Hui by five games to 0.
- **2016:** The biggest success story of the year was probably AlphaGo (Nature paper), a Reinforcement Learning agent that beat the world's best Go players.
- **2017:** Stephen Hawkins warned the emergence of Artificial Intelligence (AI) could be the "worst event in the history of our civilization." Also, China started looking like a major player in the field of AI. Facebook made a big splash with PyTorch.Tensorflow. Google released API with a stable and backward-compatible. Facebook and Microsoft announced the ONNX (Open Neural Network Exchange) open-source AI ecosystem to share deep learning models across frameworks.
- **2018:** Tesla became the first automaker to launch a self-driving vehicle. Other traditional automakers, like Audi, are poised to release their own self-driving cars in 2018. Nvidia introduced its GPU cloud, which promises to be another interesting alternative to training Deep Learning models. AI with IoT, Big Data, Data Science is the top trends of artificial intelligence.

Annexure 3
AI Terminology

- **AI bias:** The underlying prejudice in data used to create AI algorithms, and that can ultimately result in discrimination.
- **Application programming interfaces (API):** The piece of code that helps one application to connect to another.
- **Artificial Intelligence (AI):** The branch of computer sciences that is used for the development of mintelligence machines that has the ability to act rationally and to act like humans.
- **Artificial Neural Networks (ANNs):** An information-processing synthetic system made up of several simple nonlinear processing units connected by elements that have information storage and programming functions adapting and learning from patterns, which mimics a biological neural network.
- **Automatic Speech Recognition:** Machine recognition and conversion of spoken words into text.
- **Box plot:** A graphical tool used when the data is split according to its percentile throughout the range.
- **Chatbot:** A computer program that is designed to simulate human conversation through voice commands or text chats, or both.
- **Computer Vision:** A domain of AI that depicts the capability of a machine to get and analyse visual information to predict some decisions about it.
- **Computer Vision:** The capability of a machine to extract information from an image that is necessary to solve a task.
- **Convolution:** A common tool used for image editing.
- **Convolutional Layer:** The name of the first layer of a CNN.
- **Copyright infringement:** The use or reproduction of copyright-protected material without the permission of the copyright holder.
- **Corpus:** A large, organised, and structured set of texts that can be read by machines.
- **Data:** Pieces of information collected on a daily basis in the form of bits, numbers, symbols, and objects.
- **Data Mining:** The application of analytical tools and methods applied to data for the purpose of identifying relationships, patterns, or obtaining systems that perform useful tasks such as classification, prediction, estimation, or affinity grouping.

- **Data privacy:** A branch of data security concerned with the proper handling of data -consent, notice, and regulatory obligations.
- **Data privacy:** It focuses on how to collect, process, share, archive, and delete data in accordance with the law.
- **Data Retrieval:** The process of identifying and extracting data from a database based on a query provided by the users.
- **Data science:** A field of study that combines domain expertise, coding skills, and knowledge of mathematics and statistics for extracting meaningful insights from data.
- **Espionage (spying):** The disclosure or theft of many types of information, especially secrets, political, military, business, or industrial information.
- **Evaluation:** A process of understanding the reliability of an AI model, which is based on outputs by feeding the testing dataset into the model and comparing it with actual answers.
- **Flow chart:** A diagrammatic/graphical representation of a sequence of steps to solve a problem.
- **Grayscale images:** The images that have a range of shades of Gray without apparent colour.
- **Identity theft:** The use of an individual's personally identifying information by someone else (often a stranger) without that individual's permission or knowledge.
- **Information:** Organized data, which is pre-processed, cleaned, arranged into structures, and stripped of redundancy.
- **Intelligence:** The capacity of humans to learn and solve problems.
- **Interpersonal Intelligence:** The ability to communicate with others after understanding other people's feelings & influcnce on the person.
- **Intrapersonal Intelligence:** How high the level of self-awareness someone has started from realising weakness, strength to his own feelings.
- **Kinaesthetic Intelligence:** The ability that is related to how a person uses his limbs in a skilled manner.
- **Linguistical Intelligence:** The language processing skills both in terms of understanding or implementation in writing or verbally.
- **List:** An important data type of Python containing items that are separated by commas and enclosed within square brackets ([]).
- **Machine Learning:** A subset of Artificial Intelligence that enables machines to improve at tasks with experience (Data).
- **Machine perception:** The ability to use input from sensors to deduce aspects of the world.
- **Margin:** The gap between two lines on the closet data points of different classes.

- **Mathematical & logical reasoning:** A person's ability to regulate, measure, and understand numerical symbols, abstraction, and logic.
- **Matplotlib:** A Python library meant for plotting the data and has NumPy as its numerical mathematics extension.
- **Musical Intelligence:** A person's ability to recognize and create sounds, rhythms, and sound patterns.
- **Natural Language Processing:** A machine's ability to read and understand human language.
- **Naturalist Intelligence:** An additional category of Intelligence relating to the ability to process information on the environment around us.
- **Neural Machine Translation:** The use of a neural network to translate low-impact content by a machine to speed up communication with its partners.
- **NLTK:** Natural Language Toolkit- one of the leading platforms for building Python programs that can work with human language data.
- **NumPy:** Numerical Python- the fundamental package for Mathematical and logical operations on arrays in Python.
- **OpenCV:** A tool that helps a computer extract the features from the images.
- **Package:** A directory of Python modules containing an additional application environment.
- **Pandas:** A software library that provides data manipulation and analysis tools in the Python programming language.
- **Pooling layer:** The layer in CNN makes the image smaller and more manageable.
- **Pseudocode:** A plain language description of all the steps of an algorithm.
- **Python:** A high-level, case-sensitive and interpreted programming language.
- **Quantitative Data:** The data that can be expressed as a number and can be measured by numerical variables only.
- **Script bot:** A set of predefined tasks once triggered and cutting-edge software.
- **Seaborn package:** A Python data visualisation library based on matplotlib.
- **Sensor (Transducer):** A device that converts real-world phenomena, like force, temperature, and movement to voltage or current signals used as inputs.
- **Smart-bot:** A cohesive bot development platform that designs, develops, validates, and deploys AI-powered conversational chatbots that suit the user's unique needs.
- **Spatial Visual Intelligence:** The ability to perceive the visual world and the relationship of one object to another.
- **Spreadsheet:** A computer program that is used for accounting and recording data using rows and columns into which information can be entered.
- **SQL:** Structured Query Language- A programming language.

- **String:** A continuous set of characters represented in the quotation marks.
- **Supervised Learning:** The set of learning algorithms in which the samples in the training dataset are all labelled.
- **Text Analytics:** The process of extracting useful and structured knowledge from unstructured documents to find useful associations and insights.
- **Unsupervised Learning:** A learning algorithm that tries to identify clusters based on a similarity between features or between instances or both but without taking into account any prior knowledge.
- **Unsupervised Learning:** The set of learning algorithms in which the samples in the training dataset are all unlabelled.
- **Variance:** The numerical values that describe the variability of the observations from its arithmetic mean.
- **VLSI:** Very Large Scale Integration- the process of creating integrated circuits by combining thousands or millions of transistor-based circuits into a single chip.
- **Web Scrapping:** The collection of web data from websites on the internet using a web browser.

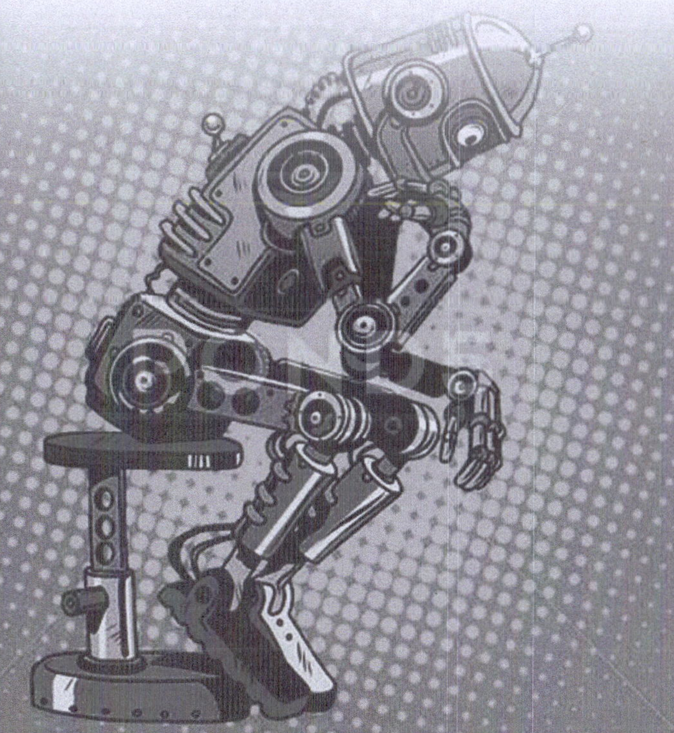

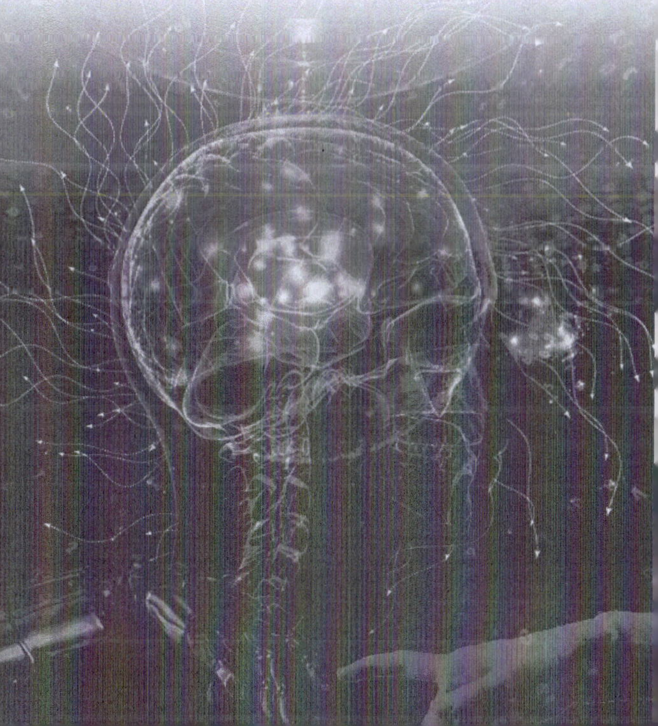

Notes

Notes

Notes